Massacre
in West Cork

Massacre
in West Cork

The Dunmanway and Ballygroman Killings

Barry Keane

MERCIER PRESS
IRISH PUBLISHER – IRISH STORY

For Louise and Ella

MERCIER PRESS

Cork

www.mercierpress.ie

© Barry Keane, 2014

ISBN: 978 1 78117 203 2

10 9 8 7 6 5 4 3 2 1

A CIP record for this title is available from the British Library

Printed and bound in the EU.

CONTENTS

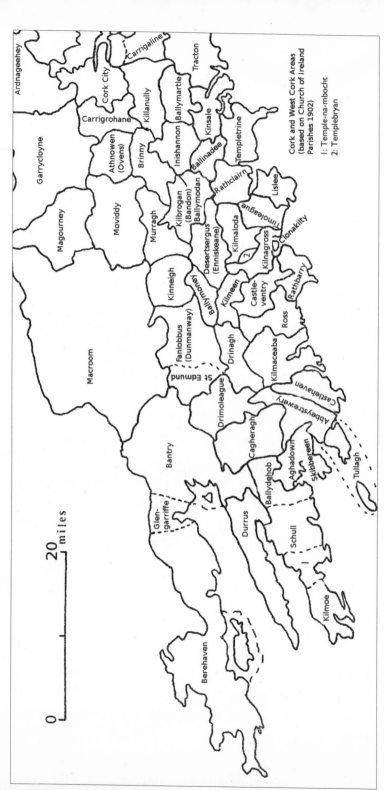

The geography of West Cork © Barry Keane

Cork and West Cork Areas
(based on Church of Ireland
Parishes 1902)

1: Temple-na-mbocht
2: Templebryan

Ardnageehey
Cork City
Carrigaline
Carrigrohane
Killanully
Ballymartle
Tracton
Athnowen (Ovens)
Brinny
Inishannon
Kinsale
Templetrine
Garrycloyne
Moviddy
Murragh
Kilbrogan (Bandon)
Ballymodan
Ballinadee
Rathclairn
Lislee
Magourney
Kinneigh
Desertsergus (Enniskeane)
Kilmaloda
Timoleague
Clonakilty
Ballymoney
Kilmeen
Kilnagross
Rathbarry
Macroom
Fanlobbus (Dunmanway)
Drinagh
Castleventry
Ross
Kilmaceaba
St Edmund
Drimoleague
Cagheragh
Castlehaven
Abbeystrewery
Bantry
Ballydehob
Aghadown
Skibbereen
Tullagh
Glengarriffe
Durrus
Schull
Berehaven
Kilmoe

20 miles
0

Acknowledgements

No book is ever written by one person and this book is no different. I first was encouraged to pursue this subject while a postgraduate in the Geography Department of University College Cork and, even though it took a little longer than planned, I owe a deep debt of gratitude to Emeritus Professor W. J. Smyth, Professor R. J. N. Devoy and Dr K. Hourihan for their help at that time. More recently Dr Andy Bielenberg, Dr John Borgonovo, Dr John Regan, Pádraig Óg Ó Ruairc, Dr Gerard Murphy and Niall Meehan have all been generous in sharing their research with me. Many of the more knotty problems have been resolved by their input.

The staffs of the Cork City Library, Cork County Library, Cork City and County Archives, UCC, National Library of Ireland, National Archives of Ireland, National Archives UK and the Military Archives of Ireland are often not acknowledged, but in this story it was their encouragement, courtesy and unfailing kindness which made many of the linkages possible. Their knowledge of what they had in their boxes of dusty documents, and their willingness to make them available, made the hard slog of raw research much easier than it might otherwise have been. My colleagues and friends in Coláiste an Spioraid Naoimh also deserve praise for listening and contributing to the story as it developed. To each and every one I am deeply grateful.

Other people deserve special mention. Thomas Hornibrook's great-grandson, Martin Midgley Reeve, provided a wealth of new information which forms the core of this book and was willing to engage with a story which could only have been painful for him to revisit. My great friend Henry O'Keeffe both listened to the story as it developed and critically read the documents along with me as they were found. Seán Crowley, Dr Martin Healy, Donal O'Flynn and Nora Lynch all took time and energy to tell their version of the story on more than one occasion when they had better things to do; they deserve special praise for their willingness to help. The photographs of Herbert Woods and Michael O'Neill provided by Donal O'Flynn are especially important as they rescue these men from being forgotten by time.

Mary Feehan and the staff of Mercier Press have proved to be exceptional publishers. Wendy Logue deserves special praise for her sterling editorial work and immense patience. Initially, this book was only 35,000 words long and it was a great risk for Mercier to take it on as a project. I am delighted that Mary had the vision to see behind the initial manuscript to what was hidden and was able to get me to tell the entire story.

Last, but not least, my family, Louise and Ella, have been fantastic supporters of this project. Research eats into all parts of family life and there has been more than one weekend wasted driving around the graveyards of West Cork looking for the right headstone. Ella has spent many 'happy' afternoons in the County Library, with all the patience of a six-year-old, and without Louise's help this book would never have got past the initial stages.

Permission for use of images was given by Dr Martin Midgley Reeve, Cork City Library, *Irish Examiner* Publications, the Military Archives of Ireland and Donal O'Flynn.

FOREWORD

MARTIN MIDGLEY REEVE (GRANDSON OF MATILDA
WOODS, GREAT-GRANDSON OF THOMAS HORNIBROOK)

As you may know much better than I do, trying to research Irish history is not easy, especially when you don't live in Ireland. My mother died on 12 June 2004, shortly before her eighty-fourth birthday. Amongst her papers I found a number of menu cards that had been on the tables of her wedding breakfast in 1939. The backs of these cards contained the signatures of all, or I assume most, of her guests. Some of the names were very familiar to me and others brought back vague memories of people I had met many years before. I set about trying to discover who the people were and if any were relations of mine. I contacted distant cousins of my father and some of my mother's relations, and slowly I started to build family trees. Finding my English relations was relatively easy, but my Irish relations have been much more difficult.

On 6 May 1928 my English grandfather, Dr H. Midgley Reeve, died of a heart attack, and in the following months his large house was put on the market. It was bought by Edward Woods, who had been born in Bandon, County Cork, and his family. The Reeve family then moved to a smaller house nearby and a friendship arose between the two families. In 1939 Beryl Woods, the third daughter of the late Edward and Matilda Woods (daughter of Thomas Hornibrook), married Bernard, the second son of Dr H. Midgley Reeve and his wife, Mabel.

I am one of the five grandchildren who are descendants of the four daughters of Edward and Matilda Woods. Sadly only four of us are still alive and none of us ever knew our Irish grandparents. My Irish grandfather died in 1933 and my grandmother died just over a year later, in 1934. She was aged forty-eight, and it was said that she gave up living after her husband's death. My mother was daughter number three. She was born in Cork city in August 1920, some four months before my Irish grandfather's shop was burned to the ground during what is known as 'The Burning of Cork'. My Aunt Doreen was the youngest daughter and she was born in Essex, where the family first moved when they had to leave Ireland; she was the last of the four daughters to survive and she died in January 2012.

Apart from my mother and her sisters, the only other Irish relation that I have met and been able to talk to about family history was one of the sons of Fred Nicholson, a cousin of Matilda Woods. His son's knowledge about my family history was very limited. In more recent times I have 'met' other relations on the Internet and they have helped to fill in many of the gaps in my knowledge.

It has been a difficult journey for me to find out about my Irish heritage, but visits to Ireland and reading have helped to fill in a few small pieces of a very large jigsaw. This new book by Barry Keane has greatly added to my knowledge of these events and the jigsaw puzzle is starting to take shape!

INTRODUCTION

On 26 April 1922, at 2.30 a.m., Captain Herbert Woods fired a single shot from his Bulldog 45 revolver at Irish Republican Army (IRA) Commandant Michael O'Neill on the stairs of Ballygroman House, Ovens, County Cork, during the Truce period following the cessation of the Irish War of Independence, and killed him. Later that morning Thomas and Samuel Hornibrook, along with Captain Woods, were taken from Ballygroman and almost certainly killed by the anti-Treaty IRA. Over four nights, from 26 April to 29 April, ten local Protestants were shot in their homes by unknown men and four British soldiers were shot in Macroom. These killings have been cited by some modern commentators as a sign of sectarian 'ethnic cleansing' by the IRA in Cork, yet many of the details surrounding the deaths remain shrouded in mystery and numerous questions remain unanswered.

Who exactly was Herbert Woods and why did he shoot an unarmed man? Who was Michael O'Neill and what was he doing inside the house at that hour? What connection had this event with the killing of ten Protestants in West Cork over the next four nights in what are commonly known as the Dunmanway killings? Are these killings linked with the shooting of three British intelligence officers, their driver and a dog in Macroom during the same period? What exactly happened to Herbert Woods, Thomas Hornibrook and Samuel Hornibrook, who were arrested by the Irish Republican Police and disappeared, undoubtedly killed by members of the anti-Treaty IRA? What was the effect on the local Protestant minority? Did thousands of people flee West Cork as a result of these killings, driven out by a rising tide of sectarian hatred?

My aim is to tell the story of what happened over the course of these events honestly and fairly, presenting the various strands of evidence and inviting the reader to draw their own conclusions. I examine the origins and history of the two men at the centre of the incident, Michael O'Neill and Herbert Woods, and show that many of the claims surrounding these linked events have little basis in fact. I also introduce newly uncovered IRA evidence from the Bureau of Military History (BMH) collection and from various British archives, which throws new light on the Dunmanway killings.

Having taken a chance in contacting Martin Midgley Reeve, the grandson of Thomas Hornibrook's daughter, Matilda Warmington Woods, I was delighted when he responded. Martin provided a wealth of details which were able to clear up any doubts about the accuracy of my research and were essential aids when I was looking at the history of the Hornibrook family after they left Ireland. Without his input many of the details in this book simply would not have been uncovered.

It must always be remembered that these events involved real people, some of whose children are still alive. It is not my intention to cause offence or hurt through the writing of this book, but the true history of these events needs to be revealed. If anybody has information that can add to our knowledge of these happenings I would be glad to hear from them.

SOURCES AND STRUCTURE

Everything about the killings carried out over those four days in April 1922 is contentious – even the names of things are different depending on which 'side' of the divide people are on. As the majority of readers will probably have been brought up in the Irish nationalist tradition, I have chosen to use the language that they will be familiar with. For example, the term 'War of Independence' is used in preference to any of the other equally valid terms used to describe this period of Ireland's history, such as 'the Anglo-Irish War', 'the Irish Revolution' or 'the Irish revolutionary period'. I have tried to avoid the old cliché of Protestant equalling unionist where possible. It does occur on occasion, for example when 'Protestant unionist' appears in some of the quotations and cannot be avoided. The terms 'loyalist' and 'nationalist' are preferable, but even these will be problematic for some readers. Another problem is that the term 'IRA' is used over the period 1919 to 1923 to mean different groups. The differences in usage pivot on the 'Articles of Agreement for a Treaty between Great Britain and Ireland' ('the Treaty'), signed in December 1921 to bring the Irish War of Independence to a formal end. Up to the vote on the Treaty in January 1922, the term 'IRA' referred to the military arm of the independence movement. After this, in most documents, it referred to the part of the IRA that was against the Treaty ('the anti-Treaty IRA'), which is how it is used in this book. Finally, the name 'Black and Tans' is often used in popular culture as the blanket term for the militarised police in Ireland during the War of Independence. However, it was the Auxiliary police ('the Auxiliaries'), a distinct section of the Royal Irish Constabulary (RIC) at this time, who dominated the story in West Cork.

Place names are given as they appear on the Ordnance Survey maps and refer to townlands, district electoral divisions or parishes. As the Roman Catholic and Anglican Churches often use different names for the same place, I have tried to ensure that both names are given where necessary. For example, the Roman Catholic parish of Kilbrittain is called Rathclairn by the Church of Ireland. Personal and family names are given as they appear in the documents, but if different documents spell the same person's name differently this is mentioned.[1]

In recent years the digitisation of the BMH's collection of witness statements and other documents relating to the period 1916–1923 has allowed researchers to search these sources using keywords, allowing them to find previously unseen references to events such as the Ballygroman and Dunmanway killings. This has allowed a new consideration of these events. The sources collected by the BMH provide a unique and priceless window into the mind of the local IRA volunteer and a detailed history of one side of the conflict.[2] As with all primary sources, the collection has to be treated with caution, as the witness statements were collected many years after the events they recall and can include half-remembered facts and some obvious self-justification.[3] However, I have read, referenced and cross-referenced more than 900 of these statements. In most cases what is surprising is the accuracy of people's recollections, rather than the opposite. Statements may get dates wrong, miss people out, or sometimes gild the lily, but generally when a statement has been cross-checked against an available independent source it has proven to be broadly accurate. For example, comparison of the Cork IRA Monthly Reports in Piaras Béaslaí's papers against the later witness statements shows that these statements are very accurate in these cases.[4] It should be noted though, that the sources held by the BMH present only one side of the argument and more work needs to be done in UK archives to reveal the British side of the story of the War of Independence and the Truce period.[5]

Given that both sides in the War of Independence were very adept at propaganda, researchers need to be highly cautious when using primary sources, which often have different agendas behind them. For example, information about the Dunmanway killings was carried in the nationalist *Southern Star* and the loyalist *Cork &*

County Eagle & Munster Advertiser (*Cork & County Eagle* hereafter) and both have differing opinions on what actually happened.

Researchers should not allow personal prejudice to dismiss sources simply because they appear unbelievable. A good example of this was my own initial reaction to Kathleen Keyes McDonnell's *There is a Bridge at Bandon*. What appeared to be one of her more incredible claims concerned 'the sack of Castletown-Kinneigh' and initially I dismissed this as exaggerated. McDonnell claimed that Lord Bandon evicted tenants of the village and five townlands for electing a member of parliament (MP) named Fergus O'Connor instead of his own chosen candidate. These Roman Catholic tenants were replaced by Protestant tenants from Bandon.[6] Most researchers would be sceptical of this account, but when I checked the sources it became clear that the facts of the story are actually correct, even if the linkages between one event and the other are not necessarily so. Fergus O'Connor was elected for County Cork in 1832 in the first election in which Roman Catholics had a vote, ousting Lord Bandon's candidate. In 1837, when the middleman landlord of Castletown-Kinneigh died, his lease on the four townlands, along with 247 under-tenants, reverted to Lord Bandon. Without warning, troops appeared at the doors of the houses and evicted the tenants. They were replaced with twenty-four farms of between 50 and 200 acres.[7] Unusually, the story made the House of Lords, and Lord Bandon was criticised for his heartlessness by the Earl of Mulgrave.[8] Among the families cleared were the Murphys, Nyhans, Hurleys, Crowleys and Sullivans. All these became leading names in the IRA's West Cork Brigade.

It is now possible to access archival material online, including newspapers from across the globe (such as the extraordinary Trove Collection of digitised Australian newspapers for the entire period covered by this book), printed and manuscript census data, cabinet minutes and situation reports, House of Commons and Dáil debates, individual letters, church histories, 25-inch Ordnance Survey maps of Ireland showing individual houses, and previous research. This access represents a revolution in historical research; it liberates the nuts and bolts of history, allowing researchers wonderful freedom to follow a story in a way that was not possible even ten years ago. As a result much new information about incidents has been discovered. Of course, much information has not been digitised and still requires trips to the archives, but the task is now much easier than was once the case.

Generally, I have referenced only those sources which are easy to access for other scholars, are referenced in previous works, or are in my personal possession. I have a preference for primary sources, where possible including documentary, taped and filmed evidence, rather than second-hand oral testimony. However, where the only sources are secondary or oral history I have included these. I have also included information gathered from local historians; in every case, I have either seen the documentary evidence upon which their story is based or recorded an interview with the historian. If information is in anyway dubious or unsupported, I have mentioned this in the text, usually using the phrase 'it is suggested'. This does not mean that I am willing to go beyond the verifiable facts. I am satisfied, for example, that, based on circumstantial evidence, I know who one of the people who committed the Dunmanway killings is. However, as there is no direct proof, it would be entirely improper to publicly 'out' him.

For clarity, the structure of this book works from the national perspective to the local. I consider the broad history of the period as a background to the main focus of the book: the April 1922 massacre and its consequences. Up until July 1921 the Irish were fighting the British Empire, and if this is forgotten some of the action and inaction by the leading players is difficult to understand. It is very easy to see the Irish War of Independence and its aftermath as central to British concerns at the time, but the truth is that the British prime minister spent much of this time at the Versailles conference and subsequent meetings which only ended in the Treaty of Lausanne, signed in 1923. In the weeks before the Truce the British cabinet was working incessantly to stave off a general strike and resolve the British War Debt to the USA.[9] Ireland was only third on their agenda.

It may seem strange initially that I have chosen the somewhat obscure 'Curragh Incident' or 'Curragh Mutiny' in 1914 as the beginning of the story. However, the importance of this event for our story is that it demonstrated to all sides in the 'Irish Question' that the British government could be forced into concessions by a threat. Combined with gun-running at Larne and Howth, it changed the dynamic of the Irish question by bringing the physical force tradition back to the centre of politics.[10]

1

PRELUDE TO WAR: 1914–1919

I ask that, no matter what pleas are addressed to them, every man who can be proved to be guilty of murder shall suffer the death penalty. I ask that particularly because I have a case before me at this moment – it has come to me from two quarters in Dublin within the last two hours – where a person responsible for the direct shooting of a police constable in cold blood has been reprieved.

Lord Midleton, 10 May 1916[1]

It is the first rebellion that ever took place in Ireland where you had a majority on your side. It is the fruit of our life [*sic*] work. We have risked our lives a hundred times to bring about this result. We are held up to odium as traitors by those men who made this rebellion, and our lives have been in danger a hundred times during the last thirty years because we have endeavoured to reconcile the two things, and now you are washing out our whole life work in a sea of blood.

John Dillon, MP, 11 May 1916[2]

Irish society was on the verge of civil war in 1914. Nationalist Ireland was just about to accept its place within the British Empire in much the same way that the Scottish parliament operates today. However, unionists utterly opposed this Home Rule, fearing that a Dublin parliament would be neither culturally nor economically beneficial to them and would lead to the break-up of the United

Kingdom as national demands in Scotland and Wales would be impossible to resist. They were in open revolt and had created all the elements of a provisional government, but had not yet taken the final step and activated it. This direct opposition to the will of the imperial parliament created a British constitutional crisis as great as that of 1653, when the army had deposed the Rump parliament and established Oliver Cromwell as a dictator.

The chosen ground for this very British 'civil war' was Ulster and the issues were relatively simple.[3] Irish nationalism ultimately demanded that all of Ireland be allowed to govern itself free from the interference of Britain and, in particular, England. Home Rule was seen as a first step. The Ulster unionists were prepared to oppose this step by any means necessary, even through armed revolt. The problem for Britain was that what was essentially a local problem had much wider implications in a changing world. The outcome of these events could have serious repercussions for the rest of the empire. Could Ulster, that most loyal of all British possessions, be coerced out of the British Empire into a United Ireland, and, if it could, what were the long-term implications for the rest of the empire and its possessions? In parliament the Conservative and Unionist parties were fighting to keep the status quo, while Liberals, the Labour Party and the Irish Parliamentary Party combined to try to work out a way of providing for national demands within the empire. The eventual solution was the creation of an informal empire, which survives today in the form of the Commonwealth, but when nationalist Ireland was seeking its independence this piece of creative brilliance was still only a dream in the eye of its leading advocate, Lionel Curtis.[4]

A full understanding of how Ireland separated from Britain makes it necessary to begin at the first point of true crisis: the Curragh Incident of 14–23 March 1914, often referred to as the

Curragh Mutiny. In early March 1914 the Ulster unionists were facing a desperate political problem. The third Home Rule Bill had been introduced into the House of Commons in April 1912 and inevitably rejected by the House of Lords on 30 January 1913 by a vote of 326 to 69. As the Parliament Act had reduced the Lords veto to a two-year suspensory clause, this meant that Home Rule would become operable in Ireland no later than 1915. The unionist campaign against this would fail without guns, as otherwise they could do nothing to stop the British military from imposing the rule of law.

Early in March 1914 intelligence reports reached the British government that plans were being made to seize army arsenals in Ulster, which could allow Edward Carson and James Craig to set up a provisional government in Belfast. No state could allow this to happen. On 14 March British Prime Minister Herbert H. Asquith's Liberal government took preventative action and a cabinet subcommittee ordered regiments from the main army base at the Curragh Camp in Kildare to go north to protect military installations and to support the civil power in restoring order if need be.

However, as the upper echelons of the 1914 British Army contained more than its fair share of wealthy Ulster and Irish Protestant aristocrats, these men instinctively supported their province and their class rather than their King's government.[5] Many were descended from Cromwell's officers and had a much better understanding than their political opponents of how far they could push the government. On 20 March the officers in the main British Army camp at the Curragh offered their resignations rather than impose Home Rule on Ulster. Asquith, concerned that some of the Liberals who made up their majority might switch sides if the government forced the issue, immediately backed down.[6] On 23 March General

Gough, who commanded the Cavalry Brigade at the Curragh, was called to the War Office and was handed a clarification:

> His Majesty's Government must retain their right to use all the forces of the Crown in Ireland, or elsewhere, to maintain law and order and to support the civil power in the ordinary execution of its duty. But they have no mention whatever of taking advantage of this right to crush political opposition to the policy or principles of the Home Rule Bill.[7]

The last two paragraphs of the clarification, including these destructive lines, had been inserted by Colonel Seely, the Secretary of State for War, without the approval of the cabinet. Lord French, then Chief of the Imperial General Staff, initialled the document, and this meant in effect that the army guaranteed it would not coerce Ulster. Because the addition of these two paragraphs meant that the guarantee went beyond what the cabinet had agreed, which was that Ulster officers could reasonably expect not to have to coerce Ulster, and had been revealed by the resigned officers' friends in the House of Commons, the Secretary of State for War resigned on 25 March 1914.[8] When the cabinet then disowned the document, French resigned on 6 April.

While leader of the opposition Bonar Law and his Conservative Party criticised Asquith for his stupidity in attempting to coerce Ulster, James Ward, the Labour MP for Stoke-on-Trent, hammered home the real significance of the crisis for the British aristocracy. Their 'democracy' was not a democracy and would have to be changed. In a fiery response to the brainless upper-class goading of Earl Winterton, he said of General Gough and his officers:

> We workmen have had an illustration in the Debate today ... that the

21

moment we get the authority to impose our will on the country in the shape of law then the aristocracy are prepared to use force in the shape of the Army or anything else to maintain their position. The law and force are for us only; the privilege is for hon. Gentlemen who sit opposite and the class they represent in this House.[9]

The debate also brought into focus the political problem for the Liberal Party. Why should working people trust them to face down the aristocracy when it came to a fight between classes? After all, workers could guarantee their position by voting for their own Labour Party. (This is what happened between 1922 and 1931, and the great Liberal Party would not return to power in Britain until 2010.) It took junior Liberal Hamar Greenwood, a man who was to become inextricably linked with the 'Irish Problem', to dissect the treason at the heart of the 'Curragh Incident':

The Crown never acts personally, but acts through the Government of the day, and anyone who does not know an elementary proposition of this sort should not be in the House at all. If an officer is to fix terms upon which his allegiance depends, if he at any time fails to carry out the commands of the Executive Government, I cannot believe that such officer should be allowed to draw the pay of the nation.[10]

Because the Conservatives had used the aristocrats in the army to block the will of the British people, they exposed the democratic deficit at the heart of the British government.[11] The rise of the Labour Party in the House of Commons over the next ten years might have led to a desperate confrontation if many of the aristocracy had not been destroyed in the Great War, which broke out soon afterwards.

Two groups came out of the Curragh Mutiny and the political

crisis it provoked as victors, no matter how effectively Asquith tried to cover over the mess. The generals had proved their political mettle – a terrifying development in any democracy. The Ulster unionists had added to their ranks of supporters among the British decision-makers, had faced down the Liberals and the nationalists, and, although Home Rule remained on the Statute Books, it seemed clear that they would never be forced into a United Ireland. The appropriateness of the guarantee, and the reasoning behind it, overshadowed Irish history for many years. A month after the guarantee, on 25 April 1914, the Ulster Volunteer Force landed 37,000 guns and 3,000,000 rounds of ammunition at Larne,[12] which gave teeth to those who had declared in the Ulster Covenant:

> Being convinced in our consciences that Home Rule would be disastrous to the material well-being of Ulster as well as of the whole of Ireland, subversive of our civil and religious freedom, destructive of our citizenship, and perilous to the unity of the Empire, we, whose names are underwritten, men of Ulster, loyal subjects of His Gracious Majesty King George V., humbly relying on the God whom our fathers in days of stress and trial confidently trusted, do hereby pledge ourselves in solemn Covenant, throughout this our time of threatened calamity, to stand by one another in defending, for ourselves and our children our cherished position of equal citizenship in the United Kingdom and in using all means which may be found necessary to defeat the present conspiracy to set up a Home Rule Parliament in Ireland. And in the event of such a Parliament being forced upon us we further solemnly and mutually pledge ourselves to refuse to recognise its authority.[13]

The lack of proper ammunition for the Ulster rifles landed at Larne meant that they were not as useful as they might have been.[14]

On 24 June 1914 the nationalist Irish Volunteer Force (the Volunteers) landed 900 Mauser single-shot rifles and 29,000 rounds of ammunition at Howth in response to the Larne gun-running.[15] Although the Ulster unionists had guns but little useful ammunition and the Volunteers had ammunition but few guns, the gun had now returned with a vengeance to Irish politics. The chances of working through the problem of Home Rule around the negotiating table were dramatically reduced. Then, just at the point at which it looked as though this cold war could turn hot, a small incident in an obscure town in the Balkans changed the world forever.

During a visit by Archduke Franz Ferdinand of Austria and his wife, Sophie, to Sarajevo in June 1914, a bomb was thrown at their car, but it bounced off and failed to injure the royals. Bosnia had been annexed by Austria in 1908, and despite neighbour Serbia's agreeing to a small territorial concession to settle its demands for Bosnia to be independent, Serbian nationalists had remained incensed, leading to this attack on the Austrian royal family. The failed assassin, Čabrinović, swallowed a cyanide pill and jumped into the Miljacka River, but the pill only induced vomiting and as the Miljacka was just thirteen centimetres deep, police dragged him out. He was severely beaten by the crowd before being taken into custody. As the motorcade sped away, three other assassins, including Gavrilo Princip, missed their opportunity to kill Ferdinand.

The angry Archduke berated the unfortunate Mayor of Sarajevo who, unaware of the bomb attack, presented him with an address of welcome. Although neither royal was hurt, twenty other people had been injured in the attack. Following the reception at the City Hall it was decided to abandon the visit, but for some reason the motorcade retraced its earlier steps, giving Princip, who was still nearby, his opportunity. He fired two shots from a distance of about one-and-a-half metres at the car, which eyewitness accounts say had either slowed to take a sharp turn or was reversing after taking a wrong turn. The first bullet wounded the Archduke and the second hit the Duchess. Both died before they reached the hospital.[16]

The resulting row between the Austro-Hungarian Empire and Serbia, and their allies on both sides, led to the outbreak of war. Slightly more than one month after the assassination, the *Manchester Guardian* reported that the United Kingdom of Great Britain and Ireland had declared war on Germany at eleven o'clock the night before:

> Owing to the summary rejection by the German Government of the request made by his Majesty's Government for assurances that the neutrality of Belgium will be respected, his Majesty's Ambassador to Berlin has received his passports, and his Majesty's Government declared to the German Government that a state of war exists between Great Britain and Germany as from 11 p.m. on August 4, 1914.[17]

By the end of August all of Europe was at war. Most people believed that this war, like many others, was just a small one and would be over by Christmas. Instead the war would last four years and be a mincing machine that claimed millions of lives.[18] Soon after this declaration of war, Irish Home Rule and Welsh Church Disestablishment were enacted and then shelved on 17 September.[19] However, when the war broke out there was much enthusiasm for the fight. The Irish Parliamentary Party leader, John Redmond, urged the Volunteers to:

> Go on drilling and make yourself efficient for the Work, and then account yourselves as men, not only for Ireland itself, but wherever the

fighting line extends, in defence of right, of freedom, and religion in this war.[20]

Eighty thousand new Irish recruits signed up in the first six months of the Great War. They were formed into three divisions and first saw action in 1915. The 10th Irish Division will always be associated with Gallipoli, while the 36th Ulster and the 16th Irish Division served in France. Both took part in the Battle of the Somme, with the 36th going over the top on 1 July 1916, the first day of the battle. In twenty-four hours the division suffered 5,500 killed, wounded or missing out of a total of about 15,000.

The mostly nationalist 16th Irish Division was introduced to trench warfare in early 1916. Out of 10,845 men, this division suffered 1,496 deaths (13 per cent) in the relatively quiet Loos Sector between January and June 1916. As well as this, 345 were gassed at the Battle of Hulluch between 27 and 29 April. In late July the division moved to the Somme Valley to draw the Germans away from 'bleeding the French white' at the great French fortress of Verdun, but the cost in men was appalling.[21] Some 224 officers and 4,090 men of the 16th Division were killed or injured between 1 and 10 September (40 per cent), while capturing and holding the towns of Guillemont and Ginchy. Despite this huge attrition rate the division gained a reputation as first-class shock troops.

However, in the new nationalist Ireland there would be no triumphant welcome home for the troops. Listening to the reports of the Easter Rising in Dublin in 1916, Tom Kettle, a nationalist MP who would later be killed on the Somme, had correctly predicted: 'These men will go down in history as heroes and martyrs; and I will go down – if I go down at all – as a bloody British officer.'[22]

The Rising surprised the British administration in Dublin

Castle as much as everyone else in the country. However, as the Volunteers, the Irish Citizen Army and the Irish Republican Brotherhood (IRB) were confused by a series of orders and counter-orders issued by Eoin MacNeill and Pádraig Pearse about the start of the Rising, whatever slim hope it had of succeeding quickly slipped away. Although MacNeill had ordered the Volunteers not to turn out on Easter Sunday, it was decided by Pearse and his comrades to start the Rising on Easter Monday instead. The small turnout in Dublin and the lack of action in the rest of the country meant that there was no hope of a favourable outcome.

The British government suppressed the Rising, but not without loss – 132 dead with more than 350 injured. Sixty-four rebels died. In total, 450 people died, 2,614 were injured and 9 were missing, almost all in Dublin. Military casualties were 116 dead, 368 wounded and 9 missing, and the Irish and Dublin police forces had 16 killed and 29 wounded. A total of 254 civilians died; the high figures were largely because much of the fighting had occurred in or near densely populated areas.[23] Almost 3,500 were arrested; of these, sixteen leaders were executed at Kilmainham. Leader James Connolly had to be strapped to a chair for his execution as he was too badly injured to stand.

The Rising had little support from the Irish public, who blamed the rebels for the civilian deaths in the conflict. Dubliners jeered the prisoners as they were being transported to Frongoch internment camp in Wales. However, the executions shocked Ireland and public opinion swung behind the rebels. Asquith, who visited Dublin to see for himself what had happened, sacked the military governor Sir John Maxwell, which was taken as a signal that the response of executing the leaders had been too harsh.[24]

There is no doubt that the Easter Rising was an enormous shock to the British government and at any other time it is likely that its savage response might have been tempered by cooler heads. Within weeks the intelligence community in Ireland observed that 'subsequently a feeling of sympathy with the rebels was entertained by many who had previously condemned the movement'.[25] This included John Dillon, the future leader of the Irish Parliamentary Party, who on 11 May told the House of Commons that he was proud of 'these men'.[26]

Such was the confusion among British officials at their head-quarters in Dublin Castle that a small nationalist party, Sinn Féin, was blamed for the Rising and catapulted from obscurity to the vanguard of the revolution when public opinion swung behind the executed rebels. It was not necessarily in control of the Irish Volunteers, but in British minds the two were linked. Yet despite the Rising's iconic place in Irish history, it was not until the British government's attempt to extend conscription to Ireland in January 1918 that the young men of the countryside flocked to the banner of the Volunteers. Many of the BMH statements note a large rise in membership at this time, which fell away when the immediate crisis passed in June 1918.

After the end of the Great War many returning soldiers across the world felt disillusioned. The sense of pointless sacrifice was particularly strong in nationalist Ireland, and the emotional double blood-sacrifice of the Somme and the Easter Rising destroyed the political centre ground where compromise might have been achieved.[27] Irish nationalists gave up on the British parliament as it repeatedly failed to break the impasse. The parliamentary arithmetic in the British House of Commons meant that no deal that threatened the empire could be put on the table. Every line of the 1912 Home Rule Act was fought over by 'die-hard' Conservative members of the House who were not willing to modify the 1801 Act of Union in any way. In *The Unresolved Question*, Nicholas

Mansergh, writing of David Lloyd George, Liberal British Prime Minister from 1916 to 1922, observes: 'He desired, of that there can be little doubt, an Irish settlement, but not one at the price of his own and, what had become much the same thing, the Coalition's survival.'[28] As neither side was willing to compromise, war became inevitable.

As it happened many of the Curragh 'mutineers' had become leaders of the British Army both in the Great War and, following it, back in Ireland. Their unionism and their class consciousness had a bearing on their understanding and prosecution of both these wars. Evidence from the latter part of the Great War and late 1920 in Ireland suggests that after their victory at the Curragh this lethal military–conservative coalition was able to win the battles that mattered with the politicians who were nominally in charge of them. For example, in his memoirs Lloyd George clearly states that he felt intimidated by the military pressure into changing his mind and allowing the Battle of Passchendaele (in 1917), even though, when he had visited the Front just before the Battle of the Somme (in 1916), he was able to see for himself the folly of sending cavalry to face machine guns.[29] The Cabinet Secretary, Maurice Hankey, later said that Lloyd George was afraid the coalition government would have fallen, so he 'funked it' over Passchendaele.[30] The same happened in December 1920, when Lloyd George was persuaded by the generals, against his better judgement, to continue repression.

Many of these generals also moved effortlessly from the military to the political arena after the Great War, and the evidence shows that the military advice they were providing to the government over issues like Ireland was clouded by their personal politics.[31] It is hard not to conclude that they had a wanton disregard for human life, and this dynamic should be borne in mind when the Irish War of Independence is discussed.[32]

2

THE POLITICS OF WAR

The Irish War of Independence officially began in Soloheadbeg, County Tipperary, on 21 January 1919, the day that the first Dáil Éireann was convened.[1] This war was different to what the British were familiar with. They were used to fighting with people who openly showed themselves, but the Irish appeared, then disappeared back into the crowd, and the British forces failed to cope with this.[2] It was not until after the Jews had humiliated them in the creation of Israel in 1948 that they started using the lessons the Irish war had taught them.[3] Two years later in Malaysia they stopped the communist insurgency using their new tactics of isolating the insurgents by winning civilian 'hearts and minds',[4] and these methods have been constantly refined since then.[5] Yet, because such tactics are now not working for the US Army in Afghanistan, the merits of this British strategy are coming under renewed scrutiny.[6]

In 1919 the British Army was mainly a counter-insurgency force: it was too small to be anything else. The Army's handbook for dealing with insurrection had been published in 1896 by Colonel C. E. Callwell and reprinted three times by 1906.[7] It remained on the curriculum at Staff College in Sandhurst until 1923 and was the British officers' 'playbook' for how to prosecute the Irish war.[8] Its central theme was that in wars against 'savages' anything was acceptable, but when dealing with civilised opposition behaviour had to be toned down.[9] Where the Irish came on this scale is unclear. Later reports to the cabinet by General Nevil Macready in July 1921 and Major Whittaker in September 1922 shine some light onto the imperial mindset. For example, General Macready, writing to Ian MacPearson, had revealed a vehement hatred of the Irish as early as 1919: 'I loathe the country you are going to and its people with a depth deeper than the sea.'[10] This was an interesting perspective, considering the fact that Macready's grandfather was Irish and his wife was the sixth generation of her family living in Ireland. If the unconscious racism of these British military officers regarding subject races is typical, then it explains some of the behaviour tolerated on the British side during the war.[11]

The army did not have as free a hand in Ireland as it would have liked. When General Lord French arrived as viceroy in 1918, he wrote a memo to the cabinet explaining how he intended to enforce conscription, including a suggestion that aircraft should machine gun and bomb Sinn Féin ambush parties. The cabinet did not allow him to follow up on this suggestion.[12] Ireland's proximity to London had in previous centuries been a disadvantage, as the army could quickly move troops to quash rebellion. However, in a modern propaganda war, this close proximity actually worked to Ireland's advantage, as the 'enemy' could stand up in the House of Commons and use information not in the possession of the relevant minister as a propaganda weapon. The stunning performance of a tiny opposition of 42 Labour, 5 Irish Nationalists and 36 Asquith Liberals in the House of Commons – which brought an enormous government coalition of 435 to account – was an essential, and often overlooked, part of the war. Ministers were often forced to reply to awkward questions about Irish issues without full knowledge of the facts, and made to look foolish when the real sequence of events emerged.

Much of the opposition's information was supplied by war correspondents, many of whom went native and helped change perceptions of the struggle, both in Britain and around the world. Maurice Walsh's well-sourced analysis of the British failure to control the news from Ireland during the war explains that it was only long after the British had lost the propaganda battle that they thought of putting measures in place to rein in the correspondents.[13] Most of the war journalists could get the mail train from London at 11 a.m. and be reporting from Dublin by 8.30 that evening. More importantly, photojournalists – whose role was just coming to prominence – became central to the coverage. For instance, five days after the Kilmichael ambush of 28 November 1920, the *Daily Sketch* carried photographs of a burned army truck from the ambush scene. The photograph of the nearby farmhouse burned out as a reprisal, which appeared on the same page, would have generated as much sympathy.[14] While the British *Rules of Engagement* allowed houses to be destroyed if British forces were attacked from them, the stark evidence of what this meant to ordinary people was not an image they would have wanted to appear publicly.[15] Despite the fact that this tactic of burning property had been counter-productive in the Boer War and savagely condemned by English MPs for its stupidity and barbarity, the British forces used it again in Ireland, with equally disastrous results, as it strengthened support for the rebels and reduced support for the British.

When the House of Commons met two days after the burning of Cork, Sir Hamar Greenwood was questioned in minute detail about the events of that night and his efforts to blame them on the IRA were laughed and jeered out of the chamber.[16] The British Labour Party report from its members who were in Ireland at the time of the fire put the blame firmly on the Auxiliaries. When the official report by General Strickland, Officer Commanding the 6th Division of the British Army in Cork and Military Governor of Munster from December 1920, was suppressed by the government in February 1921, there could be no further doubt as to who the guilty parties were.[17] The speed at which the details of the burning of Cork emerged is in contrast to what happened at Amritsar in the Punjab on 13 April 1919, when troops under the command of General Dyer opened fire on an unarmed crowd of men, women and children, killing at least 349 and injuring more than 4,000. The first mention in the House of Commons was a two-line answer to a parliamentary question on 28 May.[18] But it took a year for the full facts to come out.

For the Irish combatants there was absolutely no doubt about what was allowed and, more importantly, why many civilians were targeted. On 13 March 1920 New Zealand's *Auckland Star* ran a report from its London correspondent about a series of warning notices that had been posted all over County Cork. Two examples will serve to show what was expected of civilians:

Civilians, who give information to the police or soldiery, especially such information as is of a serious character, if convicted, will be executed, i.e., shot or hanged (Catholic Church at Mitchelstown, County Cork).

On and after August 24, 1919, every person in the pay of England (magistrates, jurors, etc.), who help England to rule this country, or who assist in anyway the upholders of the Foreign Government of this North-East Riding of Cork, will be deemed to have forfeited his life ... (Knocklong, Co. Tipperary).[19]

No exceptions were made. Anyone could become a target, and the IRA was merciless in dealing with informers. Even to be seen talking to, or drinking with, the RIC was punishable by deportation or death, despite the fact that in some cases this was unjust. The logic was simple: a colonial power can govern only with the assistance of the colonised. Once those who assisted the colonial power could be compelled to stop, then, without complete repression, the coloniser would be compelled to leave.

When targeting government officials, the IRA made a distinction between ordinary civil servants and political civil servants. Police, revenue and legal officials like sergeants-at-arms were seen as legitimate targets. However, according to the statement of Richard Walsh, who was on an IRA committee to decide how to attack the British state during 1919 and 1920, the Land Commission, the Department of Education and the Post Office were off limits, because these departments did things that benefitted and provided funds to the general public including IRA supporters.[20] As a result of this targeting, and especially the killing of Alan Bell, who had been investigating the whereabouts of Sinn Féin funds, many of the higher civil servants and the senior police moved their families into Dublin Castle, which became so crowded that wives were soon not allowed inside.[21]

From surprisingly early in the conflict, there were moves made on both sides to see if it could be ended through peaceful means. As early as 23 July 1920, a conference with the officers of the Irish government held at Downing Street had worked out that the absolute minimum the Irish would accept was what was eventually offered a year later – Dominion Status with fiscal autonomy and the permanent exclusion of that part of Ulster where the majority of the inhabitants wished to remain part of the United Kingdom. The people arguing most strongly for this settlement were the Irish, including W. E. Wylie, law adviser to Dublin Castle, and Sir James Craig, who provided evidence of loyalists in the south and west going over to the Sinn Féin side because it was running the country fairly.[22] As was the case with any such meeting, views at this 23 July meeting ranged from the wildly pessimistic (Sir John Anderson's 'There would be a massacre of Protestants in the South and West'), to the optimistic (Major General Hugh Tudor's 'Given the proper support, it would be possible to crush the present campaign of outrage').[23]

Initial peace moves began three weeks before 'Bloody Sunday' (21 November 1920), when the IRA killed suspected British agents in Dublin and the British fired into the crowd at a football match in Dublin's Croke Park sports ground, killing fourteen people including the Tipperary player Michael Hogan, after whom the main stand in the modern stadium is named.[24] While the negotiations were continuing, Lloyd George and Michael Collins were publicly talking up the war, proving yet again that great politicians may never lie but they certainly can omit a large amount of the truth.[25] In a book published posthumously in 1923, Collins would claim:

Seven months before England granted the Truce of July, 1921, she wanted very much to withdraw the Black and Tans from Ireland and end the murderous war which she had begun to realise could never be won. A truce would have been obtained after the burning of Cork by the forces of the Crown in December, 1920, had our leaders acted with discretion ... although terms of truce had been virtually agreed upon, the English statesmen abruptly terminated the negotiations when they discovered what they took to be signs of weakness in our councils. They conditioned the truce, then, on surrender of our arms; and the struggle went on.[26]

There is a large amount of evidence to support this claim. Galway

Michael Collins

David Lloyd George

businessman and IRB member Patrick Moylett left a detailed account of his dealings in London, on behalf of Sinn Féin founder Arthur Griffith.[27] Equally, there are two documents in the Bonar Law and the Lloyd George papers from British civil servant C. J. Phillips which record his meetings in Downing Street with Moylett.[28] Moylett claimed that Lloyd George took advantage of a telegram from Father Michael O'Flanagan, Vice-President of Sinn Féin, claiming to represent the party, and a motion from Galway County Council seeking a truce, to publish an impossible demand that arms be surrendered as a condition.[29] He also said that a letter from Hamar Greenwood threatening his resignation if this demand was not included in any truce also persuaded the Prime Minister to tough it out for a little while longer. The Prime Minister told Greenwood on 1 December that the cabinet had agreed to his proposals of the night before (30 November), but the demand for the surrender of arms first appeared in public on 5 December.

Lloyd George's statement to the House of Commons a week later is candid about the working out of these peace negotiations. When he spotted an apparent weakness on the Irish side he gambled that military advice of imminent victory was correct and drew back from a domestically difficult deal. Even though he had worked out what needed to be done, he decided to 'haggle over the price'.[30] Two days later, with the pictures of a smouldering Cork burned by a rampaging mob of out-of-control Auxiliaries and British soldiers splashed all over the newspapers, he must have felt very foolish indeed.

Despite these negotiations, in late 1920 the British military in Ireland were so convinced that they were winning that they had delayed the traditional winter concentration of their troops in large central barracks from the start of October to 1 December. However, thirty-three soldiers, out of a total of 162 killed in the war, were then killed in these months, and this excludes the much larger RIC and Auxiliary casualties. This upsurge in the number of deaths in winter 1920 was one of the reasons that the British Military High Command in London ignored their generals in Ireland to recommend a truce as the most sensible option.

By late 1920 the analysis of the British Military High Command was that while the British could win the current phase of the rebellion, it could break out again at any time. They would have to station far too many troops in Ireland relative to its value to the empire.[31] Strategically, how much of a threat was a partitioned and independent Ireland actually going to be in an era of air power? Chief of the Imperial General Staff Sir Henry Wilson had a different view, but he was unionist to the core and had been a leading member of the Curragh Mutiny. However, ultimately a choice had to be made in response to the sustained challenge presented by Sinn Féin and the IRA: complete repression or freedom.

Lloyd George had a far better understanding of what was at issue for the British than most. When members of the cabinet wished to amend the Government of Ireland Act in October 1920 to give the

Irish power over Customs & Excise, he dismissed this by pointing out that to concede taxes meant that they would have nothing left to negotiate with. Taxes meant independence.[32] The alternative to conceding 'independence' was military repression, and if force failed he would have to concede independence in all but name rather than threaten Britain's other possessions. This was real politics.

The subtlety of the war in its later stages can be seen from an attempt by General Strickland, the British commander in Munster, to secure his northern flank by proposing a local armistice for County Kerry in February 1921. This would allow him to turn the hammer fully on West Cork. As with any such offer the intelligence officer in Kerry decided to pursue it and asked Collins in Dublin for instructions before he took the offer to Paddy Cahill, Officer Commanding the Kerry Brigade. Collins replied:

> Armistice – This sort of thing is going on a good deal. It would be very easy for General Strickland to get rid of his troubles by giving such a guarantee, after which the Black and Tans would be quite free to murder; and as for flooding the place with troops, it can be conveyed to General Strickland that we know he can do no such thing, for he is continually begging for more men from his own Headquarters. The General seems to be a good propagandist, and a good bluffer. It might also be suggested to him that if they cannot restrain the Black and Tans, they can remove them.[33]

It is clear from this exchange that neither Strickland nor Collins were fools and that they had both become very good at their jobs by this stage.

By the start of 1921 the British had improved their military position by structural changes in their intelligence network. Pieces of information which had been going to three separate groups of people in Dublin were now concentrated in the hands of the local intelligence officer, who could react more quickly to relevant facts.[34] Between February and May 1921 one pro-establishment paper, *The Irish Times*, reported no less than five major finds of republican documents. A *Cork & County Eagle* report of 5 March gloated that the proceedings of an IRA meeting involving the Cork, Tipperary, Kilkenny and East Limerick Brigades, held on 6 January 1921, had been captured; the reporter believed that this showed the IRA was in disarray and on the point of defeat in Cork.

This optimism seemed to extend to the British government. In April 1921 when the Lord Chancellor, Lord Birkenhead, met a 'peacenik' delegation, including the Archbishop of Canterbury, to work out a way forward, he made it clear that the cabinet believed that the British were winning the war.[35]

However, the IRA was just as effective as its opponents in the intelligence war. Perhaps one of the most extraordinary documents in the BMH collection is the witness statement of East Limerick IRA intelligence officer Lieutenant Colonel John MacCarthy, which includes a copy of the British *Military Summary for May 17th 1921* for Munster.[36] The capture of this report meant that everything the British knew about IRA activity for the early weeks of 1921 became known to the IRA. Three good examples of what the report contains show how much accurate information was available to the British, as the details are confirmed by many BMH witness statements, but they also reveal an element of wishful thinking:[37]

> Rebel Flying Columns are suffering heavily from scabies. In order to cure this disease men are returning to their homes and lying up there for a week or two. It is essential that these men be kept on the move by frequent visits to their houses [p. 4].

A big drive was carried out by the Crown Forces in the Kilmacthomas [County Waterford] area on the 6th inst. The drive failed to round up the I.R.A. unit which has been operating in that area, yet there is no doubt that will have a good effect in a part of the country where Crown Forces are seldom seen. One old loyalist farmer made remarks to this officer and said that such a parade of troops would make the hooligans going round the country look very small [p. 5].

The Brigade Mobile Column returned on Thursday 12th, May after a tour of a part of the Brigade area. No armed body of rebels was encountered but the local company at Aherla was rounded up almost to a man. Frank Hurley Commandant No. 1 battalion (West) Cork Brigade and a prominent leader of the Flying Column was shot. It is hoped to obtain information as to whether the Brigade Column made any difference to rebel plans for attacks on Barracks, and caused them to be postponed. [p. 6].

The British report also shows the prevalence of British informers within the rural population.

Other documents in MacCarthy's statement include the minutes of the January divisional meeting, which can be cross-checked with the *Cork & County Eagle* report mentioned earlier, and various other intelligence reports from East Limerick. Most noticeable in these documents is the amount of detailed information both sides had gathered about each other. All these reports show that the war was a far more open and fluid affair than is generally suggested. The boundary line between 'them' and 'us' appears to have been impossible to draw.

The British had also improved their military position by the middle of 1921. The first deployment of the Auxiliaries in Ireland as an aggressive raiding force in September 1920 had increased the intensity of the war[38] and forced it to a conclusion, though not in the way intended. In 1921 the combination of the long summer days and the introduction of large, highly mobile British Army flying columns also meant that it was harder for the IRA flying columns to gather together, or to plan ambushes, without being attacked. The ground was dry from a drought, and this meant that the British could take to the fields and drive around the IRA's favourite defensive tactic of trenched roads.[39] Potential ambushes had less chance of success as the area could be quickly flooded with British troops and (to a much lesser extent) aeroplanes, once the IRA was detected. In some cases the British could almost sneak up on the IRA, as happened at Crossbarry on 19 March 1921, one of the largest engagements of the War of Independence;[40] on this occasion, however, the West Cork IRA flying column escaped the attempt by, according to Tom Barry, more than 1,300 British troops to encircle it at this rural crossroads between Cork and Bandon.[41] The troops had converged from their main barracks at Cork, Ballincollig, Bandon and Kinsale during the night and nearly caught the column off guard. William Desmond, who was captured in the first engagement, noticed that the troops 'had bags or sacking twisted around their feet to deaden the sound'.[42] The ferocity of that fight and the discipline and order of the escape from a very tight trap are credited on the Irish side as being one of the main catalysts for the Truce on the British side.

If the British Army had only had Ireland to deal with, it could easily have contained the Irish insurgents although it could not actually defeat them. If insurgents retain sufficient popular support, it is possible to keep low-level wars going for generations: for example, the Vietnamese fought a thirty-year war of liberation against the French and the Americans (between 1943 and 1973), and the Algerians defeated the French between 1954 and 1961. In both cases the weaker side could not necessarily win, but was impossible to defeat. The events of the later Irish Civil War during 1922 and 1923 proved this in the negative: once the anti-Treaty side lost popular support, it would lose that war.

Senior members of the British military understood just how difficult and expensive continuing the war would be. In his statement to the BMH, Captain Edward Gerrard, who was aide-de-camp to Sir Hugh Jeudwine (Officer Commanding the 5th Brigade in Ireland), described the situation from the British perspective in June 1921:

> I remember Sir Hugh Jeudwine saying that the estimate for the whole of Ireland was 150,000 men in 1921. Himself and Strickland required two Divisions each. That was 150,000 men between them. They wanted to divide the whole country into areas with barbed wire.
>
> I rode through Carlow and Kilkenny with the Cavalry Brigade, 10th Hussars, and 12th Lancers, in June and July, 1921. I was actually in Carlow when the Armistice came. Every field we got into was made into enclosures by trees cut down. I remember saying to the Major, 'if it is like this within twenty miles of the Curragh, what is it going to be like in Cork?' The Hussars could not see anyone. There was no one to attack. It was all so elusive.[43]

By July 1921 both sides seemed to realise that if the IRA survived until the long nights of winter the tide of war would once again swing back in its favour. Even the main proponents of a military solution in late 1920 had changed their mind by this time and were absolutely insistent that the war needed to be won by September 1921 at the latest. Macready told the cabinet that if the war was not won by the end of the summer 'steps must be taken to relieve practically the whole of the troops together with the great majority of their commanders and their staffs. I am quite aware that the troops do not exist to do this …'.[44] For the British, Lloyd

George's dilemma of October 1920 remained: meet with Sinn Féin and agree a settlement along the lines suggested by W. E. Wylie of Dominion Home Rule with fiscal independence in all but name, or take the advice of General Tudor that the war could be won by the Auxiliaries and Black and Tans before the end of summer 1921.[45] In October Lloyd George had chosen to follow military advice; now he chose the political solution.

While there is no doubt that the British were winning at the time of the Truce, their success was dependent on too many contingencies to suggest that this situation was guaranteed or likely to continue. After all, the first shower of rain would begin to swing the advantage back to the IRA, and Macready's self-imposed deadline of September was less than eight weeks away.

Despite this Macready was stung by the suddenness of the Truce. On 16 July he was trenchantly expressing the view that, while the IRA was talking up its 'victory', the officers on the British side were convinced that they had gained the upper hand in the struggle and were annoyed with IRA propaganda:

> I am quite clear in my own mind that the present negotiations have only been made possible by the fact that the unceasing efforts of troops and police together with the arrival of reinforcing units from England have brought home to the Sinn Féin leaders the advisability of coming to some terms before the rebellion is openly and obviously crushed … It is, therefore, most unfortunate that the desire to create an atmosphere has been carried so far as to give the appearance that Sinn Féin is being treated as an honourable foe who has got slightly the better of the Crown Forces in the field.[46]

Macready and his officers seemed lost in the fog of war by this stage.

In the end, geopolitics determined strategy on the British side. The army was overstretched after the Great War, with the need to deploy forces in Germany, Austria, Russia, India, Africa, Palestine, Mesopotamia, Persia and even Scotland at the same time as Ireland. Such were the difficulties in April 1921 that a proposal was agreed at cabinet to create a paid volunteer defence force of 30,000 civilians to cope with the threatened general strike planned in England and Wales for 15 April. The army could send only three companies to control the South Wales coal pits, which the Secretary of State for War admitted would be of no use in the 'valleys', so they were deployed in Cardiff instead.[47] The British cabinet was meeting daily to deal with the miners' strike and was in complete disarray. It was even agreed that four of Macready's fifty-one infantry battalions would be withdrawn from Ireland to shore up the situation.[48] Both Lord French and Macready were vehemently opposed to this, while Sir Henry Wilson once again gave up on the 'frocks' – his pet name for politicians.[49] Yet the 'frocks' had little other choice: they had bitten off more than they could chew by taking on the League of Nations mandate in the Middle East just as the vicious post-war recession was gathering pace.

The British naval establishment was also opposed to any settlement that did not allow it free access to Irish ports during times of war. However, as long as Britain could retain its strategic naval bases at Queenstown (Cobh), Berehaven and Lough Swilly the actual island of Ireland was of little value. If these ports could be retained and free wartime access allowed, then a negotiated settlement was the logical outcome.[50] All this possibly explains both the initial anaemic response to the Irish insurrection and why the British government went from an intention to escalate the war in early 1921 to agreeing a truce by July of that year.[51]

As the war came to a close it was easy to see how small a conflict it actually was. This is not to denigrate any of those killed or injured, but on the first day of the Somme British deaths alone were 19,000, or 27 per minute, between 6 a.m. and 7.30 p.m., when the day's action ceased.

Table 1 gives the official British tally in the War of Independence to the end of May 1921.[52]

TABLE 1: OFFICIAL BRITISH TALLY OF RECORDED INCIDENTS IN THE IRISH WAR OF INDEPENDENCE TO 21 MAY 1921

Incidents from 1 Jan. 1919 to 21 May 1921 (32 counties)	Total to 21 May 1921
Police killed	341
Police injured	563
Army killed	117
Army injured	259
Courthouses destroyed	76
Vacated police barracks destroyed	516
Occupied police barracks destroyed	25
Occupied police barracks damaged	193
Raids on mails	1863
Raids on coastguard stations	62
Raids for arms	3162
Raids on rates & petty sessions clerks	112
Civilians killed	138
Civilians wounded	166
Kidnappings	170
Killed in Ulster riots, June–September 1920	82

Between 14 June and 7 July 1921 seventeen more infantry battalions were sent to Ireland. This represented another 22,000 men and was a contributory factor to the IRA's burning of 'big houses' to

prevent their use as barracks. All other large accommodations – workhouses and the like – were already occupied.[53] Five days later the Truce was agreed.

Speaking from within the prism of the West Cork Brigade, Charlie O'Donoghue had a different perspective from the British as to why the war ended:

> A special check, after the Truce, revealed that only 37 rounds of .303 rifle ammunition were left on that date. The strength of the 1st Battalion at that time was 1,023 officers and men. Morale, training and organisation were never better.
>
> Were it not for the ammunition position, the fight, in my opinion, could go on indefinitely. No arms were being lost to the enemy and arrests were being offset by young Volunteers coming in. The battalion organisation had stood up to everything the British had put up. The fight at Crossbarry seemed to have been the turning point.[54]

West Cork Brigade quartermaster Tadg O'Sullivan put the entire brigade strength at 5,750 at the time of the Truce. Of course, not all of these were on active service, but the British had a maximum of 3,000 troops in the brigade area, so the Irish had a tactical advantage, at least on paper. They had one other advantage: even if the British had captured all of them, what could they have done with them? As they could not have been held indefinitely, they would have had to be freed to start again, and this was only one brigade.[55]

In his analysis of the war, J. T. Broom observes: 'Militarily far stronger than the IRA could ever hope to be, the British government, in the end, sought to secure only what was truly vital to British interests: domestic tranquillity within Britain itself, the independence of the unionists, and the semblance of imperial unity.'[56]

At the imperial conference in June 1921, this strategic analysis was reinforced by the dominions, led by Jan Smuts of South Africa. Smuts had an excellent understanding of the Irish position as he had received a letter from Roger Casement's brother Tom at Madeira while en route to the conference at the end of May 1921.[57] As the two were personal friends from fighting in the Great War, the documents were not 'thrown overboard' as Tom feared they might have been.[58] According to both George Berkley and P. J. Little, contact was made by Colonel Moore (once Inspector General of the National Volunteers) and others with the South African government to ensure that Smuts brought a message seeking a truce without preconditions from Éamon de Valera.[59]

As early as 30 September 1920, Smuts had telegraphed the British cabinet offering to mediate a truce.[60] And Smuts would write much of the conciliatory speech King George V made at the opening of the new Northern Irish parliament at Belfast City Hall on 22 June 1921. This speech, combined with adverse public opinion at home, even from government supporters and Liberal grandees like Asquith, pushed the cause of truce over escalation – the Truce would begin three weeks later at 12 noon on 11 July.[61] Equally, the replacement of Bonar Law, 'an Ulsterman by descent & in spirit',[62] by Austen Chamberlain in late March as leader of the Conservative Party and Lord Privy Seal was crucial to the outcome of the War of Independence. Chamberlain played a much overlooked and central role in dismissing the outrage of Craig, soothing the King's panicked private secretary and tempering Smuts' enthusiasm during the final drafting of the speech.[63] Once the King had nudged things along in June 1921, Smuts attended the cabinet to 'discuss' the King's suggestion and travelled to Ireland to ensure that Lloyd George's offer of talks was explained and accepted. His aim was to create a free association of independent states instead of an empire, and he believed that if Ireland joined the club it would only help his cause and that of the dominions other than South Africa.[64] His calculations proved correct, as the Irish worked tirelessly with the other dominions in their first imperial conference to change the form of the British Empire into the British Commonwealth of Nations.[65]

While imperial unionist diehards, including Sir Henry Wilson, described the Treaty settlement of December 1921 as 'a shameful and cowardly surrender to the pistol', Lloyd George told the cabinet, with no hint of irony, 'that the freedom of Ireland increases the strength of the Empire'. Lord Curzon went so far as to claim it was 'an astonishing victory'.[66] But the obvious question needs to be asked. If the settlement was such a resounding success, what then was the purpose of the prolonged war? Was it over the concept of a republic? Apparently it was, as Lloyd George told the cabinet on 6 December:

> The attention of the Cabinet was drawn to criticism which might be expected on the lines that the settlement now effected might equally have been reached some time ago. It was generally agreed, however, that a year ago Sinn Féin would not have entertained or even agreed, to discuss proposals similar to those which the Irish Representatives had now signed, and that the change in the attitude of Sinn Féin was mainly attributable to the rough treatment to which the Irish extremists had been subjected during the last twelve months.[67]

As British imperial interests were best served by peace with partition in Ireland, that is what the British conceded. According to Lloyd George's rewriting of history, the latter part of the war was nothing more than a softening-up exercise and in the early months of 1921 the British had not actually persuaded themselves they were going to win. As a piece of historical bunkum this is hard to beat, but it was the line to be spun out in public. After they lost the propaganda war, the politicians – like politicians everywhere – compromised, declared victory on all sides and moved on.

The frank comments of Michael Collins about how the end of the war came about, published after his death in 1923, agree with the British political analysis contained in the cabinet papers. Ever the politician, he quoted anti-Treaty Robert Barton's admission in *The Republic of Ireland* of 21 February 1922 that:

> … it had become plain that it was physically impossible to secure Ireland's ideal of a completely isolated Republic otherwise than by driving the overwhelmingly superior British forces out of the country.

Collins used this to support his claim:

> What it was never possible to make the more extreme of our conferees appreciate was that we had not beaten AND NEVER COULD HOPE TO BEAT THE BRITISH MILITARY FORCES. We had thus far prevented them from conquering us, but that was the sum of our achievement.[68]

Effectively Collins was pointing out the inconsistency in Barton's logic. Barton had willingly signed the Treaty, but later repudiated it, claiming that he had been forced by a threat of 'immediate and terrible war' to sign. This was particularly robust politics on Collins' part, because he destroys Barton's credibility by using his own words against him.

Collins also explained the British imperatives for a settlement, and his view is supported by the subsequent evidence from all the sources. He summed it up:

The important factors in the situation were known to all of us. We knew the Dominion Premiers were in England [for the imperial conference] fresh from their people. They were able to express the views of their people. The Washington Conference was looming ahead.[69]

Lloyd George's Cabinet had its economic difficulties. England's relationships with foreign countries were growing increasingly unhappy. Recovery of the good opinion of the world had become indispensable.[70]

Overall, one of the strangest things about the Irish War of Independence is that few modern historians actually examine it as a war. The traditional Irish history is the simplistic one of the gallant men of the 'Old Brigade' driving the British before them out of Ireland by force of arms alone. The quotation above shows that Collins knew that he had soldiers and no ammunition by July 1921 (or should have done if he was reading the reports from West Cork). The various attempts to land ammunition for the weapons had so far not come to fruition, and the ongoing manufacture of home-made rifle shells was never going to be sufficient to take the war outside a campaign of ambush and assassination. While the IRA would always hurt the British forces, it could do no more. The Irish could not be defeated, but neither could they win; there was therefore no benefit to continuing the war. Equally, some historians have recently tended to downplay the capacity of the IRA to maintain the war. In the face of the flood of primary evidence from both sides, including the witness statements and documents in the British archives, this argument cannot be sustained either.[71] Even if the IRA ran out of ammunition for a time, all it needed was one large shipment to restart operations. This was the essence of the problem for the British.

There were many elements to the war, and the Irish did enough to bring about a settlement, no matter how unsatisfactory it was. In the end this is all they had to do.[72] It was the decisive phase in the long struggle of the disenfranchised Irish to regain parity with the English, who had conquered and subdued the country finally in 1651. Irish intellectuals at the heart of the struggle, like Terence MacSwiney, deduced that the only way to defeat British rule was to peel back its layers until all that was left was the military.[73] To retain Ireland the British would have to use the military, and the closer the IRA got to an inevitable confrontation with the British military, the more intense the war became. The RIC did not put up a serious fight in defence of the status quo and the people were encouraged to turn away from the British courts system. The taxation system also broke down, much to everyone's delight, and was symbolically cremated with the burning of the local tax offices in April 1920. The collection of the myriad of statistics, requiring the almost daily involvement of the British state with the people – from the number of potatoes planted in each parish to the number of people emigrating from the ports – also ceased, as this was part of the RIC's job. By the middle of 1920 the British had become practically irrelevant, and the Irish revolution was over unless the British made a stand. Logically, they had no choice if they wished to keep their empire. However, because they lost control (or allowed themselves to lose control) of the forces they had sent to quell the Irish, they lost the propaganda war, and it was this that led to the Treaty.

AFTER THE WAR: ENDINGS AND BEGINNINGS

There are difficulties in discussing the year between the Truce and the accepted starting date for the Irish Civil War – the day of the attack by pro-Treaty Free State forces on the anti-Treaty garrison that had occupied the Four Courts in the centre of Dublin.

One aspect of this is Northern Ireland, which had been set on its own course before the Truce with the Government of Ireland Act 1920, but it was not until later that the separation between north and south became formal. There was never any doubt as to the outcome, and Sir James Craig had made it clear that this was going to be the case in July 1922.[74]

One of the biggest difficulties is the problem of deciding when the Truce actually ends and the Civil War starts.[75] From April 1922 the IRA officers had split and were engaged in a 'hot' war long before the shelling of the Four Courts.[76] Did the Civil War start when a volunteer decided to take up arms against the Free State, when the firing started, or was it necessary to wait until historians 'blew the whistle' for the official off in June 1922?[77] General Adamson of the Free State Army was shot in Athlone by republican forces on 24 April 1922, but because negotiations to stave off civil war were still going on in Dublin, this shooting is seen as an unfortunate incident and not as the opening engagement of the Civil War. According to Lady Augusta Gregory, the Civil War in Gort was effectively over by the middle of May 1922, having been won by Seán MacEoin in a preemptive strike on Galway.[78] Speaking for the army, Seán O'Hegarty warned Dáil Éireann on 1 May that what was needed was a truce, yet the Civil War started in June, didn't it?[79]

Even Winston Churchill, the highly experienced and notoriously volatile Secretary of State for the Colonies, couldn't seem to understand the fundamental change he had made by signing the Treaty in December 1921.[80] Despite having met with the envoys plenipotentiary of the elected government of the Irish Republic on 11 October 1921, Churchill was still issuing a diktat to the Irish in the House of Commons ten months after the War of Independence had ended in July. On 12 April 1922 he told the House:

Whatever happens in Ireland, however many years of misfortune there may be in Ireland, whatever trouble; the Treaty defines what we think should be the relations between the two countries, and we are prepared, and will be prepared, to hand over to any responsible body of Irishmen capable of governing the country the full powers which the Treaty confers. Further than that, in no circumstances will we go, and if a republic is set up, that is a form of government in Ireland which the British Empire can in no circumstances whatever tolerate or agree to.[81]

While he was technically correct, the only way he could enforce his views was by an extremely difficult re-conquest. Yet, despite the slaughter of the previous six years, and with the situation in Dublin on a knife-edge, the British minister with direct responsibility for Ireland failed to temper his language sufficiently to give the pro-Treaty Provisional Government some breathing space.[82] What Churchill was telling the Commons was that Irish independence was in the gift of the British parliament and could be taken away again. Churchill was claiming 'the right to fix the boundary of a nation ... Thus far shalt thou go and no further.'[83]

Although this may have gone down well with the House of Commons, the message was not lost on the Irish. Even the *Southern Star*, a newspaper that had a relentlessly local focus, reported the speech on 15 April.[84] Central to the Irish agreeing to the Treaty negotiations had been the principle that the Treaty would be an agreement between two equal nations. At the time of Churchill's speech, Collins was trying to sell the Treaty on the basis of it being a stepping stone to real freedom. In this speech, Churchill was repudiating this. These comments, intentional or otherwise, had put Ireland back in its little box, and plans were being made in London for a re-invasion if necessary.[85] Is it any wonder that on 14

April 1922 republican forces, led by Rory O'Connor, in opposition to the Treaty, occupied the Four Courts?[86]

The main compromise imposed by the Treaty that led to the point of civil war in Ireland was the imposition of an oath to be faithful (not loyal) to the king of England.[87] The settlement also meant that the ancient kingdom of Ireland was no longer united, and nationalists had not succeeded in gaining their republic. Many nationalists were caught on the wrong side of the border with Northern Ireland, and there was a great shame among members of the IRA that they had failed to defeat partition. Southern unionists had equally been betrayed and were bitter that their political allies had cut them off, although some made the best of the situation. One letter in the Siobhán Langford papers points to the delicacy of the situation and the uncertainty of the future. It was written by Rev. George Sydney Baker to the IRA on 27 January 1922 seeking the return of a gun 'requisitioned' in 1920. His form of address is a significant concession to the new authorities, even if he cannot quite bring himself to acknowledge their legitimacy:

> A Cara,
>
> I wish to make application for the return of a shot-gun … I have learned that guns and other property have been restored in several cases to their owners and feel sure that under the new regime in Ireland it is desired that all should be treated equally.
>
> Mise A Cara
>
> G. S. Baker
>
> Kilshannig Rectory.[88]

While Rev. Baker was willing to make his accommodation with the new reality, the War of Independence and its resolution had created great bitterness and fear on all sides. There was also great anger among the young men of the IRA – who had sacrificed lives, futures, friends and families – when they looked at what they had actually achieved. This anger had to find its way to the surface. Did it contribute to the Dunmanway killings? To understand fully the origins and context of the massacre, it is now necessary to examine how the war was fought in West Cork.

3

WEST CORK'S WAR

While the main theatre for operations during the War of Independence was in Dublin, the West Cork IRA Brigade took part in two of the most famous and significant actions of that conflict. The first was at Kilmichael, when an IRA flying column ambushed two lorry loads of 'invincible' Auxiliary police on 28 November 1920, killing sixteen, with three casualties on the IRA side.[1] This forced Lloyd George to recognise that the rebels had moved from assassinations to full-scale military operations, and he proclaimed martial law in the south on 10 December. Truce contacts were recommenced within days of Kilmichael. The second action was the escape of 100 members of the flying column from encirclement by 1,300 British troops at Crossbarry.

An understanding of how the War of Independence was fought in West Cork is crucial in explaining what happened at Ballygroman and Dunmanway in April 1922. The people most likely involved in the killings were also involved in the War of Independence, and the conduct of the war in the Bandon Valley had a major bearing on why the killings were carried out.

Nowhere outside Dublin was the War of Independence fought with such intensity as it was in Cork city and West Cork. There were good reasons for this. First, the terrain suited guerrilla warfare. Second, there was a long British military tradition in County Cork and this created a reservoir of talent and experience which was available to manage the rebellion there. Tom Barry, who led the IRA column in West Cork, had fought in the British Army in Mesopotamia during the Great War. Third, there was a larger imperial loyalist community in West Cork than in the rest of southern Ireland, and as they were expected by both sides to support the British rather than remain neutral, the IRA had to contend with a greater range of potential opponents. Fourth, many Cork loyalists were intermarried with the British and had strong links with the regiments sent to quell the rebellion. For these families the war was personal, as defeat would lead to the loss of prestige, power and money. (The fate of the Earl of Bandon – he lost his mansion, his servants, his judicial functions, the use of his estate, his prime position as Lord Lieutenant of County Cork and his coronet – explains why the stakes were so high for him.)[2] Fifth, many West Cork loyalists were English born and viewed a war against their fellow countrymen with disbelief and horror.[3] To succeed, the IRA had to neutralise this group.[4] Sixth, arms, and more importantly ammunition, were relatively easy to acquire from the large British Army bases in Cork.[5] Seventh, while County Cork as a whole was target-rich for the IRA – with a peacetime British military presence of over 7,000 and more than double that during the war – inland West Cork was virtually empty of the enemy, except the RIC, 500 Essex Regiment soldiers stationed in Bandon and 100–200 Auxiliaries. This comparative emptiness allowed all-important safe zones, where the guerrillas could rest and recuperate, to survive throughout the war; this situation was unique to West Cork and set it apart from the rest of the country. Military strategists have identified the need for these insurgent 'safe zones' as critical to the success of any rebellion, and to concede this advantage to the IRA without a fight was an enormous tactical and strategic blunder by the British.[6] Finally, there was a long tradition of Fenianism, agrarian struggle and general lawlessness embedded in West Cork culture, which lent it to be 'agin the government', no matter who was governing.[7] It didn't take much to persuade *these* rebels to rebel.

The topography of West Cork is overlooked in most studies of the War of Independence and yet this was crucial to the success and survival of the insurgents. It consists of a series of long, level ridges running east–west, with a series of wide valleys with the best land and all of the urban centres. At the western end of the county the land rises to almost 1,000 metres and is heavily glaciated, with plenty of exposed rocks to act as hiding places – the war was mainly fought around ditches, hedgerows and bends in the road. It is often forgotten that there is a direct line of sight from the site of Cork Airport as far west as the Paps mountains, sixty-five kilometres away outside Killarney, and the Galty mountains, fifty kilometres to the north. Similarly, in the Bandon Valley, Nowen Hill, just to the west of Dunmanway, can also be seen from the airport. If the British left Ballincollig, for example, and headed towards Macroom to the west, all local IRA commanders knew this in seconds from scouts blowing bottles or waving from hilltop to hilltop.[8]

As the main IRA travel-and-information route was the long ridge to the south of Cork city, stopping movement here should have been an absolute priority for the British commanders. Yet, while the Macroom Auxiliaries were frequent raiders along the 'communications route from Newcestown to Kealkill', the British never attempted to control this high ground.[9] They set up their bases in the towns to the north and south of this ridge (Ballincollig and Bandon), but never stationed troops in Newcestown, where they could have completely disrupted IRA activity. Had they done this, their rate of attrition and difficulty of supply would have been higher, but if they had been serious about winning the war it would have been worth it.

They were warned about this by the increasingly strident and panicked calls of the RIC Divisional Commissioner for Cork West Riding in Bandon. Throughout the early months of 1921 he called for the area to be 'flooded with troops stationed everywhere in strong detachments with every equipment for war, aeroplanes etc. etc.', so that 'the rebels could not dominate large tracts of the Riding completely, as really is the case now'. His March report ends: 'Hence, the IRA is rampant and meets with little opposition.'[10] If he was correct, while the IRA had 'not been able to drive the enemy out of anything but a fairly good-sized police barracks', it appeared to have driven them out of large parts of West Cork and was winning the war there.[11]

In response the British eventually created their own flying column of around 100 lightly equipped soldiers who moved from village to village. They also instituted occasional week-long mass sweeps by up to 5,000 troops brought in from Cork, Kinsale and Ballincollig. While this was a little more successful in disrupting IRA communications and ambushes, it still failed to deal with the topography. Led by Major Percival of the Essex Regiment, it was also rarely able to achieve surprise.[12] At the Crossbarry ambush, which was the last major engagement fought by both sides, the encirclement began, and was spotted, at 1 a.m. IRA Brigade Commander Charlie Hurley was shot at approximately 3.30 a.m. and the IRA column was in defensive position at 5.30 a.m. Two-and-a-half hours later the first main action took place; the amount of time between detection and action gave the defenders a major tactical advantage.

It would be very easy to say that there are no rules in a guerrilla war. Yet the notion of playing by the rules is central to the interpretation of the war in West Cork. Generally, both sides were trying to work within their interpretation of their law as best they could. The obvious exceptions were the uncontrolled British paramilitary forces. (Based on their experience in both Ireland and Palestine, the British now accept that these forces can have a negative effect, due to a lack of proper control structures and discipline.)[13] Both sides set out their rules in 1919, and much of the debate in both Dáil Éireann and the House of Commons revolved around breaches of the 'rules' of the war. Women, clergy and children were generally off-limits, but combatants on both sides could expect no mercy. The only problem was identifying who was a combatant.

Both sides also decentralised a good degree of tactical flexibility to local commanders and this led to different interpretations of what was allowed. In many cases it came down to the personality of individual commanders, who sometimes became irritated by attempts at central control. Many of the disputes between IRA Chief of Staff Richard Mulcahy in GHQ in Dublin and the field commanders stemmed from Mulcahy's insistence on receiving prompt reports of actions so that they could be analysed for mistakes or possible improvements, and the field commanders' view that this was too much bureaucracy. The fact that Mulcahy inadvertently became a major source of British intelligence finds after a series of raids on his headquarters did not improve relations.[14]

Overall, in West Cork the War of Independence was a short, sharp, savage affair. While there were incidents in early 1919, the war turned increasingly 'hot' with the arrival of the Black and Tans in early May 1920,[15] the appointment of Tom Barry as leader of the flying column in September,[16] and the banishment of K Company of the Auxiliaries to Dunmanway after they burned Cork on 12 December 1920.

The 'old' RIC was effectively neutralised in West Cork by

the middle of 1920.[17] Most barracks had either been burned or besieged by then, rendering them useless as British control centres. Carrigadrohid Barracks was burned in January 1920. Inchigeela was attacked on the same night but survived, only to be 'surrounded by barbed wire entanglements for a depth of ten yards' to prevent inevitable attack.[18] (It would be evacuated days after the assassination of Sergeant Maunsell in late June.) Allihies Barracks was destroyed on 12 February 1920 and the police evacuated it the following morning; this meant a large area of the Beara Peninsula was empty of British forces and was a safe area for recuperation and training for the IRA. Farther south, Timoleague and Courtmacsherry Barracks were destroyed by the end of April 1920, leaving only the navy to watch the coastline. Ballyvourney was also destroyed in April, and Farran Barracks was burned on 21 June. Most importantly, the obscure but strategically crucial stations in the heart of the Newcestown safe zone at Farranavane and Kilmurry were burned in June 1920. After this the IRA held the countryside and the British held the towns; the force that had been the eyes and ears of the British in every parish became mostly irrelevant in West Cork's war.

John Ainsworth has argued that British security policy degenerated into a desperate attempt to hold on to Ireland and initially many of the main players were tolerant of Auxiliary excesses. By the time these players accepted the advice of Macready and Wilson that the Auxiliaries were doing far more damage to the all-important propaganda war and British military discipline than they were doing to Irish solidarity, it was too late.[19]

While there is ample evidence presented by the Irish of Auxiliary brutality and reprisals, there are few actual records of any Auxiliaries or Black and Tans being brought before a court for misbehaviour.[20] Much of the Irish evidence was, of course, disputed, denied and deliberately 'blackened' by the Dublin Castle propaganda department.[21] However, the available evidence suggests that the Auxiliaries' reputation was well earned.[22] For example, in an infamous April 1921 shoot-out at Castleconnell in County Limerick, they raided a hotel and ended up fighting with other RIC and Auxiliaries who had stopped for a drink. Three people were killed in this incident, including the owner, Denny O'Donovan, originally from Skibbereen, who was killed in the yard ten minutes after the shoot-out. There is no doubt that he was shot out of hand by the Auxiliaries:

> It was a most harrowing spectacle. No one could see the yard, the scene of the shooting, or the bar, blood smeared about the wood-work and passages damaged in the firing – no one could witness these things without the sickening sense of horror which the spectacle pre-sented.[23]

Lord Parmoor's brother, who was a guest in the hotel on the night, witnessed all this.[24] Lord Parmoor read three letters from his brother into the record of the House of Lords a week later; the de-tails included the Auxiliaries using a Lewis machine gun inside the hotel. As the writer was pro-government, there can be no doubt about his impeccable British credentials.[25]

Further confirmation of the Auxiliaries' behaviour was pro-vided by Major Whittaker, who interviewed locals during his fact-finding mission for Churchill in 1922:

> Of the methods adopted by the British Government there is strong and undying criticism. Some of this may be due to a natural dislike for efficient methods and a definite policy, but the greater part of the criticism and hate has been caused entirely by the 'Black and Tans'

[Auxiliaries] whose conduct was undoubtedly often reprehensible. Ill-considered killings, very frequent drunkenness and bad discipline are the chief reasons why the 'Black and Tans' failed to link respect with the definitely produced fear ... Old women too stupid to temper the truth with the national propaganda say that on many occasions British regiments saved them (in some cases by a display of force) from outrage by the 'Black and Tans'.[26]

Two days after the burning of Cork city centre during the night of 11/12 December 1921, K Company of the Auxiliaries was posted to Dunmanway.[27] The government suppressed the subsequent British Army report on the burning of the city.[28] There is no doubt that K Company started the fires in revenge for an ambush at Dillon's Cross, 200 metres from British headquarters at Victoria Barracks in Cork, during which bombs had been thrown into two Auxiliary

K Company, Auxiliaries, at Kent Station, Cork (courtesy of Mercier Archives)

trucks, killing Temporary Cadet Spencer Chapman and wounding twelve other Auxiliaries.[29] On the same night IRA volunteers Jeremiah and Cornelius Delaney were shot while unarmed in their bedroom at Dublin Hill just north of the city. The men who carried out the ambush had been tracked to their house (apparently by bloodhounds) but had left before the Auxiliaries arrived.

In Dunmanway, the Auxiliaries took over the workhouse and dispatched the inmates to the dispensary. After the regal comfort of Victoria Barracks, the cold, damp and draughty building was a big comedown. Once half the company had recovered from bronchitis, they amused themselves by burning corks and sewing them into their caps in honour of their success at Cork.

If they wanted to announce their presence in Dunmanway, they could not have done so in a more effective way than they did, on 15 December: Cadet Hart shot Tadg (Timothy) Crowley and Roman Catholic parish priest Canon Magner at Ballyhalwick, while K Company was on its way to Cork for the funeral of Hart's friend Cadet Chapman.[30] Hart stopped where Crowley was helping the resident magistrate in Bantry, Mr Brady, whose car had broken down.[31] Hart pistol-whipped and shot Crowley. He then forced Canon Magner, who happened upon the scene, to the ground and shot him in cold blood.[32] Hart's comrades made no serious attempt to intervene until after the priest was shot. Mr Brady testified at the subsequent trial that he had run away through the fields back into Dunmanway, a mile to the west, after Canon Magner had been shot.[33] He said that the Auxiliaries had fired after him. At the trial it was also said that Hart had been drinking all day because one of his best friends had been killed at the Dillon's Cross ambush – this was confirmed by Sir Hamar Greenwood during a tetchy exchange in the House of Commons on 17 February 1921: 'Yes, Cadet Hart was a chum and companion of Cadet Chapman, who was massacred in an ambush a few days before in Cork, and undoubtedly that had an effect on his mind.'[34]

Even after the Truce, O Company of the Auxiliaries, which was now stationed in Dunmanway, was involved in a number of aggressive actions against the IRA, in direct contrast to the attitude of the Essex Regiment and Black and Tans in Bandon. During Christmas week 1921, four IRA members called into a pub in Devonshire Square in Bandon and found three Black and Tans inside. Michael O'Donoghue recalled:

I called for a drink but before it could be supplied one of the Tans, a small thick-set Cockney, butted in. 'Have a drink on me, matey. Do you mind?' I agreed, so did the rest. He asked us individually what would we have. A glass of brandy was mine. He looked a wee bit startled. Mick Crowley chose likewise. Price and O'Connor had small whiskies. The Tans had beer. The drinks were filled and the Tan proposed the toast of 'Peace in Ireland'. We all drank heartily. A second Tan then called for the same again, and after a little demur we all drank again – this time to each other's health.[35]

The situation was so different in Dunmanway that Peadar Kearney, the senior IRA officer in the town, decided the Auxiliaries needed to be taught a lesson:

With two other men I patrolled Dunmanway town in a motor car one evening after dark. After passing to and fro on a few occasions, some of the Auxiliaries endeavoured to stop the car and, as we did not halt, they struck the windscreen with ash-plants. We retaliated with one revolver shot. They fired back half a dozen and with the aid of a carbine we drove them off the street. They brought out armoured cars and patrolled the town and, naturally, we retreated to the country.[36]

Three regiments of the British Army were stationed in West Cork during the war. The Manchester Regiment was based in Ballincollig, nine kilometres west of Cork city, and patrolled north-west Cork. The Essex Regiment was the first to arrive and was tasked with patrolling all of West Cork from December 1919 until the arrival of the King's Liverpool Regiment in late 1920. After this the Essex was split between Kinsale and Bandon and generally patrolled as far west as Dunmanway. The King's Liverpool Regiment occupied Bantry and dealt with the western end of the county.[37] There was a marked difference in the way each of these regiments was viewed by the locals. One of the greatest puzzles of the war is why the Essex Regiment seems to have prosecuted its campaign with an aggression that made it infamous and the King's Liverpool Regiment did not.

The Essex Regiment had a wealth of experience dealing with insurgents.[38] It was always at the cutting edge of empire building and the first of its eighteen campaigns began in India with the Assam War in 1824. By the time the regiment arrived in Bandon it had fought for 100 years against peoples whom British military doctrine stated should be repressed with any means necessary. Callwell, Britain's expert on dealing with insurgents, had long made it clear that 'uncivilised races' needed to be 'thoroughly brought to book and cowed or they will rise again'.[39]

Major Percival of the Essex Regiment had quickly gained notoriety for robust action against the IRA: on 27 July 1920 IRA men Tom Hales and Pat Harte had been tortured by officers of the regiment.[40] Hales said he was beaten and had his fingers and other parts of his body crushed with pliers in an effort to get him to talk.[41] He also lost four teeth after both he and Harte were caned and then beaten by two of the officers for refusing to divulge information. He received five years in prison in England and was released after the Treaty was signed.[42] Harte broke down as a result of his torture. After the Truce Dr Vincent Ellis collected Harte from Broadmoor Criminal Lunatic Asylum and brought him to Grangegorman Mental Hospital in Dublin before his transfer to Cork. He reported, 'I found that Harte was in a very bad state mentally, that he was almost in a state of dementia, refusing food and not co-operating in any way.'[43] Harte's great friend Michael Collins had him placed in a private ward of the Cork Mental Hospital after this.[44]

Percival is a uniquely monstrous fig- ure in the BMH witness statements, but this does him a disservice, as this culture permeated the entire regiment. William Desmond, who was picked up as an uni- dentified British prisoner at Crossbarry, provides not only a unique insight into the battle from the British ranks, but a detailed account of his brutal imprison- ment while held in the Essex headquar- ters at Bandon Barracks. The key point is that at the time of this treatment the

Major Arthur Percival (courtesy of Mercier Archives)

British were not sure that he was in the IRA. In the following extract he discusses what happened in the first couple of hours:

We, the less fortunate ones, found ourselves in Bandon in the hands of the enemy. On the way in in the lorry I was beaten with the butts of rifles and threatened with a nasty end if there was any attack along the road. When the lorry stopped on the barrack square the four dead Volunteers were just thrown out on to the ground. I was kicked out after them and fell on the bodies. All the soldiers standing around swore and cursed at me ... I was handed a pen and told to sign my name in a book … I was just about to do so when I received a blow across the bridge of my nose from a revolver held by a soldier. My blood spurted and spattered all over the book … All the prisoners were together in the one cell and all showing signs of ill-treatment. Humphrey Forde had a very bad black eye.[45]

Desmond's true identity was confirmed after two weeks. He was brought before Percival, who informed him that he was to be shot the following morning. However, the prisoners were taken to Victoria Barracks in Cork, where the physical abuse stopped. He noted that when he was then transferred to Cork Prison his treatment improved.

Another volunteer, Frank Neville, describes an incident that occurred in December 1920, in which he was arrested by Percival in Knockavilla. It was ordered that he be taken to Cork. The two others captured were sent to Bandon. On Neville's journey to Cork, the lorry stopped and he was forced out at gunpoint. One soldier:

… urged me on up the boreen at the point of a revolver until the two of us were out of sight of the lorry on the road. I knew what was intended and that the excuse for what was about to be done would be 'shot while attempting to escape'. At the critical moment, as if by instinct, I turned sharply and he fired at the same moment. I could see a flame from the muzzle of the revolver almost touch my chest and I made a spring.[46]

Neville was surprised that Percival had so much knowledge about him, including the 'jobs' he was involved in, which suggests that Percival had good-quality sources of information and it is likely that some came from within the IRA. However, Neville believed that a Mr Jagoe was the culprit, as the man left the area shortly afterwards.[47] Neville's evidence also suggests that Percival knew what was intended for him by putting him alone in the lorry for Cork. Historians must take care with any testimony, but in this case Neville knew that both he and Percival would be dead before this testimony came out, so he had no reason to lie.

One of the first detailed accounts of the Essex Regiment in West Cork to become available was that of Kathleen Keyes McDonnell in 1972.[48] She came from a well-off nationalist family and her father-in-law was a JP. McDonnell's account is not only a detailed record of what happened to her, but is also a key source for many of the other incidents of the War of Independence in the Bandon area.

McDonnell's home at Castlelack outside Bandon – with only McDonnell, her nurse and her children inside – had been raided on eleven successive nights after an ambush at Toureen in September 1920. On the eleventh night she had stood in the hall being questioned and insulted by the raiders while the clock struck 4 a.m. Her description of what happened might once have been claimed to be greatly exaggerated propaganda, but now – in the light of the admissions of the Palestinian police in their oral history – it seems more far more plausible.[49] According to McDonnell, on 29 November 1920 – the day after the Kilmichael ambush – the Essex Regiment visited her home at Castlelack yet again. She wrote:

> The Essex broke into Castlelack ... The safe was rifled, the deed box stolen. Furniture had been smashed and set alight, business records and valuable books feeding the flames. Bathroom flooding had brought down the dining room ceiling ruining the room and its contents.[50]

She was in Glengarriff at the time, meeting with Violet Annan Bryce, an English woman who had been arrested at Holyhead under the Restoration of Order Act and deported to Ireland to prevent her speaking to a public meeting about reprisals in Ireland.[51]

On 7 December McDonnell's solicitor, former MP Maurice Healy, wrote to Major Neave in Bandon looking for the return of the deeds to the house. An appointment was arranged, but Major Percival arrived instead of Major Neave. McDonnell's sister, Miss Healy (no relation to the solicitor), accompanied her, and Percival berated the women in the corridor of Bandon Barracks to such an extent that Ms Healy 'burst into tears! Percival was stunned! So taken aback he simply gaped at us, with never another word! ... After this incident Percival made himself noticeably scarce at Castlelack.'[52] It appears even monsters know shame.

As a result of his activities Percival became a prime target for the local IRA. A number of attempts were made on his life, and he had an extraordinary escape when shot in the chest by Jack Ryan, who explained that when Percival had captured him Ryan had whipped out two revolvers and fired at point blank range. One gun had failed to go off, but the second shot had knocked Percival to the ground. Unbeknownst to Ryan, Percival had been wearing a chain mail vest, so had lived.[53]

Not all members of the Essex Regiment were monsters; some of those stationed in Kinsale had a less vicious attitude. Denis Collins of the Ballinadee IRA was captured in February 1921. Having witnessed a mock execution, he was taken to Kinsale:

We were ... brought to Charles' Fort. All the time we were here ... a Sergeant and some Tommies, all belonging to the Essex, could not do enough for us ... The Sergeant said he had the greatest sympathy for anyone who was a prisoner as he had been one for four years in Germany during the War ...

We appreciated this N.C.O.'s attitude and that of the men under him. They seemed to be permanently on garrison duties and didn't go round the country making war on the people like the majority of their regiment.[54]

What the Essex did in Bandon was not a frustrated reaction to IRA violence, as has been claimed by many over the years, but was designed to intimidate and terrorise the local people into submission.

Hughes, in his study of the Palestinian police and military during the British Mandate from 1921 to 1948, observes that, unsurprisingly, records of army brutality are rarely kept, and if brutality is alleged it is vigorously disputed by the army and routinely downplayed by the government and their supporters in the media. In Palestine the protection of the rule of law was shredded as military tribunals could ignore evidence; newspapers were suppressed for 'preaching sedition' or were so heavily censored that they became worthless as records of events. All this was designed to allow the police to root out 'terrorists' with a free hand and many of the same individuals and regiments fought in both Ireland and Palestine.[55]

What happened later in Palestine, Malaysia and Kenya shows that the Essex Regiment's brutality in Bandon was neither unique nor unusual, but part of 'normal' activity. It is hard not to conclude that the regiment simply brought to West Cork the tactics long employed when slaughtering 'savages' on punitive expeditions (an essential component of British rule in India).[56] As the Annan Bryce and McDonnell cases show, the Essex Regiment and the Auxiliaries did not seem to understand how close London was and what the impact of their actions would be at home. It was perfectly fine for Rudyard Kipling to write about the bravery of the Fuzzy Wuzzy during their annihilation by the British outside Khartoum in 1898 when nobody could see it, but with more than 500,000

Irish living, and more importantly voting, in Britain in 1921, even the coalition government was concerned about the impact these actions were having on public opinion.[57]

The savagery in and around Bandon was in direct contrast to the 'civilised' campaign conducted by both sides in the extreme west of County Cork. Ted O'Sullivan's witness statement shows that after the IRA had attacked Drimoleague RIC station, the IRA understood that the Bantry military were very different to the Dunmanway Auxiliaries:

… strong forces of military arrived from Bantry (10 miles) while a force of Auxiliaries arrived from Dunmanway (10 miles). The military were apparently first on the scene, otherwise it is likely that Drimoleague would have been burned out that night by the Auxiliaries.[58]

On another occasion four members of the IRA captured by the RIC in Durrus were protected from serious injury or murder by the intervention of the local British Army commander, Colonel Hudson of the King's Liverpool Regiment. Hudson famously returned a trench coat to Tom Barry after it was captured during a raid on a brigade meeting in Skibbereen. Barry had written to him asking for it.[59]

Lieutenant Colonel Jones of the King's Regiment had set the less aggressive tone earlier when he had written to Violet Annan Bryce's husband – in response to a letter she had written to Jones – in relation to a reprisals notice that had been handed in to the Eccles Hotel in Glengarriff, which she had bought in 1915, and which would be occupied from 1920 to 1921 by troops of the Essex Regiment:[60]

J. Annan Bryce, Esq
Eccles Hotel, Glengarriff.

In reply to your letter of September 17, 1920, addressed to O.C. Barracks, Bantry. It appears that slips similar to the one to which you evidently refer are being distributed about the country. On investigation I find that an officer of my battalion picked one of them up. This officer having seen similar slips in Bantry and other places thought it would be a good thing to hand it in to one of the hotels in Glengarriff as he passed through. As yours was the most convenient, being close to the road, he put it in an envelope and addressed it to the manageress and handed it in as he passed.

L. M. Jones, Lieutenant-Colonel, Commanding Troops, Bantry and commanding 1st Battalion, The King's Regiment. Bantry, September 20, 1920.[61]

However, their area was not immune to retaliation. After two RIC men – Thomas King and James Brett – were killed, the Auxiliaries in Bantry shot an invalid called Con Crowley. On the same night the business premises and garage of a Mr Biggs and a number of houses were burned.[62] The former was in clear revenge for Biggs' writing to *The Irish Times* as a 'neutral loyalist' complaining about the previous behaviour of Auxiliaries.

How could things be so different between one regiment and another? It appears the King's Regiment knew the Irish and had no tradition of brutal suppression. Formed in 1881, the 1st Battalion of the regiment was based at the Curragh from 1882 to 1893, then Nova Scotia and the West Indies, both relatively quiet postings. This is not to suggest that the regiment was soft. In 1902, during the Boer War in South Africa, the battalion was besieged at Ladysmith for 118 days. After this it spent three years in Burma and two years in India before returning to Fermoy in Cork in 1908. It seems clear that the regiment saw the enemy more as individual people and this was central to their different approach to the insurgents.[63]

On the other side of the war was the West Cork Brigade. If the British had defeated the IRA in Cork, then the War of Independence would now be called the second Sinn Féin rebellion, and people like Michael Collins, Tom Barry, Ned Young and Seán Hales would be footnotes in history. There is no doubt that Barry would have been tried and executed. In *Guerilla Days in Ireland*, he is brutally honest when he says that in response to the Bandon-based Essex Regiment: 'They said I was ruthless, daring, savage, bloodthirsty, even heartless. The clergy called me and my comrades murderers; but the British were met with their own weapons. They had gone in the mire to destroy us, and our nation, and down after them we had to go.' While Barry regretted the effect of some of his actions on the families of those he killed, his view was that 'From February 1921 terror would be met with counter terror.'[64] This is the essential logic of guerrilla warfare, and he never apologised for anything.

By the end of the war some members of the Bandon IRA were far more inured to amoral behaviour than those anywhere else in the West Cork Brigade. The BMH witness statements make clear that the shock of the Kilmichael ambush had badly affected some who had taken part; Peadar Kearney claims that local officers had to be replaced.[65] Barry states in his reply to criticism of Kilmichael in 1974 that after the ambush he only wanted those who understood that they were expected to kill face to face if necessary.[66] Ned Young, who took part in the Kilmichael ambush, makes a point in his witness statement: 'I should have mentioned that between the date of Kilmichael (28 November) and December 8th, 1920 the column O/C. (Tom Barry) paraded us on several occasions and asked anybody who desired to leave the column to step forward. All present maintained their positions.'[67]

After Kilmichael the core IRA fighters were hardened professional soldiers, used to following orders without question and
to killing without compunction. Yet, even late in the war, there
is little suggestion that their violence was random. If they killed
people, they did it for a logical reason. What other explanation
can there be for the famous incident in Bandon on 23 February
1921? In this incident four members of the British military were
captured and Jack Hennessy recalls:

> [They] shot two of the Essex at the Laurel Walk ... They also cap-
> tured two British Navy ... The Navy men were released and handed
> a letter addressed by Tom Barry to the O/C of the Essex in Bandon
> warning him that in view of the fact that the Essex had murdered and
> tortured prisoners, he (Barry) had given orders that the Essex were to
> be shot at sight whether armed or unarmed.[68]

Yet the savagery of some members of the column had shocked
Michael O'Donoghue when 'hardened and envenomed by the
ferocity of the fight in West Cork' they were going to shoot a 'love
struck' Black and Tan in February 1922.[69] There should be little
doubt that, after their War of Independence experiences and their
habitual response to orders, this group would have carried out any
order they were given.

Caught between both sets of forces, as always, were the civilians.
In early January 1921 the British commander in Munster, General
Strickland, issued a proclamation stating that 'anyone who had
information about ambushes, the carrying of arms and so forth were
duty bound to provide it to the military on pain of prosecution'.[70]
Both Cork unionist papers, the *Cork Constitution* and the *Cork &
County Eagle,* complained bitterly about the impossible position
in which local loyalists were now placed. If it became known that

loyalists 'intended to comply with the government's order their lives would not be worth 24 hours purchase'.[71]

The 'respectable' citizens of the towns now had a problem. If they did not help the military, then they risked having their homes looted and burned (or worse) by the Auxiliaries, and if they did help, then the IRA would shoot them. Denis Lordan gives a perfect example of the civilian dilemma:

> ... the Auxiliaries stationed in Dunmanway had ordered a number of shopkeepers and residents of Ballineen and Enniskeane [sic] to act as Civic Guards ... These people were instructed to send at once any information they may get regarding the movements of the Column or members of the I.R.A., to the British Military or police. They were threatened with various penalties if they did not comply ... It was discovered by the I.R.A. that these men attempted to comply with the orders of the British Auxiliary police. The local Dispensary Doctor in Enniskeane had refused to attend the Brigade O.C. when he was wounded at the Upton train ambush and had also refused to attend other wounded men. Both the Dispensary Doctor and those appointed as Civic Guards ... were arrested by the I.R.A., and tried by Courtsmartial on Tuesday, 15th March [1921]. They were ... fined and ordered under threat of further action to desist ... The Dispensary Doctor was ordered to leave Ireland within twenty-four hours. The fines were paid and the Doctor left the country within the time specified.[72]

The IRA was also demanding, rather than requesting, loyalty by January 1921. Most of the 'hostile' civilian trouble focused on the collection of the IRA levy from September 1920, as this was to be used to buy arms to fight the British. Tom Barry said in *Guerilla Days in Ireland* that as long as Protestants and loyalists remained neutral they were left alone. He does not seem to have understood that asking loyalists for money to buy guns to fight the British Army was forcing them to take the side of republicans against their own beliefs and, in many cases, their own families. Picking a safe course through these conflicting demands required fine judgement on all sides, and clearly there was an absence of this on many occasions.

Tadg O'Sullivan was the quartermaster of the 3rd Cork Brigade. In his witness statement he outlines the extent of the levy, with '£12,000 being secured in the period November, 1920 to June, 1921'.[73] It is clear from his statement that the levy was *not* voluntary in West Cork.[74] There is no doubt that loyalists were subject to intimidation and harassment by the IRA as a result of their refusal to pay the levy. The case of William Sweetnam – a Catholic in Lissangle, Caheragh, to the east of Skibbereen, who claimed £100 compensation – was reported in the *Cork & County Eagle* in January 1921.[75] He had refused to pay the IRA levy of £7 on 20 November and was summoned to appear before the republican court. He refused. When his sister (who actually owned the farm) attended the republican court, she was informed that he had been fined £2 for non-payment. The overall claim was £13 by January, and hay ricks were burned in an effort to enforce the judgement. He was visited by up to twenty armed men on a number of occasions, who threatened him, and early in January he was kidnapped, terrorised, beaten and threatened with shooting at an IRA court-martial on the side of a mountain. Sweetnam's solicitor, Jasper Travers Wolfe, noted that the issuer of the Sinn Féin judgement was Fee McCarthy from Corliss, who was 'a mark', that is he had the money to pay the £100 compensation that Sweetnam was now claiming. This case shows a clear escalation in intimidation and also that the republican courts were functioning as efficiently as the petty sessions, despite repeated British claims that they had been closed down.[76]

In some cases the IRA simply seized the property of people who refused to pay. John McCarthy of Bridge Street in Skibbereen lost a horse from just outside the town because he had refused to pay the levy. The same week Mrs Townshend of Myross Wood lost a hunter for the same reason, but this was returned as being of much higher value than the original levy.[77]

Evidence from the Bandon area confirms that there was a sizeable hostile loyalist community there and reveals the apparent difficulty faced by the IRA when attempting to collect money in Inishannon, at least according to Cornelius O'Sullivan:

> During the months of October and November we were mainly engaged in the collection of the Arms Fund Levy from friendly people resident in the area. There were a large number of British loyalists in the area who were hostile to us and the collection of the levy in their case was deferred to a later date.[78]

In contrast, Patrick Cronin of Aherla, according to his witness statement, had no difficulty in collecting the levy. Interestingly he notes that Protestants had to pay more. This could be interpreted as sectarianism, but the point he is making is that the Protestants had the best land or the largest farms: 'We collected money for general purposes for the Volunteers and we taxed householders 1/6d in the pound according to the valuation. The Protestants' valuation was always higher but they never grumbled at having to pay the levy. There never had to be seizures.'[79] However, there is really no suggestion that the levy was voluntary.

Another source, in the Florence O'Donoghue papers, suggests that many people paid up out of fear, no matter who they were. Jeremiah Keane of Crookstown, writing to O'Donoghue in 1927, said: 'The Army levy was compulsory – at least in the country –

and the majority subscribed more through fear than love.' He owned a substantial business premises in the village, and while there is no doubt that he actively supported the IRA, his letter gives an unvarnished view of the times. It is also noteworthy that he acted as a republican judge in a case involving an ex-JP who had 'condescended to recognise' them. While the fact that the plaintiff was wearing his best clothes amused the 'judges', they found in his favour 'as he had right on his side'. Keane also complains that 'people who would have been openly hostile at the time had they dared' were 'better off than we are today'.[80]

The IRA levy was not the only problem that loyalists faced. The following testimony from Richard Collins in Schull deals with the problem of private enterprise and explains not only the breakdown in law but also the climate of fear that can be created during any period of civil strife:

> ... individuals in our area formed themselves into a gang to carry out several robberies. They always operated at night and raided only the homes of Protestant families. To make matters worse, the raiders always informed their victims that they were acting for the I.R.A. threatening dire penalties should the victims inform anybody of the raids ... However, one of the men – Thomas Love, Crookhaven – whose house had been raided, mentioned the matter to Con O'Reilly ... In conjunction with the officers of Lisagriffin Company, I undertook an investigation of the report and, within a few days, we had discovered and arrested the culprits. They were tried by court-martial.[81]

There is no doubt that loyalists found themselves in a terrible position. In *Guerilla Days in Ireland* Tom Barry made it clear that there was a deliberate policy of burning the houses of loyalists in reprisal for the burning of republican houses, in an effort to force the British to stop using this tactic.[82] Percival, on the other side, recognised the problem: 'in a struggle of this nature the existence of a large number of loyalists among an otherwise hostile population is, and always will be, a powerful weapon in the hands of the rebels'.[83]

Michael J. Crowley of Kilbrittain Company was a member of one of the main IRA families in the area. His brothers, Pat and Con, are central to the story at the heart of this book and they were neighbours and close personal friends of the O'Neills, whose family member Michael O'Neill would be shot at Ballygroman House. In his BMH witness statement, Michael J. Crowley shows that while loyalist houses were initially targeted for arms raids, this had changed by 1921. He states: 'At the latter part of the campaign, we billeted when possible on the wealthy "loyalists", or forced contributions from them of cattle, which were killed and dressed by the column butcher and distributed to billets.'[84] Crowley claims that the flying column 'lodged' with their perceived loyalist enemies in an effort to spare the poor among their own supporters.

These examples suggest a much greater (and believable) nuance in attitudes within the loyalist and nationalist, Protestant and Catholic, Planter and Gael communities towards the IRA than is suggested by some scholars. Clearly they were not supported wholeheartedly by the entire Roman Catholic community, nor were they actively opposed by the entire Protestant community. Given the difficulties of telling who was friend or foe, it is unsurprising that some innocent people were swept up in the storm along with active combatants.

Perhaps the most exceptional example of this confusion of identities within members of the population is illustrated by Lady Albina Broderick. In June 1921 Castle Bernard was burned and Lord Bandon abducted as a hostage against British executions.

Following this, Lady Broderick, his first cousin, arrived in Bandon to seek his release.[85] Albina Broderick, who was English-born, had joined Sinn Féin as early as 1917 on the grounds that it promised equality for women. Her revulsion at the poverty she found in Kerry when she moved there in 1901 had radicalised her; she built a hospital for the local Kerry people and lived in profound poverty herself. She is better known in Ireland as Gobnait Ní Bruadair and was not alone among her class in taking the nationalist side.[86]

Broderick had probably walked from her home in Derrynane, West Kerry, to visit Lady Bandon. She was a most unwelcome visitor, as this extract from Mary Gaussen's diary recalls:

> The following Sunday evening, Lord Bandon's cousin Albina Broderick arrived on a visit. She was dressed as a nurse as she was looking after IRA wounded and giving shelter to men on the run in her cottage hospital in Kerry. D. [Lady Bandon] finally consented and that terrible woman came in.[87]

According to Major Percival, Broderick warned Lady Bandon that Lord Bandon would be shot unless the British gave in to IRA demands.[88] Mary Gaussen, who witnessed the conversation between the two women, was outraged at a suggestion from Broderick that Lady Bandon should put pressure on the British government for a truce and told Broderick that this was blackmail. Despite the low opinion of her within the Bernard family, Broderick's mission to the IRA in Coomhola was successful.

According to Anna Walsh, whose brother Frank had been arrested and shot by the British Army in May:

> Shortly after the date of the Truce, a lady called to the house to see me [she is mistaken about the date here]. It was the Hon. Albina

Broderick, a strong friend of the National movement. She was the sister of the Earl of Midleton and first cousin of the Earl of Bandon. The latter had been captured at Castle Bernard some time before the Truce and was still a prisoner. I brought the little lady in and gave her a cup of tea and she explained that she had walked the whole way out from Bandon to ask me to put her in touch with the Column as she wished to intercede for the safety of her cousin. She had been directed to me by the Cumann na mBan in the town and that was good enough for me, so while the Hon. Albina was having her tea I arranged for a pony and trap and driver to bring her on her way to Coomhola where the Column was at the time. She set off and eventually, travelling by relays of traps, she got to her destination away beyond Bantry and there interviewed the Brigade Staff.[89]

The Earl was released from captivity in Rathbarry and returned to the gates of Castle Bernard the day after the Truce.

To understand the events of April 1922, it is also necessary to examine the overall quality of IRA intelligence gathering in West Cork during the War of Independence. One of the best examples of the IRA's ability to break into British lines of communication can be found in a statement from Denis Lordan, which not only explains why the Peacocke house was burned in June 1921, but also shows how well the IRA had infiltrated the enemy communication system by that stage:

A residence overlooking Innishannon [*sic*] Bridge on the Bandon river, which was the property of Lieut.-Colonel Peacock [*sic*] (this Lieut.-Colonel Peacock had been executed by the I.R.A. for conveying information to the British Forces) was to be occupied by a force of the Black and Tans at 6 o'clock in a morning in May.[90] A coded telegraph order was sent to the Black and Tans in Bandon on the previous evening and a copy of the code message was passed out by our agent in the Bandon Post Office and reached Brigade Headquarters about 7 o'clock that evening. Orders were immediately issued to the Officer Commanding, Ballinadee Company; to mobilise sufficient of his men and to proceed to Peacock's house and destroy it. These orders were carried out and on the following morning when the convoy of Black and Tans moved out from Bandon to Innishannon for the purpose of occupying Peacock's residence they only found smouldering ruins.[91]

If this source is correct, then IRA intelligence capacity in West Cork was astounding. Its veracity is supported by the following examples. According to Thomas Reidy, intelligence officer in Bantry and Skibbereen, the IRA was reading all British military communications from early in 1920:

About this time, R.I.C. and military messages being transmitted through the Post Office were sent in code. The Brigade I.O. (Seán Buckley, Bandon) supplied me with a copy of the key to this code so that messages could be deciphered. At the time I had an arrangement with the members of the staff at Bantry Post Office (Jim O'Sullivan and Patrick J. Lynch and Seán Buckley) whereby copies of all messages for military or R.I.C. were sent to me by messenger before they were dispatched to the addressees. This information was, in most cases, sent to me at least 30 minutes before it was transmitted through official channels to the appropriate addressee. This interval of 30 minutes enabled me to transmit necessary instructions to I.R.A. personnel affected by the messages or to communicate the details of the message to my superior officers ...[92]

In Clonakilty the telegrams and letters were delivered to Intelligence Officer Ted Hayes 'by — Heaphy, who was a sorter in the local post office and who collected all items due for delivery from me each evening. He was working in co-operation with C. All-cock, who was an assistant in the post office.'[93]

In Macroom the intelligence officers proved how effective the system was:

On June 1st our two Intelligence Officers at Macroom Post Office, Mr. Curtin and Miss Rice, succeeded in deciphering enemy messages pertaining to a large scale round-up of the Macroom-Ballyvourney area ... Confirmation was received from [Auxiliary] Cadet [Patrick] Carroll at Macroom Castle ... and this big enemy round-up, wherein over two thousand men took part and which lasted over five days, proved abortive. Not even one active Volunteer was arrested.[94]

While everyone knew that the IRA was getting much of its information from stealing and censoring the mails, nobody seems to have seriously suspected the staff in the post office. Even more impressively, in Dunmanway, K Company messages were being read and passed along by Flor Crowley, the clerk of the workhouse, in whose office the intelligence officer had his desk.[95]

Finally, in Ballincollig, according to Tim Herlihy: 'there was an Intelligence System in operation in the Barracks, carried out by the local Volunteers, which nipped them in the bud, by sending out word prior to their moving out of Barracks'.[96]

If people were passing information to the British in secret, it was getting to the IRA. In many cases as soon as this information was passed on through the encrypted telegraph service, the IRA would have that information before the British intelligence officers, and this allowed the IRA to avoid trouble. In a way, it is hardly surprising that Collins was able to infect the British post office network so completely with his intelligence officers. After all, as an ex-post office clerk he had more experience of the post office system than most and was intelligent enough to recognise its potential.

Another intelligence stream were the British forces. Auxiliary Cadet Carroll was a prime asset in Macroom. The local RIC officer, Cahill, in Dunmanway is regularly mentioned in the witness statements of IRA men from the area as being an excellent source of information about the raiding plans of the Auxiliaries. On one occasion a planned attack on an intelligence officer was called off, as the IRA would have hit that RIC officer as well.

As information gathered in 1921 was apparently used to target people during the 1922 Dunmanway killings, it is important to examine how the IRA gathered the information to provide a context for these later killings. To put it simply: could the IRA have drawn up a list of names containing the members of an Anti-Sinn Féin Society or a Protestant Action Group? If the IRA had such a list, how likely was it to use it after the War of Independence was over? There is sufficient evidence to suggest strongly that one of these groups existed, so the identification of spies and informers by the IRA during the War of Independence is central to the story at the heart of this book.

If a proper judgement is to be made about whether the April 1922 killings were random or targeted, then a close examination of the West Cork IRA's professionalism as spy hunters is necessary. If their evidence gathering against suspects is shown to have been poor, then it is more likely that the Dunmanway killings were sectarian; the reader will have to make up their own minds on this.[97]

The IRA was convinced that some members of the loyalist community were actively supporting the British attempt to quash the revolution by giving information to the authorities.[98] According to the British Lord Chancellor, Lord Birkenhead, in April 1921, there was truth in this.[99] This is supported by the county inspector of Bandon, who reported in January 1921 that information was being 'given freely'.[100]

The early months of 1921 proved the most deadly for the locals during the war in West Cork. Thirty men were shot and killed. Eleven of these casualties were IRA members, killed by the British Army and Auxiliaries in the first twelve days of February 1921. Not one enemy soldier was shot. This was almost a third of all 3rd Brigade losses in the entire war.[101] The IRA shot some of the civilian casualties as spies; Tom Barry put the figure at thirteen in a month.[102] Most of the deaths occurred within ten kilometres of Bandon, with a few in Skibbereen and Clonakilty. At the same time houses of nationalists and unionists across the area were burned, either as reprisals for other burnings or to prevent them from being used as barracks by the British.[103]

On 21 January 1921 the local IRA accidentally discovered a spy at Cahoo named Denis Dwyer, from Castletown-Kinneigh. He was an ex-soldier and a Roman Catholic. Dwyer was waiting on the road to meet the British forces and mistook the IRA soldiers for them. He started giving them information about the local IRA. Having questioned him, the IRA shot him there and then, leaving his body exposed to lure the Essex Regiment out of their barracks three kilometres away in Bandon to investigate. As the Essex had failed to take the bait by the following evening, the flying column decided to billet with local farmers while they waited. All BMH witness statements make it clear that while a hostile reception might be expected in some loyalist houses, a refusal to assist would be ignored.[104] When some of the column members called to Thomas J. Bradfield, he mistook them for Black and Tans and started telling them about an IRA hideout nearby. Denis Lordan describes what happened next. He records Bradfield as saying, 'I'm not like the rest of them round here at all. The Reverend Mr Lord

is my man, and I give him the information. You fellows should
come round at night I'd show you round.'[105]

Lordan says that he was 'used as a football by the lads' while
they waited for orders from Tom Barry. He was shot on 24
January as the column departed for their next rendezvous. The
Essex Regiment arrived shortly after the column had left, having
travelled to the area by a roundabout route.[106]

Thomas J. Bradfield's admission is significant as, according to
the IRA, he confessed that he was involved in a conspiracy with,
at least, Rev. John Charles Lord, Church of Ireland rector of
Kilbrogan (Bandon North). This suggests a sort of Anti-Sinn Féin
Society gathering and passing information to the Black and Tans
and Essex Regiment in Bandon. There may have been only two
people in this group, but surely its existence cannot be in doubt.[107]

Any competent IRA intelligence officers would immediately
have been looking at the known associates of the dead men.
On 1 February, a week after discovering Thomas J. Bradfield's
activities, the IRA called to the house of his cousin (also named
Thomas Bradfield). There was suspicion that he too was providing
information to the Essex Regiment. Having accidently tricked
Thomas J. Bradfield, they tried the same strategy – dressing like
the Auxiliaries – on his cousin. James 'Spud' Murphy recalled what
happened next:

> The remainder of the column, under Tom Barry, moved into Clona-
> kilty battalion area. We were in the Ahiohill district on the night
> of 31st January 1921, when the column O/C asked Dan Corcoran
> and myself to accompany him to the house of Thomas Bradfield,
> Desertserges. We were driven there in a horse and trap by Tim Coffey,
> Breaghanna, Enniskeane [sic]. Tom Barry approached the house and
> asked the maid whether Mr. Bradfield was at home. She said that he

was out in the fields. Dan Corcoran accompanied the maid to the field to call Bradfield and to inform him that the officer wanted him. We were all wearing Sam Browne belts outside our trench coats and Bradfield assumed that we were members of the British forces. When Bradfield came in he welcomed us and invited us into the sitting-room where he gave us some refreshments. He sat down and began to talk to Tom Barry about the activities of the I.R.A. in the area, giving a number of names of prominent officers. At this stage I had taken up position at the front door and Dan Corcoran was likewise at the back door. When Bradfield had given sufficient information, Tom Barry disclosed his identity and Bradfield was certainly shocked. We immediately placed him under arrest and removed him on foot to Ahiohill area. He was tried that night and when we were moving from Ahiohill to Burgatia House on the night of 1st Feb. 1921, Bradfield was executed. His body was labelled as that of a spy and was left on the roadside.[108]

Denis Lordan also notes the execution took place on Tuesday 1 February while the column was marching to take over Burgatia House in Rosscarbery, where they tried and deported Tom Kingston for informing on the IRA in the district. This was also the scene of a pitched battle between the column and the army, who surprised them. During the fight the IRA placed Kingston, his family and servants in the safest part of the house after his trial.[109]

The *Cork Constitution* blamed General Strickland's new order (that loyalists had to hand up information on pain of arrest and punishment) for the killing of Thomas Bradfield. It asked, 'In short, is it an offence to remain neutral?'[110] Given its strident unionism since its foundation 100 years before, this is an extraordinary comment.

Retaliation was swift and merciless. On 15 February the *Cork Constitution* noted the killing of brothers Timothy (Tim) and James Coffey in Breaghna, Desertserges (Enniskean). It noted that

Thomas Bradfield had been shot in the same locality two weeks previously and suggested that the Coffey brothers were shot in response. The *Cork & County Eagle* was not so coy. It gave many more details in its report of the family's compensation claim in April.[111] According to the brothers' parents: 'The head was nearly shot off one of them, and the other was shot in the neck. On a card on one body was written *Revenge*. On the other body was – *Convicted Vide Bradfield Anti-Sinn Féin – of murder*.'[112] It is possible that Tim Coffey had been recognised driving Tom Barry and the others to the Bradfield house, as they were neighbours.

According to Thomas Bradfield's wife, Elizabeth, in her compensation claim on 25 June 1921, armed men had come to his home at Knockmacool House near Desert(serges) railway station, taken him away and shot him three miles away. His farm and goods were confiscated as a spy's. Bradfield's daughter had married a Mr (Joseph) Stokes a few days before the killing. When the family attempted to sell the farm with the help of Mr Stokes on 10 March, the IRA had warned off all prospective purchasers. One of the warnings posted around the farm stated, 'Take notice that any person or persons having dealings or holding any communication with spies or the relatives of spies do so at their own risk.'[113] The IRA confiscated the contents of the farm and stated that the lands were confiscated in 1921, but on 29 May 1926 Elizabeth sued Cork County Council for charging her rates after the land was sold. The judge's decree makes clear that the Bradfields were the legal owners of the farm until they sold it in February 1925 for £600 for the seventy-one acres, and that they were liable for the rates from 1921 to March 1924.[114]

Elizabeth Bradfield was a sister of John Good, of Barry's Hall, Timoleague, who was shot as a spy on 10 March. His son William – who returned from Trinity College in Dublin to settle his father's estate – was shot on 28 March. He was a reserve officer in the British Army and a note was left on his body warning spies that they would be shot.

The killings of John and William Good were related to the shooting dead of IRA man Denis Hegarty, who worked for the Goods, by unknown masked men some time before. He had been taken from his house in the Goods' farmyard and shot at the end of their lane.[115] John Good told Hegarty's inquest that he had heard movement on the night but understandably had not gone out. Whether the IRA suspected or knew he was in any way involved in the killing of Hegarty, or he was shot simply because he looked the other way, is never made clear in any of the BMH witness statements. The Good family killings are unique in the Cork statements as no explanation or evidence is given, other than that John was a spy. His son William was also labelled a spy, but no evidence is presented.

A *Southern Star* report on 25 June mentioning the Good killings reported that Tom (aka William) Connell and Mathew Sweetnam of Skibbereen were also shot for giving evidence against IRA men who were collecting the IRA levy. Connell was a cousin of the Bradfields. William Kingston, in his memoir, recalls that Skibbereen loyalists and Protestants took the Connell and Sweetnam killings as a warning not to get involved in the war by taking sides.[116] However, he makes it clear that he felt that as the War of Independence was a much less savage affair in the western part of County Cork, there was little need to take sides.[117] It is also notable that the Mizen and Durrus peninsulas had the greatest percentage concentration of Protestants in West Cork, but there is much less evidence of informing or IRA attacks on suspected informers west of Dunmanway.

In February 1921 Alfred Cotter was shot in his mother's house in Ballineen.[118] The IRA targeted the Cotter family because it believed that the family were watching Tim Warren and Jack Hennessy. Both had been severely beaten by members of the Essex Regiment in July 1920 after they had placed posters in Ballineen calling for a boycott of Cotter's Bakery. Hennessy had had a revolver pushed into his mouth and the hammer clicked while being questioned, and had been certain he was to be shot in the back when he was ordered to walk away from the military after his beating. He escaped by diving into the River Bandon. Hennessy later recalled:

> Early in my statement I referred to the case of Alfred Cotter of Ballineen who was supplying the R.I.C. with bread. The case of Cotter had been continually before the battalion and there appeared to be evidence to connect him with spying. After the O/C, Tim Warren, and I went on the run Cotter continued his contacts with the R.I.C. The case was dealt with by the Brigade when they were cleaning up the British spy ring in West Cork in the early days of 1921. Alfred Cotter was executed on brigade orders on the 27th February, 1921.[119]

Tim Warren had no doubt that the Cotters were spying on him:

> They appeared to have been kept well informed of my movements as they had associated me with the fight at Manch. I got away to the back of the post office and escaped in the darkness. Cotter's, the bakers, were keeping the British informed of our movements.[120]

However, another reason for the shooting seems to have been because the Cotters refused to stop supplying bread to the army in Bandon. This might seem appalling to the modern observer, yet there was a vicious logic to it: if the supply of food to the occupying power can be cut off, then that power cannot function and has to leave. The same reasoning applied to railwaymen's refusal to move army supplies around the country. A boycott had failed to stop the Cotters, so more drastic action was taken.

In a claim for damages for the death of a horse, the Cotter family give a very different picture about the start of their troubles.[121] According to Mrs Cotter, the youngest brother, Herbert, was studying in Trinity College, Dublin, and on a visit home had been keeping company with the military. Mrs Cotter and two of her sons, Patrick and Pierce (a veteran of the Great War), ran the business. Alfred worked for his brothers in the bakery. They were at pains to point out that they had nothing to do with Herbert and therefore the boycott of their business was unjust. However, they continued to supply the British military during the entire period in direct opposition to IRA policy.

The case of Lieutenant Colonel Warren Peacocke is different to the others, in that if anyone was going to be an active loyalist it should have been him. He came from a military family and his father had been a major in the British Army before him. The family came originally from Limerick, having bought land there after the Cromwellian confiscations, and lived at Skevanish House, Inishannon. There seemed to be little doubt within the IRA that he was a spy. He was shot on 1 June 1921.

His death was discussed in the House of Commons on 2 June, and Sir Hamar Greenwood suggested, 'The only motive that I know is that this gallant officer was a loyalist and an ex-officer of His Majesty's Army.' Lieutenant Colonel Willoughby asked if 'this officer was known to have ever given any information to the Government as to any action of the Sinn Féin party?' Greenwood replied evasively, 'He had no connection whatever with the Government or any public office or with any political movement in the county in which he lived.'[122]

The IRA claimed that Peacocke was working with the Essex Regiment in the area, and he had become secretary of the Cork Branch of the hardline Irish Unionist Alliance in 1920.[123] Tom Barry does not name him in *Guerilla Days in Ireland,* but gives enough details to leave no doubt that the informer he labels 'C' is Peacocke.[124] According to Barry, four Black and Tans were guarding the house on the night of the killing but, although they opened fire on the two members of the IRA, the killers were not pursued.[125] On 12 December 1921 his mother, Ethel Peacocke, wrote from Coombe House, Bruton, Somerset, England, and protested at the Treaty. She outlined a litany of suffering and concluded, 'Is there no statesman left to say a word for the despised and persecuted loyalists?'[126]

Richard Russell, one of the Inishannon IRA, provided exceptional detail as to why Peacocke was targeted and how he was killed:

I think it was on June 1st 1921 that Lieut-Colonel Peacocke, a 'retired' British army officer who resided at Innishannon [*sic*], was shot. He had been operating in the area as an intelligence agent and had guided raiding parties of military in the area. His identity had been established some time prior to Xmas 1920, when during the course of a raid the mask which he always wore on such occasions slipped. From the date of this incident, Peacocke lived in Bandon military barracks and only visited his home in Innishannon on odd occasions. Information was received on May 31st (I think) that he had been seen at his home. Tom Kelleher and Jim Ryan – two members of the Column were sent to Innishannon to shoot Peacocke. They were scouted by Jack Murphy, Ml. McCarthy and Tom O'Sullivan of the local company (Innishannon). The men detailed to carry out the shooting (Tom Kelleher and Jim Ryan) hid in the laurels outside the house, and when Peacocke came to the hall door he was approached by them. He attempted to draw his gun but was shot by our men, who were fired on by Peacocke's guard of Black and Tans. Our men, including scouts, withdrew without casualties and returned to their H.Q. in Crosspound area.[127]

According to the British, Warren Peacocke was a Great War hero, but to the IRA he was the primary eyes and ears of the Essex Regiment in its raids around the Bandon area. Neither side mentioned his religion. He was a combatant in a covert war and his bravery deserves to be acknowledged as such. The men who shot him did so because they believed he was their enemy and this was the only way to get him to stop his activities.[128]

On the surface it appears that the West Cork IRA was generally careful to gather evidence against suspected informers before making a decision. The BMH witness statements make it clear that people who were suspected of being informers, but against whom there was no evidence, were initially warned. If they persisted in 'anti-national' activities, then they were shot.[129] To cast all IRA victims as defenceless, innocent civilians is a greater insult to their memory than to acknowledge that they believed in their cause. The Delaney brothers were shot in their beds as a reprisal for the Dillon's Cross ambush in Cork city in December 1920. Nobody would dream of suggesting that they were not in the IRA, that the Auxiliaries who shot them got the wrong men or that their sacrifice for their cause was of any less value than that of Pearse and Connolly. Why should the same not apply to the other side?

In his post-war lectures to Staff College, Major Percival states that his main sources of information were loyalist farmers and that he kept a six-inch map which identified the individual houses of those known to him on his office wall. This seems bizarre behaviour, given the probability that the wrong eyes would see it.[130] The British *Record of Rebellion* shows the consequences for the loyalists who provided information where it says:

> ... in the Bandon area where there were many Protestant farmers who gave information. Although the Intelligence Officer of the area was exceptionally experienced and although the troops were most active it proved almost impossible to protect those brave men, many of whom were murdered while almost all the remainder suffered grave material loss.[131]

This quotation is often cited when these murders are discussed, but the actual quotation is rarely considered on its own merits. Its provenance is beyond question, and it clearly says that even though the intelligence officer (Major Percival or Captain Kelly) was highly experienced, many of the Protestant farmers who gave information were killed and almost all suffered material loss.[132] They were killed for providing Major Percival of the Essex Regiment in Bandon with information and, therefore, the IRA's targeting of these farmers was strategically correct.[133]

As I have said, in many cases the person was ordered to leave, while in other cases a warning as to future conduct was deemed sufficient. Tim Herlihy of the Ovens Company gives direct testimony of what happened in his area:

> Thompson and the Herons, senior and junior, must have been the first prisoners to have been expelled from Ireland by a Republican Court. They were strongly suspected of being spies for the British but there was not sufficient evidence to convict them, so, instead, they were expelled from the country. They had been passed on from the III [3rd] Brigade for safe keeping while awaiting trial. Another prisoner,

MacGibbon, against whom suspicion was not so strong, was given the benefit of the doubt and was released.[134]

This first killing of spies, such as Thomas Bradfield in February 1921, annoyed the British, and in Dunmanway and Bandon K Company of the Auxiliaries posted a notice, which included the following:

> In order to prevent outrages by strangers taking place in Dunmanway and district, it has been decided that six male inhabitants shall be held responsible for each week for informing the O.C. Auxiliary Police at the Workhouse, Dunmanway, of any suspicious stranger arriving in the Town, or of any occurrence or circumstance which points to contemplated outrage. This plan is further intended to protect other inhabitants from intimidation and to render it possible for any LOYALIST to give information without the rebels being able to trace its source.[135]

Given that Flor Crowley was telling the IRA everything that was happening in the Auxiliary barracks, it is likely the IRA knew about this statement before the ink was dry.

However, there was an inherent risk in the structure of the IRA, or any military force for that matter, in the making of decisions on who was a spy/informant. Once the brigade commandant was convinced of a person's guilt, then, quite often, nobody higher up the chain of command reviewed this decision until after punishment had been carried out.[136] This seems to have happened in the case of Thomas J. and Thomas Bradfield, both of whom were shot on orders from Tom Barry.[137] Writing in 1924, P. S. O'Hegarty stated in his book, *The Victory of Sinn Féin*, that this had the potential to lead to miscarriages of justice. O'Hegarty was a member of the IRB and a brother of Seán O'Hegarty (the IRA commander in Cork city after Terence MacSwiney).[138] He took the pro-Treaty side in the Civil War, and while this coloured his view of the leaders of the anti-Treaty side, his description of IRA controls agrees with that of Tom Barry. In a chapter titled 'The Moral Collapse', O'Hegarty says, 'The eventual result of that was a complete moral collapse here ... it was open to any volunteer commandant to order the shooting of any citizen, and cover himself with the word "spy".'[139] He blames this moral collapse for the events of the Civil War and states that by the end of the War of Independence, and especially during the Truce period, the local commander became supreme.[140] Effectively, 'the man with the gun had become a law unto himself.'[141]

Virtually the same language is used by Michael O'Donoghue in describing what happened to his brother, who had been demobbed from the RIC at the end of March 1922. O'Donoghue recalled, 'The local I.R.A. police had promptly arrested him and ordered him to leave Cappoquin within 24 hours under threat of death. He had gone back straight to Gormanston R.I.C. H.Q.' O'Donoghue was angry at the treatment of his brother, but he recognised that at this stage he was powerless to intervene:

It certainly was galling for me, an I.R.A. fighter in North and South, to dash home to see my parents and family and to find that my brother, a demobbed R.I.C. man, returned home, had been driven away as a dangerous criminal at the point of the gun by the local Republican Police in Cappoquin. It was just one of the many acts of bullying and brutal tyranny indulged in at that time by petty local Republican 'warriors' to show their arrogant authority and self-importance. These acts resulted in the name of the I.R.A. police becoming obnoxious in many districts. In many places, the local Battalion Commandant claimed supreme authority in his area and ruled like a feudal baron.[142]

Yet it appears that the IRA in West Cork maintained discipline throughout the Truce period. In January 1922 Tom Barry sentenced to death the man who had admitted he 'spilled the beans' before the Crossbarry ambush but, because it was Truce time, the man was subsequently banished rather than shot.[143] Other evidence in British records shows that West Cork had surprisingly few IRA Truce violations up to the signing of the Treaty. During the week ending 19 November 1921, Mayo recorded sixteen incidents, while Cork West Riding recorded none.[144] Once the occupation of Colonel Peacocke's property, which was a breach of the terms of the Truce, was raised by the British authorities with Tom Barry, the IRA liaison officer for West Cork, he was able to report that it had been evacuated a week later.[145] This action went against his own views that these properties should be broken up and their lands given to landless people without compensation and shows that Barry, at least, did not see himself as another feudal baron.[146]

Yet during the week of the Dunmanway killings there was a breakdown in this discipline. The local commanders in Bandon went to Dublin and left Michael O'Neill in command. When Michael O'Neill was shot, the remaining people in the command structure failed in their duty to protect the citizens of the area from arbitrary and unlawful killings. How, and more importantly why, did this happen?

4

THE BACKGROUND
TO BALLYGROMAN

There are numbers of loyalist exiles whose lives would be in danger if
they returned to Ireland.

Lord Bandon[1]

There is nothing to prevent them coming back as citizens of the Irish
Free State. They will be afforded the protection of the government in
accordance with the recent amnesty proclamation.

Michael Collins[2]

The critical event of the story of the Dunmanway killings of April
1922 happened at Ballygroman House around 2.30 a.m. on 26
April – everything that follows cascades from the shooting dead of
Michael O'Neill. Much that has been written about this killing is
not accurate, which makes it necessary to re-examine these events
to establish the true history as far as is possible. The reader will
have to decide which of the many conflicting pieces of evidence
available are valuable and which are not.

The central facts are not in dispute: Captain Herbert Woods,
who was either temporarily resident or staying at Ballygroman,
shot and killed the unarmed Michael O'Neill, the Officer Commanding the 1st Battalion of the 3rd Cork Brigade.[3] Michael

Ballygroman House today (courtesy of Donal O'Flynn and Dermot O'Donovan)

O'Neill was no ordinary IRA volunteer, having been appointed acting Officer Commanding the battalion by Tom Hales while he joined the leading IRA officers in Dublin in an attempt to work out an agreement to avoid the slide into civil war. The fact that his death happened during the Truce made it more shocking to his comrades. The man on the other side of the gun, Herbert Woods, was a hero of the Great War, having been awarded two medals for bravery for service on the Western Front.

It is also certain that senior Bandon IRA officer Charlie O'Donoghue returned to Ballygroman House later that morning with four anti-Treaty IRA men and arrested Herbert Woods. Along with his uncle Samuel Hornibrook and his grand-uncle Thomas Henry Hornibrook Snr, Woods disappeared. The three men were killed and nobody was ever arrested for their deaths nor were their bodies recovered. Over the following few days ten men were killed in the Dunmanway area.

Because they occurred in the same week, the O'Neill shooting, the disappearance of Woods and the Hornibrooks, and the subsequent killing of the men in the Dunmanway area, are now seen as one event. However, it may be wiser to separate them. A valid argument can be made that the killing of Woods was an execution in response to the shooting of a senior member of the

Irish Republican Police, and the Hornibrooks' deaths the result of their attempt to prevent Woods' arrest, but the killings that followed had no such justification. However, it should also be noted that there was a court in Bandon, so Captain Woods and the Hornibrooks could easily have been taken there and tried; there was no need for their killers to act as judge, jury and executioner.

Before looking in depth at the killings themselves, we must first look at the individuals at the centre of this story, as they have both been written out of history. In all my research, only one – blurred – photograph of Michael O'Neill has been found. Herbert Woods fares a little better, but before the publication of this book there was no known photograph of him either. What made these men so special within the history of their respective armies that one should have received both the Military Medal and the Military Cross during the Great War, and thousands of IRA volunteers should march with arms reversed at the other's funeral? What brought them together on the stairs at Ballygroman? Are their deaths special or are they nothing more than collateral damage and the inevitable casualties of war? It is now time to examine all the evidence, without prejudice.

THE HORNIBROOK/WOODS FAMILY OF CORK

The Woods family was a well-known Cork merchant family who had a wine and spirit business in Cook Street in the city. Originally from Kilbeggan, Christopher Woods moved to Bandon some time in the second half of the nineteenth century, where he married Ellen Mary Greave. In 1881 the family had opened the Glen Distillery in Blackpool, Cork, with Thomas Warren, but this failed in 1884 when Warren had to withdraw his cash, and it was sold to John Henry Sugrue, whose family still owned it in 1921. It is possible that the Woods family retained a minority shareholding.

Edward Woods (courtesy of Martin Midgley Reeve)

In 1908 Edward Woods, who had inherited the Cook Street business from Christopher, married Matilda Warmington Hornibrook of Ballygroman House and they moved into Crosses Green House next to their bonded warehouse. Her father, Thomas Henry Hornibrook Snr of Kinsale, had married Elizabeth Warmington of Ballygroman in 1885. It was his second marriage, and it is believed that Elizabeth died in childbirth in 1895. Matilda was a very good match for the Hornibrooks. Her aunt had married James Nicholson of Woodford Bourne & Co., the main wine and spirit merchants in Munster. The two businesses held the contracts for the Victoria Barracks, the Imperial Hotel and the Metropole Hotel between them. The barracks contract alone was worth more than £6,000 (€148,270 today) per annum to Woodford Bourne, and its loss in 1922 virtually wiped out all profits for that and subsequent years. In 1907 Matilda Hornibrook inherited property in London from her mother and was therefore wealthy in her own right.

Matilda's older brother Thomas Henry Hornibrook caused problems for the Hornibrook family in 1902. When a crowd was encroaching onto the field at a coursing meeting in Crossbarry, he assaulted the parish priest of Kilmurry by hitting him on the head with the butt of his riding crop. The local community, both Roman Catholic and Protestant, was incensed, and at a public meeting in Ovens it was agreed to ban the Hornibrook family from all sports meetings. Martin Midgley Reeve relates a family story about Thomas Henry: he was sent to New Zealand after a subsequent fight between members of the congregation inside Athnowen, the local Church of Ireland church.[4]

Samuel Wood Hornibrook, Matilda's half-brother, was born at Kinsale on 12 October 1872 to Thomas Henry Hornibrook and Mary Jane (Wood) Hornibrook. By 1922 Samuel was still unmarried (aged 46) and living with his widowed father. He was mechanically minded and owned a motorbike with a side-car, which was used to take his father to petty sessions courts, among other things.

Matilda's nephew, Herbert Woods, was thirty when he died.[5] He was the son of Edward's brother Christopher, who was a bank official in Skibbereen, where Herbert was born in 1892. After his death, Alice Hodder, a wealthy, English-born Protestant, writing to her mother from Fountainstown in Cork about the situation in the county, described him as a 'bit of a ne'er do well and quite mad'.[6] There is no record of his parents in either the 1901 or the 1911 census anywhere in Ireland and Herbert, his brother Charles Carbery and his sister Maud were living with their grandparents in 1901. In 1907, aged fifteen, he was arrested for stealing fruit knives

Herbert Woods,
seated centre
(courtesy of
Donal O'Flynn)

and remanded in Kilmainham Gaol. His prison record states that his grandmother is his next of kin, suggesting that he was an orphan, but it also states that he was released pending sentence on 22 July 1907 by his father.[7] Martin Midgley Reeve has discovered that he was bought out of the Royal Leicestershire Regiment a year later. Three years later he was working for his uncle in Cork, according to the 1911 census.

His unexceptional life as a clerk in Woods & Sons was changed by the outbreak of the Great War in 1914. He joined the Prince of Wales' Leinster Regiment in Fermoy early in 1915 and was a member of the 7th (Service) battalion.[8] He started the second phase of his military life as a private, but was eventually made a temporary colonel for a brief period whilst specially employed in the records section of the War Office from 4 January 1919 until 6 June 1919. By the time he, along with a host of other recipients, was awarded the Military Medal on 16 September 1916, he had been promoted to corporal. No official citation has been found in the *London Gazette* for the act that led to the award.[9] He was also awarded a 16th Irish Division citation for heroism by Major General W. B. Hickie, the commanding officer of the Irish Brigade, on 14 June 1916.[10] His Military Medal was sold at auction in London on 28 June 2000 and his medal index card stated that he had been commissioned after winning the medal as a corporal. His regiment number (2107) is engraved on the side of the Military Medal.[11]

Despite his heroism, the war took a huge toll on him. While his full service record was 'weeded' of duplicates and other documents in 1934, it still gives much important information about his war service. He was sent to the field hospital from the Passchendaele Front on 4 December 1917 and was returned to the firing line on 13 January 1918. On 15 February he is recorded as arriving in

Southampton with a scalp wound. He was a temporary lieutenant at this stage and had been awarded the Military Cross, also on 15 February 1918. On 18 February a mental breakdown was diagnosed, and he spent until 8 July in Carnarvon Hospital and then went to Holmrook House in Carlisle.[12] While at Holmrook he was court-martialled for drunkenness and it was suggested his Military Cross should be revoked. It was agreed, however, that a reprimand would be enough. His file shows that he returned to active service in the 88th Trench Mortar Battery on 16 July 1918, but according to F. C. Hitchcock, who fought alongside him, he rejoined C Company of the Leinster Regiment's 2nd Battalion and did not move over to the Trench Mortar Battery until 9 September.[13] Also on 16 July, the citation for the Military Cross was published in the *London Gazette*: 'For conspicuous gallantry and devotion to duty as a platoon commander. By his courage and skilful dispositions, he repelled an attempted surprise attack with severe casualties to the enemy and captured two prisoners.'[14]

Hitchcock also reports that Herbert took part in the fifth Battle of Ypres and was at the Front on 29 September 1918 with the Trench Mortars, trapped at the railway line between the destroyed village of Hooge and Ypres under systematic strafe and shrapnel fire from the German artillery. They were literally in the same place in which they had been in September 1915. From this battle on, however, their war became somewhat of a stroll to Cologne, which they formally occupied on 9 December 1918.[15]

His file states that he was discharged from the army on 1 November 1920 with the rank of lieutenant, and went to Homeville in Crosshaven, where Edward and Matilda were living.[16] However, a *London Gazette* entry suggests that he re-enlisted and remained in the army until September 1921, although the linkage has not been proven beyond doubt so must be treated with great care.[17] What he was doing during this later appointment does not appear in his file, so the person to whom this entry refers may not be him. What is clear is that by April 1922 he was in Ballygroman House.

THE O'NEILLS OF KILBRITTAIN

The BMH statements make it plain that the O'Neill household was central to the operations of the Kilbrittain IRA. The O'Neill family were farmers from Maryboro, south of Bandon. In the 1911 census, Maryboro was in Rathclairn district electoral division and there were ten in the family, with two servants. The father's name was Patrick and the mother's Norah (Hanora). The daughters were named Mary (Molly) and Margaret (Maud), and the sons Jeremiah, Denis (Sonny), Patrick, Daniel, John (Jack) and Michael. Their house was a newly built Land Commission house with five windows in front, a kitchen, a parlour and three bedrooms – similar to many that still dot the countryside in Ireland today. They were relatively well off, with no less than eight outhouses keeping both cattle and goats.[18]

Daniel Manning formed the Irish Volunteer company in Kilbrittain. It was a democratic, if ineffectual, army, and it was not

Michael O'Neill (courtesy of Donal O'Flynn)

until January 1918 that proper arms training was attempted. The students included Michael and John O'Neill. The family regularly provided food and shelter to the Volunteers and then the IRA, and Maud O'Neill is often mentioned as having carried dispatches, so it is clear that the whole family were involved in the republican movement. Mary was the captain of the Kilbrittain Cumann na mBan and provided a statement under her married name to the BMH.[19] Her statement is far more personal and detailed than those of the surviving male members of the Kilbrittain company and provides extraordinary details of the capture of her brother Daniel and the shooting of Volunteer Pat Crowley.

After the Kilmichael ambush, Tom Barry was taken ill at Kilmoyarne near Ahiohill with a possible heart attack.[20] Once Dr Fehily had treated him, Mary O'Neill, who was a trained nurse, nursed him there and in her own house at Shanaway, further evidence of the family's trusted role within the republican movement. She moved him on 9 December to Granure, where she handed over the patient to Bébé Lordan, also a nurse.

The reports about the Kilbrittain IRA make it obvious it was the epicentre of the War of Independence in West Cork. Charlie O'Donoghue's statement shows that twenty-four of the thirty-seven officers and men killed in the 3rd Cork Brigade were in the 1st Battalion (Bandon/Kilbrittain).[21]

Until the release of the BMH files in 2003 it was difficult to gain any clear picture of Michael O'Neill and his family. In an *Evening Echo* article, Liam Deasy explained that in the first action by the Kilbrittain IRA in May 1919 – only two of them were armed – they surprised six members of the RIC at Kilbrittain pier with the express purpose of seizing their rifles. Five of the RIC officers were successfully disarmed, but the sixth, who was a little behind the rest, managed to unshoulder his rifle and was in the act of getting ready to fire. Michael O'Neill spotted this and attempted to wrestle him to the ground, but the RIC officer broke loose and hit him on the head with the stock of the rifle, splitting open his skull. Despite this serious wound, O'Neill continued to wrestle until his colleagues could intervene; he then collapsed, semi-conscious. Having finally disarmed the six RIC men, the IRA retreated, without a shot being fired.[22]

The leaders of the Kilbrittain IRA gave a detailed statement to the BMH, which explained that Michael O'Neill remained at Ahiohill for a number of weeks while he recovered.[23] All the raiding party's houses were raided within twenty minutes of the ambush by the military garrison in Kilbrittain Castle, which was 200 metres from the village. Over the next weeks:

> ... the homes of O'Neills and Mahonys were raided on 17 occasions; those of Mannings and Crowleys on 25 occasions; those of J. Fitzgerald and J. O'Leary, 4 miles distant, were raided regularly at 7 a.m. every morning, while there were numerous raids on the houses of several other Vols., the raiders everywhere searching for a wounded man and inquiring the whereabouts of Con Crowley who had been 'on the run' since the previous March.[24]

In March 1920, after a thirty-minute firefight, the military arrested Michael O'Neill and Daniel Manning at Maryboro and they were interned.[25] Michael escaped to Ireland from Marylebone Infirmary on 8 May after a hunger strike in London's Wormwood Scrubs. Upon their return the Kilbrittain Company twice captured the Howe's Strand Coastguard Station a mile south of the village, without serious injury to either side. After the first raid the barracks was reinforced with five marines and a patrol boat, which moved out of the harbour during the day. In the second raid O'Neill smashed the door with a sledgehammer while under fire from the marines.

In October 1920 the Kilbrittain Company attended an armed training camp at Ballymurphy; while returning from this to organise the Toureen ambush, Michael O'Neill's military career during the War of Independence came to an end:

Michael O'Neill and John Fitzgerald returning from Ballymurphy to

Clonbogue where they were to arrange some matters re Toureen ambush were arrested by military raiding party soon after entering Coy. area. Held in Cork for some weeks, after which they were interned in Ballykinlar until the general amnesty, Xmas 1921.[26]

On his release in January 1922, Michael O'Neill was immediately appointed as second-in-command to Tom Hales in the 3rd Brigade, which is a good example of the esteem in which he was held. However, during a tribute to him on 5 May at Cork County Council after his death, it was also suggested that he was reckless with his own safety, and this may have contributed to the events that led to his death – entering a house uninvited in the countryside at night at any time was likely to end in a shooting.[27]

An incident in February 1922, recorded by Michael O'Donoghue, casts further light on the character of Michael O'Neill. A Black and Tan radio operator named Carley from Claudy in Derry had a girlfriend in Bandon. After the Essex Regiment had evacuated the town he returned on a clandestine visit to his 'ladylove'. The local Irish Republican Police were informed and he 'was roughly seized by [Jack] O'Neill, Con Crowley and two others and hustled out. I was aghast at the savagery of my comrades and pitied the poor shivering wretch as he was dragged away.'

O'Donoghue then relates:

The Tan was taken to the barracks. Tom Hales, Brigade O/C, convened a kind of drumhead court-martial at once in the brigade office. About nine senior I.R.A. officers were present and there was no formal prosecution, defence or procedure. The Brigadier presided. The Tan was questioned about his presence in Bandon in disguise (he was in 'civies' [*sic*], well-dressed and muffled up). He said he slipped away from Cork city (where he was now quartered) down to Bandon to meet his lady-love in her own house secretly; that he infringed his own police regulations and discipline in doing so, that he never thought that the I.R.A. – even if they did detect him – would molest him now ... Then the court-martial went into session to decide his fate. For an hour or more, we argued about what to do. Three or four of the more bloodthirsty revengeful officers – Con Crowley and Jacky O'Neill among them – hardened and envenomed by the ferocity of the fight in West Cork, were all for executing the poor Tan and burying him and no more about it.

'Why execute him?' I asked. 'What crime has he committed and been found guilty of?'

'Oh, he's a bloody Tan and deserves only a bullet. What brought him back here again?'

'Love', I said, 'but that's no reason to kill him.'

Tom Hales said that if we were to execute him, we would do it officially and that he would, openly, as Brigade O/C, take responsibility for the detention, trial and execution of the Tan if the Court decided on his execution. I asked the Brigadier 'on what charge was the fellow being found guilty'. He could not define any definite charge. I then asked him what reason would he give to the public press and the people to justify the execution. He was just as vague. I then stated that I saw no reason for the killing of the Tan except brutal revenge on a helpless and perhaps innocuous individual for the misdeeds of the Tans in general; that to execute him on that excuse would be murder and cowardly murder at that, and that by a deed like that we would bring disgrace on the name and character of the I.R.A. in West Cork. That impressed Hales. Some of the others too, especially Mick [Michael] O'Neill, Vice O/C 1st Battalion, recently released from prison, and brother of Jacky, were reasonable and fair-minded and anxious to be just in their attitude. They supported my contention that the Tan should be freed and permitted to depart without molestation. At length, Brigade O/C Tom Hales accepted our advice and decided on the Tan's release. I, accompanied by Mick

O'Neill, went to the guardroom and announced to the Tan that he was free to go.

We escorted him from the barrack, down a back-lane by a short cut to a footbridge over the Bandon and safely within sight of his sweetheart's house ... On our way back, we encountered three I.R.A. men who were laying in wait to beat him up, if not worse. When we accosted them, they admitted their treacherous purpose and, on learning that O'Neill and I had escorted their intended victim safely to his fiancée's house, they became very surly and angry. We insisted on seeing them back in barracks before us and into their own quarters.[28]

This statement by O'Donoghue gives an insight into the personality of Michael O'Neill, who was only twenty-four when he died, and shows that two of the more restrained and thoughtful members of the Bandon IRA, after the departure of O'Donoghue, were not available when they were needed most: Michael O'Neill was dead and Tom Hales was in Dublin. Their absence turned out to be critical.

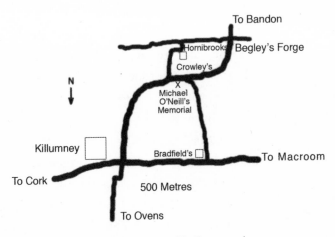

Map of Killumney (Ballygroman) area

5

THE HORNIBROOKS AND THE WAR OF INDEPENDENCE

The War of Independence was a disaster for the Woods/Hornibrook/Nicholson family. They were definitely staunch loyalists, as Matilda tells the Irish Grants Committee in 1927, and must have looked on with horror as the position of their government was threatened by the rise of Sinn Féin.[1] They were also Protestant, and the actions of Thomas Henry Hornibrook Jnr at the coursing meeting in Crossbarry when he assaulted the parish priest of Kilmurry in 1902 had led to a brief rise in sectarian tensions in Ovens, before these were skilfully defused by local councillor Jeremiah O'Mahony, who stressed that Thomas had acted alone and had been condemned by other leading Protestants in the parish.

The destruction, looting and burning of Edward Woods' business in Cook Street by the Auxiliaries during the sacking of Cork in December 1920 was the first major blow to the family. While *Guy's Almanac* records them as living in Crosses Green in 1921, Gerard Murphy suggests that they had moved in with Mr Lacy in 'Glenbrae' on the Cross Douglas Road in Cork at this time. Certainly, Matilda was living in 'Glenbrae' in May 1922.[2] The loss of the wine store left Edward without an income, and Herbert, who had finally returned from the war three weeks earlier, jobless. Although Edward claimed that he owned the Glen Distillery, which closed around this time, at the very best he was a minority shareholder.[3] According to Edward's statement to the Irish Grants Committee in 1927, it was burned, but no record of this has been found in the local papers.[4] Finding work as yet another demobilised soldier would have proved difficult for Herbert, and he was back living on the Cross Douglas Road with Edward's young family in 1921.

Perhaps the most important event in the lives of the interlinked Nicholson and Woods families occurred at the Chetwynd Viaduct in Cork at the end of November 1920, as it placed both families under suspicion of providing information to the British. An inter-rogation and execution at the viaduct was the last of a series of events that had started a few days earlier with the killing of Sergeant James O'Donoghue, a Roman Catholic from Cahersiveen who had joined the RIC in 1898. His family, as many Irish families did at the time, saw education as an avenue out of poverty. The other members of the O'Donoghue family were a doctor, a priest, a nun and a nurse, with the eldest inheriting the family farm. The RIC was a good job – well paid and pensionable – and although RIC officers were armed, their chance of actually getting shot was tiny until the War of Independence.[5] A 1920 manuscript in the Terence MacSwiney archives details MacSwiney's plans for winding up the RIC, including compulsory resignations organised by deputations visiting their homes to emphasise to their families the necessity of retiring,[6] and asking them to swap sides.[7] For Sergeant O'Donoghue to have remained in the RIC at this stage was clearly presenting himself as a target. Some 890 RIC officers had resigned across the country up to 9 August 1920, with 62 per cent of these resignations occurring from 31 May, suggesting that many resigned rather than continue to take part in the war.[8]

On 17 November 1920 Sergeant O'Donoghue was shot dead in White Street, Cork, as he was returning to his barracks in Tuckey

Street, having investigated the theft of a lorryload of bacon from Lunham and Co., which had been destined for Victoria Barracks in Cork. Lunhams was a regular target and was again raided in April 1921, when three tons of bacon ended up with the flying column in Donoughmore.[9]

O'Donoghue's killers included Willie Joe O'Brien. Later that night, during an unsanctioned Black and Tan reprisal, his brother Charlie O'Brien was shot in the mouth, leaving him seriously injured. Eugene O'Connell (brother-in-law of Charlie O'Brien) was killed. The Black and Tans also raided the house of Stephen Coleman, a relation of the O'Briens, on Broad Street, wounding Coleman and killing Patrick Hanley. Both were unarmed. The Hanley killing was witnessed by IRA intelligence officer Leo Buckley, who was hiding on the roof of the house next to Coleman's.[10] However, a member of the Fianna, George Hurley, gave a fuller account of the events:

At about 11.45 p.m. on the night of 17th November 1920, the residents of No. 2 Broad St. were awakened by the noise of the front door being broken open; a man rushed up the stairs and entered the bedroom of Mr. and Mrs. Coleman who also resided in the house. The man was wearing a policeman's uniform, cap and goggles. He came to the bedside with a revolver in one hand and a flashlamp in the other. When asked by Mrs. Coleman what in God's name brought him there, he merely exclaimed 'Hello', flashed his lamp on the bed, raised his revolver and fired point-blank into the bed. The bullet wounded Mr. Coleman in the arm. The assailant then turned and walked out of the room leaving Mrs. Coleman screaming. Paddy Hanley opened the door of his room when he heard the man rushing up the stairs. The man in police uniform had just come from Mrs. Coleman's room. Hanley, standing at his bedroom door, said: 'Don't shoot; I am an orphan and my mother's only support'. 'Very well,' replied the man, and, raising his revolver, fired at Hanley. The bullet missed him, but the man fired the second time, the bullet striking Hanley above the heart, killing him instantly. Hanley was in his night attire at the time.

This murder was by way of a reprisal by the British for the shooting of an R.I.C. sergeant named O'Donoghue by the I.R.A. earlier on the same night in the course of an I.R.A. raid on Lunham's bacon factory.[11]

The city IRA was immediately suspicious and a hunt was on for the spy in their midst. It was noticed that Din Din O'Riordan had a lot more money to buy drink than he should have had and Florence O'Donoghue investigated him. However, O'Riordan was not alone in being suspected and other IRA members were also followed at this time. In some cases they were shot. Suspicion also fell on Din Din Donovan of 2nd Battalion, Cork City IRA, but Dick Murphy, a friend within the IRA dismissed this.[12] As it turned out this was a mistake, and he was later shot as a spy.

By the end of November 1920 the IRA had set a trap for Din Din O'Riordan; once the British reacted to the information it had fed him, it had its man. He was taken to the Chetwynd Viaduct. Mick Murphy and Frank Busteed, playing on his weaknesses, promised him £50 and free passage from Ireland if he gave information about his paymaster. Din Din confessed and said that another IRA man who worked for Woodford Bourne had recruited him. This confession implicated the owner of the firm, James Nicholson, and some of the other leading businessmen in the city, including Alfred Reilly, manager of Thompson's Bakery, and George Tilson. The alleged paymaster was Charles Beale, an Englishman who had come to manage Woodford Bourne eight years previously. When Din Din had finished his confession, he was shot by Frank Busteed and buried at the viaduct.[13]

According to Busteed, letters passing through the hands of Josephine Marchmont Browne (the IRA spy in the office of Captain Kelly, the intelligence officer for the British in Cork) also identified two interlinked spy rings centred on Woodford Bourne. The first consisted of businessmen, bankers, merchants and clergymen of high social standing, and the second consisted of members of the YMCA who had been recruited by the senior spy ring.[14]

On 29 November father and son James and Fred Blemens were kidnapped separately from their home, held for a few days and then shot. James Blemens worked in Woodford Bourne. The next killing was even more shocking as it struck at the heart of Cork society:

> As the result of information received by our Brigade Intelligence Service it became known that an organisation run by the Free Masons and The Young Men's Christian Association had been formed in Cork to spy on the movements of I.R.A. men in the City and to report on them to the British Authorities. One of the principal men in this organisation was named Riley [*sic*], who was Manager (so far as I can recollect) of Thompsons [*sic*] Bakery, Cork, and lived in Rochestown, County Cork. This man was reputed to be the paymaster for the Spies.
>
> Early in February 1921 I received instructions from the Brigade to take into custody Riley and have him executed. On the evening of the 10th February, 1921, as he was returning from work in King Street (now MacCurtain Street) in his pony and trap, four of us, armed with revolvers, got into the trap and drove him to his home at Rochestown. We shot him outside the gate of his house and affixed a card to the body with the words 'Spies and Informers Beware' written on it.[15]

In the middle of January 1921 two men called to the house of Charles Beale at 7 Laurelhurst, College Road, Cork, looking to speak to the 'man of the house'. Sarah, his wife, had grown suspicious of the two men and said he was not at home, which was true. The men had left. On 16 February Beale was kidnapped on his way home from work, having been spotted on the South Gate Bridge. His body was found in a field owned by Mrs Dennehy of Dennehy's Cross, almost opposite Wilton church, then a mile outside the city. The body was face down with his arms outstretched. The head was a tangled mass of blood. On the body was a note: 'Spies and informers beware'.[16] According to the IRA, information found on Beale's body cracked the spy ring open, and the other members of the 'Anti-Sinn Féin League' were picked up and 'suitably dealt with'.[17]

It is logical to assume that Edward and Matilda Woods, as 'staunch unionists' and immediate relatives of James Nicholson, would have been kept under observation by the IRA to see if they were linked to the conspiracy. In fact, Edward later claimed that these events forced him to leave Cork in 1921, in fear of his life. The Hornibrook family lived on the border between the 1st and 3rd Cork Brigades, and the entire area around their house was the scene of many of the most famous and bloody incidents in the war. There is no doubt that they remained openly loyal to Britain in the fight, but there is no suggestion that they were active in their support. If anything, they were aggressively neutral, but Thomas Hornibrook was harassed by the IRA in Ballygroman and appears to have resigned as a JP by 1921.[18]

As early as 1919 Thomas Hornibrook had been involved in a firefight with the local IRA. Tim O'Keeffe tells the story:

Houses of loyalists which were raided were Clarke's of Farran,[19] Hornibrook's of Killumney, McGivern's of Waterfall and also Castle White at the same place. A good supply of arms was collected. When the Volunteers came to Hornibrook's house, however, he spoke out of a window to them and said he would resist. In the course of his declarations, he quoted Mr. Gladstone as having once said that every man's house was his castle and so he was going to defend his. And so he did and defended it well. He was a good shot but after half an hour's fight the Volunteers forced their way in and compelled his surrender. No one was hurt on either side but three revolvers with about 300 rounds of ammunition for them and two shotguns were secured.[20]

This statement identifies only the loyalist houses and not the many other Protestant houses in the area.

According to local historian Nora Lynch, all comings and goings at the Hornibrook house were being observed by a servant in a nearby house and reported to the IRA throughout the period up to the Hornibrooks' killing.[21] Their mail would have been censored by the IRA, as was everyone else's, and they were subjected to some intimidation possibly related to their open loyalty to the empire. On 19 January 1921 Thomas claimed for a break-in at his stable, the theft of a harness and an injury to one of the horses (which may have been accidental, according to the RIC report). Why only the harness was stolen and not the horse is another matter. Another incident, recorded in the Manchester Regiment's *Record of Civilian Arrests*, states that Jeremiah Herlihy was arrested on 7 July 1921 for cutting the tail off one of Thomas Hornibrook's horses with a saw. Jeremiah was taken to Victoria Barracks on 14 July and was interned.[22]

On 18 July 1921, after the Truce, Samuel Hornibrook's motorbike and the mudguard of the Hornibrooks' car were damaged during another break-in. On the same occasion the windows of the empty steward's house in the farmyard were smashed.[23] On 18 February 1922 Thomas H. Hornibrook claimed in the Bandon Board of Guardians for damage to a plough and the lock on an outhouse at Ballygroman, through his solicitors Wynne & Wynne of Cork.[24]

This story has one other strand that has not been discussed in detail before. At the start of April 1922 the inhabitants of Killumney, less than one kilometre from the Hornibrook house, were shocked by the kidnap of Timothy C. Hurley by armed men early one morning. According to the *Southern Star* of 22 April, this was apparently a case of mistaken identity and was thought to be linked to a wages dispute between the farmers and the labourers in the area – the post-war recession had struck with a vengeance during the middle of 1921 and across County Cork labourers were striking, occupying farms and attempting to intimidate the farmers into maintaining wages at current levels. The Hornibrook farm had been damaged in early February, and it is possible that this damage was linked to this dispute. When Matilda and Edward Woods visited Ballygroman two weeks before the kidnapping, they took the most unusual step of recording a full inventory of the furniture and farm contents – the family must have been concerned about their property, at least in relation to theft or malicious damage. This inventory was submitted as evidence in a compensation claim before the circuit court in Cork in 1926. It is possible that Herbert Woods came to Ballygroman at this time as an extra insurance policy, although there is no evidence of this.[25]

None of these incidents on their own amounts to very much, but when combined with the fact that the Hornibrooks could get few people to work for them due to the local labour dispute, they show that this must have been a difficult and troubled time for the family. These incidents are part of a long tradition of irritating agrarian intimidation and may have been the reason that an IRA guard had been placed on Ballygroman House in the second half of 1921 according to Nora Lynch.

In considering all of the available evidence, it seems that although Din Din O'Riordan had cast suspicion on the three related Nicholson/Hornibrook/Woods families, there is nothing to suggest that Thomas and Samuel Hornibrooks were suspected of being part of an Anti-Sinn Féin Society or of informing on the IRA, despite the fact that their home had a bird's-eye view of both the Lee and Bandon Valleys, and was situated directly along the safest IRA route from Cork to the west. Given where they lived, they should have been a prime asset for any British Army intelligence officer and we know that 'the Intelligence Officer of the area was exceptionally experienced'.[26]

Meda Ryan claims that 'the Hornibrooks were extremely anti-republican and in regular contact with the Essex in Bandon', but she presents no evidence for this.[27] All their dealings during the War of Independence were with the RIC, the Manchester Regiment in Ballincollig, and the petty sessions court in Farran on the north side of the ridge, so they would have had little reason to be involved with the Essex Regiment. Neither the BMH statements nor the published biographies of the war, nor any other records so far discovered, suggest that the Hornibrooks were actively informing. If there had been evidence, there is no doubt that the IRA had the capacity to find it and the ruthlessness to execute them long before 1922.

6

26 APRIL 1922:
THE SHOOTING ON THE STAIRS

Michael O'Neill, acting Battalion Commander of the IRA in Bandon, Stephen O'Neill (no relation), Charlie O'Donoghue and Michael Hurley arrived at the Hornibrooks' Ballygroman House some time after midnight on the morning of Wednesday 26 April 1922. According to the inquest, they arrived at around 1.30 a.m. on official business and knocked on the door.[1] After about fifteen minutes someone opened a window and asked who was there. They said they had business with Mr Hornibrook. Someone called out 'Sam' from the inside and the window was closed. The door was not opened, and after another fifteen minutes Michael found an open window and climbed in, along with Stephen O'Neill and Charlie O'Donoghue. Michael had a torch. As they climbed the stairs a shot rang out and Michael was hit in the stomach according to Charlie O'Donoghue.

At the inquest that followed, Dr Whelpy gave a detailed description of the wound, reported in the *Cork & County Eagle*, saying that Michael O'Neill had been 'shot in the chest 2 inches below the collarbone on a downward direction. There was no exit wound.'[2] It is likely that the shot was fired without warning, as stated by Charlie O'Donoghue at the inquest. Michael was carried out of the house, and the three men carrying him headed towards Killumney, about two kilometres away, looking for a doctor or a priest. Michael died on the roadside about 600 metres from the entrance to Ballygroman House. A small cross marks the spot, on the main Bandon–Killumney road, one kilometre to the south of the village.

Later on the morning of 26 April Charlie O'Donoghue returned to Ballygroman House with 'four military men'. According to the Hornibrooks' maid, Margaret Cronin, who saw what happened, the house was laid siege to for two-and-a-half hours and was 'riddled with bullets'.[3] Captain Herbert Woods, who admitted firing the shot on the previous night, was then arrested and taken away with Samuel and Thomas Henry Hornibrook.[4] The following day the coroner's jury at Bandon found that Herbert Woods was guilty of murder and the Hornibrooks guilty by association. As the evidence of Tadg O'Sullivan to the inquest was that he had sent Michael O'Neill to the house on unspecified official business, this was the only verdict the jury could have brought. Technically, the Bandon IRA was the legal authority at the time and if its members were there on official business they should have been allowed in, no matter the time. Whether this was a fair verdict, given the fact that only Herbert Woods had fired the shot, is a separate question.

The four 'military men' who accompanied Charlie O'Donoghue have never been identified. We know from Michael O'Donoghue's statement that there were approximately nine senior IRA officers in Bandon. Tom Hales, Liam Deasy and, possibly, Tadg O'Sullivan were in Dublin at the time. In his statement to the BMH, Tadg O'Sullivan states that he was 'Sent to Dublin with L. Deasy and Tom Hales re Pact' but he was back in Bandon to give evidence at the inquest. Charlie O'Donoghue was definitely in Ballygroman at the time of the shooting and on the following morning, when he arrested the Hornibrooks. Stephen O'Neill had been at Ballygroman when Michael O'Neill had been killed, and was in

Bandon for the inquest on Thursday 27 April, the morning after Michael's body was brought to the church, on Wednesday at 6.30 p.m.[5] Daniel O'Neill, the inspector of the Irish Republican Police at Bandon (and Michael's brother) attended the inquest. Another brother, Jack (John) O'Neill, and Con Crowley were two of the other officers recorded as IRA officers by Michael O'Donoghue in February, and Mick Crowley had replaced Michael O'Donoghue as engineering officer of the 3rd West Cork Brigade stationed at Bandon at the end of March. It would be surprising if the car that returned to Ballygroman to arrest the Hornibrooks did not include at least one of Daniel O'Neill, Jack O'Neill, Con Crowley, Stephen O'Neill, Michael Hurley or Mick Crowley, but there is no direct evidence of this. Charlie O'Donoghue could have taken four ordinary volunteers with him. Nobody knows.

IRA officers provided an honour-guard for Michael O'Neill's body on Wednesday and Thursday, and his funeral was a major military ceremony through the centre of Bandon on Friday 28 April. The chief mourners were Mr and Mrs Patrick O'Neill 'of Maryborough [*sic*, actually Maryboro]', Kilbrittain. His brothers Denis (Sonny), Jeremiah and John (Jack) also attended. Patrick Jnr is not mentioned as attending, but his sisters Molly and Maud were present. Floral tributes were sent by Tom Hales, Liam Deasy, Denis Lordan, Denis Sullivan and Con Lucey, among others. Charlie O'Donoghue and his brothers and sisters also placed a wreath on the grave. According to the *Cork Examiner*, 'his coffin was carried by his brother officers, and followed by thousands of Volunteers, and a firing party with arms reversed'.[6] He is buried beside the church in Kilbrittain in the republican plot.

What exactly happened to the Hornibrooks and to Herbert Woods is not known. Everyone in the area knows the folklore that has arisen around the kidnappings. All the known versions of the rumours are presented in this chapter. While they vary wildly in detail, they all agree that the Hornibrooks were taken to Templemartin and killed afterwards. Some suggest that Woods and the Hornibrooks were buried in Newcestown; others suggest they were buried further east or further west.

Peter Hart wrote that Charlie O'Donoghue returned to Ballygroman with rope, which implies that someone was going to be tied up or hanged. At the time at which Hart was writing there was no evidence for this, except an anonymous interview and local folklore.[7] This folklore had also suggested that Woods was dragged after the car in revenge for the same having been done to IRA 'bad boy' Leo Murphy at Waterfall in 1921.[8]

Another version of the story appeared in the *Cork Hollybough* in 2002, written by R. D. Kearney, who stated that 'a retired British Army Major named Hornibrook lived there with his wife, son, daughter and her husband Capt. Woods'.[9] He further stated: 'After some negotiations the mother, daughter and maid were allowed to go free, but the three men were reportedly subjected to violent torture before being taken to a secret location where they were summarily courtmarshalled and executed.' As Thomas Hornibrook was a widower in 1911, and his only daughter, Matilda, was married to Edward Woods, who lived in Crosses Green, this version cannot be accurate. Matilda was not in the house on the night.[10]

A different version was told to Dr Martin Healy, another owner of Ballygroman House, and his source was Father Crowley, the locally born parish priest of Ovens, who was four at the time of the shootings. He was told that Michael O'Neill had been carried on a door to the neighbouring house, where he died in the yard, and Herbert Woods was taken into the same yard the following morning and 'half hung between the shafts of a cart before being tied to the back of the Hornibrooks' car and dragged behind it'.[11]

Three similar versions of these rumours were told to local historians. Nora Lynch's main source was Mr O'Halloran of Ballincollig. Mr O'Halloran was not born in 1922, but the information was told to him by members of his family. Nora Lynch said that she spoke to Mr O'Halloran, who had lived in Templemartin[12] near to a disused forge called Lynch's Forge.[13] He told her that shortly after the disappearance of the three men from Ballygroman, a woman named Mary Horgan was passing the forge and heard men screaming.[14] She looked into the forge and saw men covered in scars. They were tied to a pig trough. Not knowing what to do, she went to the priest in Cloughduv and demanded that he return to the forge with her. Upon seeing the men, he blessed them and went to the commander of the local IRA to demand that they be moved. That night a group of IRA men arrived at the forge with carts and removed them. The O'Hallorans were told a few days later that they had been taken to Farranthomas bog, Newcestown, and made to dig their own graves. The O'Hallorans were also told that the men were not shot, but were axed into the grave and dismembered.[15]

Nora Lynch also said that another local rumour suggested that Michael O'Neill had been drinking with others in Killumney and had walked up the hill to the Hornibrooks' house to borrow Mr Hornibrook's car to get back to Bandon. Hornibrook had taken the carburettor (magneto) out of his car in case it got damp overnight. When O'Neill asked for the carburettor, Hornibrook, who had no idea who he was, refused. O'Neill broke into the house, and Herbert Woods grabbed a gun on the stairs. In the struggle to control the gun, it went off and O'Neill was shot in the stomach. The medical evidence at the inquest shows that O'Neill was shot in the chest from above and that the bullet pierced his heart, so this element of the rumour is not correct.

According to a different story also told to Nora Lynch, on the morning after the shooting a man from Ovens Bridge and two men from different families in Walshstown in Ovens, who were friendly with Michael O'Neill, went to the Hornibrooks' house. After a mêlée outside the house, in which one of the Hornibrooks received a broken nose from the butt of a rifle, the Hornibrooks were bundled into their own car and driven away to the west. The source for this was John Lucey of Grange, Ovens, who worked for the Hornibrooks. He said that when he saw his employer being attacked, he went to help him and was told to clear off if he knew what was good for him. Nora Lynch states that he told her the story when she was a young girl and he was a neighbour of hers. She also states that the killings were regularly discussed in the parish and that 'everyone knew the story'. There is no documentary evidence to support this information except that an agricultural labourer named John Lucey is recorded as living in Grange in the 1911 census.[16] When Nora Lynch went to write the story twenty years ago, she was told that she would be sued and she decided not to proceed.

Seán Crowley of Garranes, Templemartin, in his history of Newcestown published in 2005, provides another version of the story that was related to him. He states that the three men were taken to Scarriff, Templemartin, and court-martialled.[17] In his interview with me he said that while the men were held in Scarriff, Julia Hallahan and Margaret Murphy of Cumann na mBan provided tea and food for them. They were held at a disused house on Daniel Horgan's farm, which included Scarriff House. He had bought this from his neighbours, the Good family, in 1919.[18] Mr Horgan – who was in Bandon on business – was told that armed men were at his house. When he returned home he recognised some of the men holding the Hornibrooks, but he never revealed their names. According to Seán Crowley, they were being guarded by the Quarry's Cross Company (East Newcestown) of the IRA, which would have been normal if they had been arrested by the Irish Republican Police and taken into the company's area. Their 'prison' was the disused workman's house on his farm which later became known as 'the College' because Irish classes were held in it. He states that they were then seen being driven through Quarry's Cross and they were killed 'in the general Newcestown area'. He also suggests that if Michael O'Regan of the Ovens IRA had been protecting the Hornibrook house from agrarian agitation, as was normal, then the events that night would not have happened, as the Hornibrooks lent their car to him on request. However, in O'Regan's witness statement to the BMH, he makes no mention of the incident, despite the fact that the statement covered events up to May 1922.[19]

A little sketch map was drawn during Seán Crowley's interview, identifying where all the witnesses were living. The distance be-
tween Scarriff House and Horgan's original farm is about 500 me-tres. The disused work-man's house is close to Scarriff House. The tiny Methodist church building is still there today but now used as a private home.

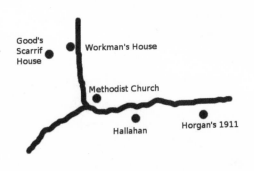

Donal O'Flynn, during his interview with me, paused and said, 'You must remember I grew up with the Hornibrooks – their story – I've known it for as long as I can remember.'[20] He was told that the bodies are buried in the locality, in the same field as two 'informers', one from the Brinny ambush (possibly Crowley) and the other a man from Bandon (whose name he was unable to provide).[21] He was also able to provide a great deal of information about the killings and the Hornibrooks, which both confirms and clarifies much of the information in the other rumours and stories.

Donal O'Flynn explained that Thomas Hornibrook was well liked and respected in the area, and was seen as a good neighbour. On the Sunday before his disappearance he had been paid nine pounds to convert the watchman's hut at Athnowen church into a bicycle shed. He was also a 'bit of a vet', and employed three people until his death. One of these was John Lucey, who worked on the farm. The cook was a woman from Macroom, whose name he could not recall (she was Margaret Cronin). On the morning of 25 April Herbert Woods went with Samuel and Thomas Hornibrook to get the train in Killumney. However, just as they reached the village, they saw the train crossing the railway bridge and so returned up the hill to wait for the next day.

That evening Michael O'Neill called with his friends to Killumney to find a car to take them back to Bandon. While there they had a couple of drinks and then after midnight walked up the hill to the Hornibrooks to borrow Mr Hornibrook's car. O'Neill was shot and carried down the hill to the main road (where his monument is now) and died there. Some of his friends gathered up the younger members of the local company and told them to watch the house. Donal O'Flynn refered to them as 'scouts' and clarified this to mean the Fianna, who were the youth wing of the IRA. The Hornibrooks had two to three hours after the shooting before the IRA had organised itself, and they could have gone to the Manchester Regiment in Ballincollig for protection in that time.

The IRA commandant in Ovens, Lieutenant Michael O'Regan, had given Thomas Hornibrook a gun to protect himself from agrarian agitators and would have intervened if he had known of the incident, but when it happened he was asleep more than three kilometres away on the other side of the parish. The first he knew of the incident was hours after the Hornibrooks had been taken away.

Donal O'Flynn stated that while Charlie O'Donoghue attempted to arrest the three men 'there was a mêlée' and Woods and the Hornibrooks were 'abused and kicked'. Herbert Woods 'had his nose broken by a blow from a rifle butt and it was practically hanging off'.[22] They were court-martialled at Ballygroman, forced into the Hornibrooks' own car and taken to 'the College' in Templemartin. They were held there before their execution. His source for this is the nephew of one of the firing party who took him to 'the College' to show him where it is. It is the same building identified by Seán Crowley. They were driven back east, where a grave was dug for them. Thomas Hornibrook threw his stick into it, saying 'Fire away.' He was 'defiant to the last'.[23]

On the following Sunday at second mass (noon) in Ovens, Michael O'Regan overheard some locals discussing a raid on the Hornibrooks' house. Initially locals had been afraid to approach the house. O'Regan went to the house and 'if you had taken a wardrobe he [O'Regan] made you put it back', so was 'not popular with the people of the locality'.[24] Some of the items taken were an oak table and six chairs, the sink and the silver service.[25]

With the exception of Margaret Cronin's evidence, there is no way of knowing which, if any, of these stories are true unless some of those involved left evidence or acknowledged their part in the disappearance of the Hornibrooks, or if the men's bodies are recovered. All the stories are based on local oral history and there are no verifiable documents to back up the claims.[26] However, these stories are far more grounded in the facts of real people in the locality than any other versions, and there is a logical cause and sequence of events. Too many people in Scarriff saw the three men after their arrest for these to be dismissed. Seán Crowley's story suggests that the Hornibrooks were openly court-martialled, held as prisoners at Templemartin and executed in the general Newcestown area. In my interview with Crowley, he explained his sources were direct family members of the people mentioned in the story and that he had no doubt as to the accuracy of their information. Donal O'Flynn's story agrees with Nora Lynch's story about having to borrow the car to get home, and confirms her comment that John Lucey worked for Hornibrook and was an eyewitness to the events.[27]

While some of the details of the rumours are different, they all place the events in the same localities of Ballygroman, Templemartin, Scarriff and Newcestown for the location of the Woods/Hornibrooks trial and execution. Donal O'Flynn alone says the trial was at Ballygroman, the imprisonment at Scarriff and the execution somewhere else. Clearly either Seán Crowley or Donal O'Flynn is mistaken about the location of the graves. O'Flynn suggests the men were driven east and executed, while Crowley suggests they were buried in the general area of Newcestown. The O'Halloran and O'Flynn stories are the most savage versions of the story that are told, and if the men in Lynch's Forge/Good's were the Hornibrook family (and it would incredible if they were not) then it seems like a straightforward revenge killing.[28]

While the execution of Woods possibly had justification, the Hornibrooks did not shoot Michael O'Neill and should not have been harmed. However, if they defended their home as vigorously as they had done during the arms raid of 1919, then, in the minds of the men who laid siege to the house for two-and-a-half-hours, they became complicit in the killing of Michael O'Neill. When I suggested that the killing of the three men was straightforward revenge to Donal O'Flynn, he stated that they were killed after an IRA court-martial because Herbert Woods had shot Michael O'Neill. However, the IRA had set up its police force (the Irish Republican Police) to ensure court judgements were enforced and fair procedures were followed. The accused had no benefit of counsel, Charlie O'Donoghue was witness and judge, clearly no defence was allowed and there was no right of appeal.

A number of weeks after the disappearances, Alice Hodder, from Fountainstown in Cork, wrote to her mother, parts of her letter giving a graphic account of what is rumoured to have happened:

> The murderers returned and caught Woods, tried him by mock court martial, and sentenced him to be hanged. The brothers of the dead man then 'got at him' as they say in this country and gouged his eyes out while he was still alive and then hanged him. I believe they also caught the uncle and aunt but I haven't heard what happened to them. The comment of all the country people around here, where the Woods lived in the summer and to whom the Woods were always generous and open-handed while here, was 'That will bring Mrs Wood's head down a bit'. As a matter of fact I believe Mrs Woods is a gentle retiring sort of woman – Does that not show the spirit of the people who are outwardly civil? Needless to say the Woods are Protestants.[29]

Much of Hodder's account seems to be based on the *Morning Post* reports of the incident, but as the *Southern Star* also reported the parliamentary question about the disappearances, she may have obtained the information from there.[30]

It should be remembered that Edward Woods said he had been ordered out of Cork city by the IRA as an alleged spy in June

1921 – before the Truce – having been caught up in allegations that he was part of the 'Anti-Sinn Féin Society' which included Blemens, Beale and Nicholson.[31] If the IRA had a report from the person they had watching the Hornibrooks' house that a person called Woods was staying there, then it is possible that it was assumed Edward Woods was staying there. This would be a reasonable explanation for Tadg O'Sullivan, Quartermaster of the IRA at Bandon, to order the Irish Republican Police to visit the Hornibrook house early in the morning on business, but in that case the men would have been armed. If Edward was expected it would explain later confusion about who was in the house.

Finally, we must turn to the previously overlooked evidence of Michael O'Donoghue from Cappoquin, who was an engineering student in University College Cork and became an engineering officer for the Cork City Brigade (his father had been a member of the RIC before retiring to Waterford, and his brother remained a member of the force throughout the War of Independence). His BMH witness statement confirms some of the details provided by the local historians in the only known comment from inside the anti-Treaty IRA. While he was not in Bandon at the time of the killings, he found out what happened from the people who had carried out the killings:

Poor Mick O'Neill: A grand chivalrous warrior of the I.R.A. Less than two months later, he called at the house of a British loyalist, named Hornibrook, to get help for a broken-down motor. As he knocked on the door, he was treacherously shot dead without the slightest warning by a hidden hand from inside the house. The I.R.A. in Bandon were alerted. The house was surrounded. Under threat of bombing and burning, the inmates surrendered. Three men, Old Hornibrook, his son and son-in-law, a Captain Woods. The latter, a

British Secret Service agent, confessed to firing the fatal shot. Why? God alone knows. None of the three knew O'Neill, or he them. Probably Woods got scared at seeing the strange young man in I.R.A. attire knocking, thought he was cornered and fired at him in a panic.[32]

Is Michael O'Donoghue's version of events any more credible than any other? He gets some of the details wrong, which is unsurprising as he was not there, but this is the only evidence we have from the side of the killers. The second part of his comments, linking the Ballygroman and Dunmanway killings, is far more important as it provides a motive for the Dunmanway shootings (and will be discussed further in Chapter 7).

Ultimately, the reader will have to decide for themselves how much of the 'evidence' presented in this chapter is to be believed. However, there is other information to be considered that may help the reader come to a firm conclusion: the Free State investigation of the Ballygroman events.

Over the following months, at the insistence of Matilda Woods, who was desperate to find out what had happened to her family, the Free State government initiated an investigation into the killings at Ballygroman. Matilda was initially moved to make inquiries by an *Irish Times* report on Thursday 27 April that 'it is understood that a member of the Hornibrook family had been arrested' for shooting Commandant Michael O'Neill.[33] What Matilda discovered concerned her deeply and she wrote to the Dublin government for the first time about the incident on 1 May 1922 from 'Glenbrae'.[34] However, the Free State investigation was hampered by the other, more important events that were happening at this time.

On 14 April 1922 the occupation of the Four Courts in Dublin by 300 armed men set in motion the train of events that led to the Irish Civil War, which officially broke out on 28 June when Free

State troops shelled the building. Among the thirty-two prisoners taken in this initial phase of the operation was Commandant Tom Barry of the West Cork IRA, who had tried to join his anti-Treaty comrades, disguised as a nurse. A suspicious Free State officer had unmasked him.

During the time of the Hornibrook and Dunmanway killings, the leadership of the pro- and anti-Treaty IRA, including Tom Hales, leader of the Bandon Brigade, had been in Dublin trying to hammer out a compromise on the Treaty, which was then rejected by the Four Courts garrison and de Valera. This compromise would have averted civil war and allowed the Treaty to be voted on in a plebiscite.[35] On rejection of their compromise much of West Cork chose the anti-Treaty side. This only made any investigation by the Free State of the killings in this area more complicated.

On 5 May the Department of Home Affairs of Dáil Éireann wrote to the Adjutant General of the army asking him to 'furnish your observations on the attached copy of a letter from Mrs M. W. Woods relative to the arrest on the 26th ultimo of her father'. On 9 May the department wrote again asking for information following a 'further urgent inquiry' from Mrs Woods. On 20 May Matilda wrote again looking for information, saying, 'I am nearly distracted going from post to pillar looking for information & nobody will give me any. I went to the local authorities here, and wrote to Bandon. They have ignored my letters …'. On 24 May the department wrote a brusque letter to the Adjutant General demanding 'forthwith … a report showing the result of your investigations in this case. It is obviously the Minister's duty to give all the information available in the matter to Mrs Woods immediately.' On 8 June the department wrote again, with no result, and on 13 June Wynne & Wynne solicitors wrote to the department on behalf of Matilda, asking for information. This letter, which confirms that Matilda, at least, had spent the previous two months trying to find information about her missing family and was still living in 'Glenbrae' at this time, was forwarded to the Adjutant General on 17 June, noting that the department had written on 5, 9 and 24 May with reminders on 9 and 24 May without success or reply.

A week later Brigadier-General Richard Colvin, a Conservative MP, raised questions about the case in the House of Commons, and the details were reported in the *Southern Star* on 3 June 1922. The full details of what happened are presented in the newspaper's report. Neither Colvin nor Mr F. Wood, who replied for the government, held out any hope for the missing men, with Wood stating that 'having regard to the time which had elapsed since they were kidnapped ... it must be presumed that they were dead'.[36] The case was again raised on 26 June during Irish Office questions by Lieutenant Colonel Archer Shee, who called for British government intervention.[37]

Once the Civil War started, all possibility of investigation ceased. It was very unlikely that people fighting against each other would co-operate as to the whereabouts of the three men. The case was taken up again only on 9 February 1923, when the Duke of Devonshire wrote to the Governor-General from the Home Office in Downing Street, stating that the office had received a request from the government of New Zealand for full particulars of the 'shooting of Mr Thomas Henry Hornibrook J.P. of Ballygorman [*sic*] House, Ovens, Cork, on 26th April last'. The request was made by a 'Mr Hornibrook, of Ngaire, Taranki in New Zeland [*sic*]'.[38] The letter was forwarded to the Department of Home Affairs.

On 15 February the Secretary of Home Affairs set out what had happened in the earlier investigation, and the fact that on 22 June 1922 Wynne & Wynne had suggested that they contact the Department of Defence instead. The Department of Home Affairs had done nothing since 22 June 1922, and it now closed its file with the classic, callous, civil service observation that: 'for reasons over which this Ministry had no control it was not possible to obtain details in the present case. As you [Cosgrave and the Governor-General] have now referred the matter to the Ministry of Defence for immediate attention there is no reason why we should communicate with him [Hornibrook] again.'

At 4 p.m. on 16 February, following a telephone conversation with W. T. Cosgrave, the Commander-in-Chief of the Free State Army wrote to the army's Director of Intelligence demanding that information about the fate of the Hornibrooks be made available before the following Saturday. The Duke of Devonshire's letter reached the Director of Intelligence on 17 February, with a comment that the President (William T. Cosgrave) was 'pressing very strongly for an answer before evening'. This eventually got results, even though the Director of Intelligence wrote back saying it was impossible to fulfil the request immediately.

Two weeks later, on 5 March, the Commander-in-Chief's office wrote again, demanding an answer to his two letters of 16 February, and his letter of 20 February.[39] A hand-written note on the text of the 5 March letter states that another reminder was sent on 7 March. At 12.20 p.m. on 7 March a coded message was sent from the Director of Intelligence to the Intelligence Officer in Cork, stating: 'Please reply at once to my radio of 17th Feb. Re: shooting of Hornibrook J.P. President and C-in-C pressing for report. *Most urgent.*' At 3.30 p.m. the Commander-in-Chief ordered the Director of Intelligence to call personally 'for my letters 16th and 17th, and 5th inst. regarding the shooting of Mr Thomas Hornibrook and see that a definite reply reaches me at the earliest possible moment about this case'. He also noted that a special reminder had been received by the Governor-General from the 'secretary of the colonies [*sic*]' in connection with the matter, and the President had 'made personal representations to this Office with a view to getting a reply'. Finally, at 8.20 p.m. on 7 March 1923, the command Intelligence Officer in Cork replied in code, which was translated in Portobello Barracks (headquarters) at 9.30 p.m. before being delivered to the Director of Intelligence at 9.55 p.m.:

> Hornibrook's daughter was married to Woods of Cork City an ex British Army Officer of Bandon. I.R.A. under Commandant Michael O'Neill for some obscure reason raided Hornibrook's about midnight April 26th 1922. Hornibrook refused to open door. Raiders entered by window of dining room. Woods was armed with Bulldog 45. Woods fired at raiders and O'Neill was killed. Hornibrook and Woods were taken prisoners and executed by raiders. Motive obscure! This report has been previously sent.

The Commander-in-Chief added his thoughts the following morning:

> The Irregulars under a Michael O'Neill, who styled himself 'Comdt', raided Mr Hornibrook's house for some obscure reason, and both Hornibrook and Woods were then taken prisoners by the raiders, and executed, probably out of revenge. The Director desires me to state that at the time this crime was committed, the perpetrators of it were in covert revolt against the Government.

No mention is made in either report of the third man, Samuel Hornibrook.

On 26 April 1922 there were technically no Irregulars (a

derogatory name for anti-Treatyites) and the Four Courts had been occupied only a week previously. The Civil War did not begin until late June, but even at this stage, divisions had emerged within the IRA. The Free State investigation concluded that members of the anti-Treaty IRA had executed the men in revenge for the killing of Commandant O'Neill.

The reply that Governor-General Tim Healy made to Devonshire in March 1923 said Woods and Hornibrook had been taken away by Irregulars and murdered in revenge for Michael O'Neill's death, which leaves no doubt about who killed them.[40] In November 1922 the British government accepted that the Irish government was unlikely to get to the bottom of some killings and that these murders would have to be dealt with by way of the Irish Grants Committee.[41] This is what happened in the Hornibrook case.

The Free State identified the killers as members of the anti-Treaty IRA, and both the British government and the Woods family accepted this. All sides acknowledged that the result was not at all satisfactory, but if the killers were unwilling to reveal themselves, then at the time there was little more could be done.

According to Martin Midgley Reeve, his aunts, who would only have been children at the time, remembered that the family left Ireland in 1922 after the shootings in Ballygroman, taking with them only a green trunk that was in the attic. They sat on the trunk while on the boat between Ireland and England. Once again there is some confusion about the date they left. According to his statement to the Irish Grants Committee, Edward Woods recalled that he had left Ireland in 1921. This is possible, but it would have been unlikely that the children went with him if he left at this time. It is also possible that he had returned after the Truce and had to flee a second time after the killings. Matilda was still living in 'Glenbrae' in April 1923 when her father's estate was probated. It is possible that the family left after this date, or she may have been staying there simply for the court case to get a court order to probate the estate.[42]

An article, with information supplied by Matilda, in the local Southend newspaper at the time of Edward's death in 1933 gives more details, although its accuracy is somewhat questionable:

> In 1922 during the Sinn Féin disturbances, Mrs Wood's father, a Justice of the Peace, her brother, and a nephew, were killed in Cork by the rebels. Mr and Mrs Woods, who lived some distance away, were given 24 hours to leave the country. They fled for their lives and the distillery business at Cork was destroyed.[43]

They left with little or nothing, no matter when they left. After all, the Cook Street business had been burned by the Black and Tans in December 1920, and little or no compensation had been paid out at this stage to the victims. Between late 1922 and 1927 they lived in Wickford in Essex, but by the time of their statements to the Irish Grants Committee in 1927 they had moved to live in 'Eastwood', Crowestone Road North, Westcliff-on-Sea. This was a substantial house, which suggests that their fortunes had improved. Matilda died in 1934 and the terms of her will were published in the *London Gazette*:

> Notice is hereby given that all creditors and other persons having any debts, claims or demands against the estate of Matilda Warmington Woods, late of Burlescoombe House, Burlescoombe Road, Thorpe Bay, in the county of Essex, deceased (who died on the 3rd day of March, 1934, and whose Will was proved in the Principal Registry of the Probate Division of His Majesty's High Court of Justice on

the 20th. day of April, 1934, by National Provincial Bank Limited, of 15, Bishopsgate, in the city of London, the executors therein named), are hereby required to send the particulars, in writing, of their debts, claims or demands to us, the undersigned, the Solicitors.

Dated this 27th day April, 1934. *Dennes, Lamb and Drysdale*, 41, Clarence Road, Southend-on-Sea, Solicitors for the Executors.[44]

When Matilda died her estate passed on to her children. Martin Midgley Reeve explained that the National Provincial Bank became trustee of the four children until they had made 'good marriages'.[45] In 1949 her remaining property in Ireland was disposed of, and Ballygroman House was sold for £120, according to a deed of probate in the Irish National Archives, and the money was divided between her daughters.[46]

No amount of compensation could ever repay loved ones for the loss of family members, and there is no doubt that both Edward and Matilda were traumatised by what happened. As part of their claim for compensation, Matilda had to submit to a medical examination by the Grants Committee doctor, who agreed that her mental condition was poor as a result of the stress of trying to find her father and brother in the years after their disappearance.

While there have been suggestions that the family's lands were seized by the Irish Free State, these are clearly untrue.[47] She and her brother, Thomas Henry Hornibrook, were given the farm and the house in 1923.[48] In 1926 Matilda and Edward returned to Ireland to see if they could track down her father and the others. They visited the house to find it burned and looted, and the fences torn down. Trees of a value of some £200 had also been cut down according to Edward in their joint claim to the Irish Grants Committee in 1927. A house unoccupied for three years was always likely to be a target, but as we have seen, Michael O'Regan's evidence suggests that the house was stripped shortly after the kidnappings. Matilda and Edward's main reason for returning was to attend the circuit court in Cork on 29 July, where Matilda claimed £1,606 12s for the destruction of the house. During this hearing she stated that the second attack on the house on the morning after Michael O'Neill's shooting was a 'fierce attack with machine gun and rifle fire'. She went on to say that the three occupants 'suffered the extreme penalty and subsequently the house was destroyed'. Her claim was granted with a 15 per cent discount for depreciation, which her architect agreed was a fair amount, and she was awarded £1,362. As previously stated, Matilda said that she and Edward had visited her father two weeks before the kidnappings.[49] A second claim for £2,654 for the furniture and farm machinery was adjourned until two days later. They were awarded for £1,963 for this claim.[50]

On 31 January 1927 the couple made a joint claim to the Irish Grants Committee (a lot of claimants made applications despite already having received compensation).[51] The graphic details that appear in Matilda's claim for damages before the Grants Commission in London are mentioned in no court report, which presumably means she did not reveal them. Matilda told the Grants Committee: 'Herbert Woods it was ascertained afterwards was hung, drawn and quartered in the presence of my father and brother. Then my father and brother had to make their own graves and were shot and buried.' The Woods were granted £6,575 in compensation between them after a protracted hearing.[52] The final payments were not made until 10 March 1929. According to the committee's terms of reference, as Matilda did not have a housing need and did not suffer any personal material loss, she would have been entitled to only a small amount of compensation for the trauma she suffered at the deaths of her family. A valuation for the Ballygroman property, by George Joyce of Cork on 18 August

1926, confirms that she was in sole possession of the burned house, the intact steward's house and a small cottage, along with the land which was not being farmed. She was in dispute with the Irish government, which wanted the house rebuilt as per the regulations for compensation, while she wanted to use the money for property elsewhere.

In a 1928 report titled 'Taken away by armed party', Matilda probates the estate of Samuel Hornibrook through an affidavit before Justice Hanna. This confirms that she was his half-sister and generally summarises what happened again.[53] It appears that Thomas Henry Hornibrook Jnr made a claim from New Zealand in 1931 for a share of the Hornibrook estate.

In the final analysis it is up to the reader to effectively act as juror and decide which of the pieces of testimony recorded in this chapter are valuable and which can be discarded.

Having spoken to Matilda Woods' grandson, Martin Midgley Reeve, I am in no doubt that what hurts him most is having no grave marker for his family and no bodies to mourn. Anyone who has searched for a missing person will understand his feelings; in my view, his wish that the location be disclosed should be granted. Other bodies from this time also lie in the bogs of Ireland, and more than enough time has passed for those who can help to recover these to do so.

However, the consequences of the Ballygroman killings did not end with the Woods and O'Neill families.

7

The Dunmanway Killings

Still, it is the primary right of men to die and kill for the land they live in, and to punish with exceptional severity all members of their own race who have warmed their hands at the invaders' hearth.

Winston Churchill[1]

The (Dunmanway Murders) are being undertaken because the Southern Irish native is a barbarous savage with a strong inherent penchant for murder which those responsible for him – his priests, his politicians and his alleged organs of enlightenment – have not only failed to eradicate from his primitive bosom, but have actually fostered.

Morning Post[2]

The Ballygroman killings were bad enough on their own, but over the next four nights (26–29 April 1922) there were widespread attacks on loyalists across West Cork. The motive for these attacks has already generated huge debate within Irish history regarding the interpretation of evidence. As the actual evidence tends to get lost in the debate, I have chosen to concentrate on that evidence here. In total, nine Protestants were killed between the towns of Dunmanway and Bandon in West Cork, one in Clonakilty and another was shot and badly injured in Murragh, on the main road between Bandon and Ballineen. If the Ballygroman killings are included, as well as those of four British soldiers who were

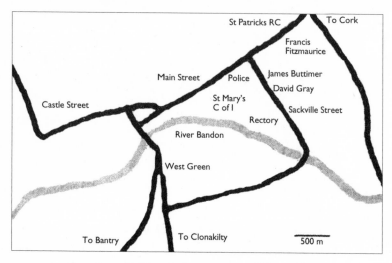

Locations of killings in Dunmanway © Barry Keane

kidnapped and executed while on intelligence work at Macroom, twenty-five kilometres north of Dunmanway, this brings the total of dead to seventeen.[3] If those who were targeted but not killed are included, the figure rises to at least thirty. In Dunmanway, for example, William Jagoe's house was attacked and if he had been at home it is probable that he too would have been shot. George 'Appy' Bryan had a gun placed to his head but the gun jammed and he fled. Local schoolteacher William Morrison also escaped from attack, as did John McCarthy and Tom Sullivan.[4] This level of attack on defenceless civilians was unheard of in the Irish War of Independence, and as virtually all the victims were Protestant it raised fears that the killings were sectarian.

Specifically, on the night of 26–27 April three men were shot and killed in Dunmanway: local solicitor Francis Fitzmaurice was killed at 12.15 a.m., chemist David Gray at 1 a.m. and retired draper James Buttimer at 1.20 a.m. All were shot on their doorsteps. According to David Gray's wife, his killers called him a

Free Stater a number of times while they were shooting him. All this took place within a hundred metres of the police station in Dunmanway, which was controlled by the anti-Treaty IRA under Peadar Kearney, who failed to stop them. During the second night, 27–28 April, John Chinnery and Robert Howe were shot in Castletown-Kinneigh to the north of Ballineen at around 1.30 a.m. according to the *Cork & County Eagle* of 6 May, or 10.30 p.m. for Howe according to *The Irish Times* of 2 May. Chinnery and Howe were next-door neighbours. The pattern was the same in both cases. Howe's wife, Catherine, gave evidence to his inquest that he was attacked in the bedroom of his house at around 10.30 p.m., having refused to harness a horse. When he refused a second time he was shot and killed. John Chinnery was shot while harnessing a horse for the raiders. On the same night Alexander Gerald McKinley, who was sick in bed, was shot in Ballineen after 1.30 a.m. His aunt was put out of the house and he was shot in the back of the head. At Caher, three kilometres west of Ballineen, John Buttimer and his farm servant James Greenfield were shot at 2 a.m.:

Frances Buttimer (John's wife) stated that she heard noise and shots – Her son said 'we are being attacked', and jumped out of bed. She became weak, but recovered quickly. She met her husband on the landing, and said 'for God's sake get out', and he said 'shure I can't'. Greenfield called on her to stay with him. She came down stairs, and met a man and said 'Where are you going?' He replied 'Where are the men?' She said 'I do not know. What do you want them for?' He said 'only very little'. She said to him 'Take my house, my money, or myself and spare the men'. She put her hand to his chest to keep him back, and he pushed past her, and went upstairs calling on her husband in a blasphemous manner to come down. She went away from the house and returned after a while and met a man and said 'You have killed them, but you cannot kill their souls'.[5] She went into the house and found her husband dead in a sitting position in Greenfield's room, and Greenfield was dead in bed.[6]

Church of Ireland curate Rev. Ralph Harbord was shot (but not killed) in Murragh on the same night. Robert Nagle was shot and killed in Clonakilty after 11 p.m. Two men called to the house and, having questioned Robert about his age, they doused the light in his bedroom and shot him. His mother, who was in the house and witnessed the events, said one of the killers was drunk. He was shot in place of his father, Tom, the caretaker of the Masonic Hall, and on the same night the Masonic Hall was burned.[7]

The final victim was John Bradfield of Killowen Cottage at Cahoo, four kilometres west of Bandon. He was killed at 11 p.m. on the night of 29–30 April in place of his brother William:[8]

Elizabeth Shorten (his sister) … stated that at 11 p.m. on Saturday a group of men called to the door to get a horse and car. Her brother got out of bed, but did not answer. They knocked on the door and broke the windows. On entering the dining room, they asked for her brother William. They entered John's room and she heard a shot. John was unable to walk without sticks.[9]

More than thirty men of both main religions were targeted, shot at or forced to flee over the same three days, but all those killed were Protestant. As the killings continued into a third night, the officer in charge of the Royal Navy based at Queenstown (Cobh) began putting contingency plans in place to evacuate loyalists and Protestants from southern Irish ports.[10] He even suggested that this might well be the start of a pogrom.

Many scholars have recognised the importance of the information contained in the inquest report into the killing of John Buttimer and James Greenfield in Caher. Others give less weight to Frances Buttimer's account. Anyone who reads her testimony should conclude that the killer was calm and focused on his mission. Her bravery – in putting her hand out to bar the way of an armed man who had broken into her home in the middle of the night looking for 'the men' – is heroic. There was a general prohibition on killing women, but it is extraordinary that the gunman did not harm her person in any way. Clearly the Buttimer family home was targeted for a reason: it was awkward to get to and was surrounded by other Protestant homes that were more accessible. If this was a sectarian attack, why did the attackers walk past those other homes and target the Buttimers? The killers knew who they wanted, and they apparently pursued the son, who escaped them, relentlessly, though the only source for this is an anonymous interview.

Theories about the 'who and why' of the events in Dunmanway have been proposed for a long time. Henry Kingsmill Moore was the principal of the Church of Ireland teacher-training college in Kildare Place, Dublin, for much of this period and was one of the first to use the term 'Dunmanway massacre', in his autobiography written in 1930.[11] He stated that the massacre was in response to the Belfast 'pogroms', and gave details of the events 'from someone who was there'.

The traditional view was that the killings 'violently in conflict with the traditions and principles of the Republican Army' were an aberration and a stain on the West Cork IRA.[12] At the time there was a dispute between Cork Corporation and Cork County Council as to whether the killing of Michael O'Neill was a possible trigger. However, in the absence of any other evidence, local people concluded that the killings were a response to the Belfast 'pogroms'.

It was not until 1993 that any serious attempt was made to challenge this traditional view. In truth, most people had forgotten about the incident. Certainly, it was mentioned to me in passing when I was talking to Protestants in West Cork in 1986–87 about migration, but details were sketchy and people were far more interested in hammering home the point that the *Ne Temere* decree of 1908 was the single greatest threat to the native Protestant community during the period.[13]

In 1990 Kevin Myers, the person who kick-started this debate, declared in *The Irish Times* that leading West Cork IRA members Peadar Kearney and Sonny Crowley were among the killers, without presenting any evidence to back up his claims.[14] Tim Pat Coogan, in his 1992 book *The Man who Made Ireland: the Life and Death of Michael Collins*, ascribed the killings to 'latent sectarianism of centuries of ballads and landlordism', also without presenting any direct evidence.[15]

It was not until Peter Hart entered the debate that a sustained challenge to the orthodoxy was attempted. Because it is not too strong a claim to suggest that civil war in Irish historical studies broke out in 1998 with the publication of Hart's book *The IRA and Its Enemies*, it is worth looking at his arguments and the counter-arguments in some detail.

At first Hart's book was received with critical acclaim and, as readers assumed that all of his assertions were supported by the copious and meticulous referencing, there was no reason not to be generous in praise of the book. Indeed Kevin Myers, writing in *The Irish Times*, was ecstatic at the publication and flagged the book repeatedly in his 'Irishman's diary'.[16] When discussing the murders of 26–29 April 1922, Hart argued that in revenge for Michael O'Neill's death, the IRA – as a result of a process of intimidation and exclusion which had increased during the War of

Independence – punished and attempted to drive out members of the minority Protestant community because they were Protestant. He concluded that 'the Catholic reaction to the murders was so muted' because Protestants had become outsiders.[17] As Hart apparently had identified a host of sources to back up his arguments, he told a seemingly accurate story of what happened both before and after the killings, and the inherent claim of sectarianism had to be accepted, no matter how unpalatable this was for nationalists and the descendants of the 3rd Cork Brigade. Despite his use of overly dramatic language, a society, brought up on the belief that the War of Independence was the final act in a long struggle to cast off the imperialist yoke, was being challenged to accept that sectarian motives were at the heart of it in West Cork and that 'they had closed ranks' against their neighbours when they had needed them.[18]

Hart explicitly, for example, rejected the possibility that the motive for the Dunmanway killings was that those shot had been part of a 'Loyalist plot'. Based on his research, common sense suggested that his fundamental argument about the Dunmanway massacre was accurate: 'In the end, however, the fact of the victims' religion is inescapable. These men were shot because they were Protestant.'[19] Hart said that Protestants had little information to give, and that if they were targeted as spies it was a result of paranoia brought on 'by a welter of suspicions and a sectarian and ethnic subtext'.[20]

Not long after publication, however, local historian Meda Ryan, Brian Murphy PhD (a Glenstal Abbey priest), the Millstreet-based Aubane Historical Society and, of course, all strands of Sinn Féin began to criticise Hart's work. They were dismissed as 'cranks' or 'republican sympathisers'[21] until Murphy showed that Hart had selectively quoted the British Army intelligence document that was central to his argument.[22] Instead of pointing out that Bandon was an exceptional area of loyalist co-operation with the authorities, Hart stated that the complete opposite was the case.[23] In more recent years other historians – including former colleagues, some of whom had previously vigorously defended him – have also questioned the accuracy of Hart's work.[24] The quotation identified by Murphy was:

> … the truth was that, as British intelligence officers recognised in the south, the Protestants and those who supported the Government rarely gave much information because, except by chance, they had not got it to give. *An exception to this was in the Bandon area, where there were many Protestant farmers who gave information. Although the Intelligence Officer of the area was exceptionally experienced and although the troops were most active it proved almost impossible to protect those brave men, many of whom were murdered while almost all the remainder suffered grave material loss.*[25]

Hart leaves out the section I have indicated in italics in the quotation above and it seems that this exclusion must have been deliberate.[26] This omission did not fatally damage Hart's analysis, but it encouraged Brian Murphy and Niall Meehan to re-examine Hart's other sources. Meda Ryan, who initially focused her research on Hart's treatment of the Kilmichael ambush, where he had called Tom Barry little more than a serial killer (language which was certain to inflame passions in West Cork), was subsequently also highly critical of Hart's analysis of the Dunmanway killings.[27]

Meehan and Murphy criticised twelve areas where they had serious concerns about Hart's work.[28] As some of the complaints are trivial, and others require reference to a relatively inaccessible thesis and a host of other articles by various authors, the key arguments tend to get lost in the forest of detail. This doesn't mean that the criticisms were wrong, however, just difficult to follow.[29]

The obvious nationalism of many of his critics allowed Hart to ignore much of their work and his untimely death in 2010 should have brought an end to the controversy, as there was nobody left to debate. However, the controversy continues. John Regan of the University of Dundee, who had been a friend and colleague of Hart's, entered the debate in recent years to criticise Hart's use of elision: the selective quotation of documents to build an ahistorical argument which is propaganda rather than history.[30] David Fitzpatrick rejected these criticisms as 'dismissible, for the most part, as the fantasies of cranks', in response to Regan's 2012 article in *History Ireland*, which summarised his critique of Hart's methodology.[31] Fitzpatrick suggested that many of the chosen examples of 'elision' are not significant or are footnotes that had gone astray. He declared that Regan's article 'adds to an unseemly chorus' of 'suggestions and innuendos [that] have long been circulated by bloggers and republican apologists with the result that the popular reputation of Hart and other historians may have been corroded'.[32]

In my view, the debate about Hart's methodology and his theory has polluted examination of the actual history. While researching this book, much of my time was taken up re-examining Hart's research on the topic. I have already published some of my detailed analysis of his work, which is freely available on Academia.edu or on my website 'Protestant Cork 1911–26'.[33] In one way Hart should be thanked for placing an obscure field of study inhabited by only dusty demographers, military historians and hagiographers centre stage in modern Irish history. Whether the subject deserves its exalted position is another matter. Hart's history and historiography have become such a battleground because they were so different to the traditional view of the war in Cork, were misused by others to pursue their own agendas and showed, when they were examined by the 'cranks', that there was a lot to be cranky about.

Hart's history of individual events in relation to Ballygroman and Dunmanway is substantially accurate; he shows that there *was* an unauthorised and illegal attempt between 26 and 29 April 1922 to punish and drive out mostly Protestant unionists (a political group) by some members of the IRA in response to the murder of Michael O'Neill. However, nationalists and Roman Catholics did not close ranks against local Protestants and divide up the spoils, as he claimed.[34] If anything, the opposite was the case. When Hart strays into speculation about motive, based on questionable use of sources, his work becomes ahistorical, and when questionable quotes are underpinned by anonymous interviews, these sections cannot be called history.[35]

Those who defend Hart's history cannot deny that he was less than fair to the reader in his work. Information which would damage his theory was omitted from the quotations he himself selected. Why he chose to do this is a separate question. None of the criticisms of Hart mean that everything he wrote is incorrect, but these criticisms force the reader to return to the sources to check that he accurately reports the facts. Sometimes he does; sometimes he does not. Sometimes it may be accidental; sometimes it cannot be anything other than deliberate. Telling the unvarnished truth is one of the cornerstones of academic research; what, then, is the reader expected to do when it comes to Hart? Ultimately, the reader will have to decide for themselves as to the value of his work.

In some ways, Gerard Murphy's view in his reassessment of the Dunmanway murders in *The Year of Disappearances*, that these were unauthorised killings, comes closest to the traditional view. However, Murphy also suggested a link with his claims of the IRA's pursuit of 'teenage boys' and also Freemasons in Cork city. He speculated that the prime anti-Treaty IRA targets were William Jagoe, the leader of the local Boy's Brigade, and William Morrison, the local schoolteacher, for being 'connected to young people' in Dunmanway.[36] William Jagoe had a slightly different interpretation of why he was targeted on the night of 26 April. Murphy also speculated that the similarity of Ballineen victim Gerald McKinley's name to that of Rev. McKinley, who left Cork city around this time, demonstrated a connection between his claims of a vendetta against Freemasons and the Dunmanway killings. However, Murphy now believes that internal church politics were responsible for the departure and that there was no link between the murder of Gerald McKinley and the departure of Rev. Harold McKinley.[37]

Suggestions by Owen Sheridan and Jack Lane that the Dunmanway attacks were carried out by British agents to prompt a re-invasion rest on the testimony of Alice Gray, who recalled that when her husband was shot the killers said, 'Take that you Free Stater', several times, and on the evidence of Robert Nagle's mother, who said that she had not recognised the killers of her son in Clonakilty, one of whom was unmasked.[38] According to this theory, ultra unionists – possibly organised by Sir Henry Wilson (the new military advisor to the Northern Irish government, who was assassinated by the IRA a few weeks later) – arrived in West Cork and carried out the killings. While there is no doubting Alice Gray's recollection, or Nagle's mother's statement, there is no evidence trail leading to the British or to Henry Wilson. It is even possible that David Gray was shot in error, as he lived next door to James Buttimer, who was shot twenty minutes after Gray, according to the inquest report in the *Cork & County Eagle*.

The second main theory about why the men shot in April 1922 were killed is the informer theory. This suggests that their names were on a list of 'helpful' citizens found in the Dunmanway workhouse after it was evacuated in late January 1922. The theory is controversial, because its main proponent, Meda Ryan, has not furnished a copy of the list for scrutiny by any other historian. As a result the theory deserves close examination. There are now three pieces of evidence of varying quality to support this theory and these will be considered in detail here. The first is Pat O'Brien's BMH witness statement, the second relates to the murder of Patrick Cronin in Dunmanway in August 1921, and the third is the Dunmanway Dossier discussed by Meda Ryan in her biography of Tom Barry, *Tom Barry: IRA Freedom Fighter*.

Pat O'Brien's BMH statement from Dunmanway shows that the IRA had obtained direct evidence as early as 1921 from the Auxiliaries' own list as to who was pro-British in this area:

> The Auxiliaries' C[ommanding] O[fficer] was de Havilland and Brownie was the I[ntelligence] O[fficer]. He instituted a very perfect intelligence system and ... drew up lists of all the houses in the Dunmanway Battalion area, both friendly and hostile to the British régime ... However, any of his investigations ... were with us just as soon, thanks, to Florence J. Crowley, the Clerk of the Union.[39]

There is a similar story in the *Southern Star*'s 1971 'Black and Tan diary' series about how Crowley gathered and passed on the information to Pat O'Brien.[40] As the clerk of the workhouse and a 'friendly' angler, who drank in the workhouse with the Auxiliaries, Crowley aroused no suspicion when he regularly went fishing at Manch Bridge. Once there, he left the information in O'Reilly's cottage and Pat O'Brien would pick it up.

This means the IRA had a list of 'friendly' houses before the end of the War of Independence, and there is no doubt that the Auxiliaries were not loved in Dunmanway. On the face of it, Pat O'Brien's evidence shows that the April 1922 victims may well have been identified as friendly to the British interest during the War of Independence and this is why they were targeted, but unless an actual list is discovered there is no direct evidence to connect one set of facts with the other.[41] Headquarters in Cork regularly asked for lists; for example, on 2 June 1921 headquarters requested the very discreet collection of the names and current addresses of all resident magistrates, justices of the peace, crown solicitors and petty sessions clerks, and there is no doubt that some of the victims would have appeared on this list.[42]

One list may be of particular significance. Without attempting to create another conspiracy theory, J. Buttimer from Sovereign Street in Clonakilty was named as an enemy agent by the West Cork Brigade in July 1921. James Buttimer, who was shot in Dunmanway, was this man's uncle. As this has been the least understandable of these murders (the man was eighty-two and a member of the pro-Home Rule All for Ireland League), this information provides a possible explanation for his death. It may be only a coincidence or it may be highly significant that two of the murdered men were called J. Buttimer. In my view it suggests that once a family had been identified as 'hostile' by the murderers, then a male member of that family was shot in reprisal for Michael O'Neill's death. While this provides a motive for this killing, any reasonable person would have to conclude that this was no justification for it.[43]

William Jagoe, a Dunmanway merchant, provides further information about IRA targeting of individuals identified as informants after the Truce. William had been sought out to be murdered on 26 April. He discusses the murder of Patrick Cronin in Dunmanway in August 1921 as part of his compensation claim in 1927. Jagoe had been told on the night Cronin was killed that 'Truce or no Truce he [Jagoe] was one of seven men marked down for assassination' in the town for collaborating with the British. Patrick's murder was also the subject of a compensation claim by Mary T. Cronin in 1927. Patrick Cronin's parents, who had been dependent on him, were awarded £400.[44]

Meda Ryan's core claim is that an Auxiliary intelligence diary (notebook, actually) left behind in the Dunmanway workhouse along with other documents identified all but two of the men shot in 1922 as 'informers' or 'helpful citizens'.[45] Photographs of the diary were donated to the BMH by Flor Begley in 1947 and are easily accessible to any visitor at the Military Archives in Cathal Brugha Barracks in Dublin.[46] In 1971 Flor Crowley, when writing a series of articles for the *Southern Star*,[47] got this diary on loan from 'a man whose IRA rank in 1921 and earlier entitled him to hold and preserve all enemy documents coming into the possession of the IRA of those days. This one came into the possession of the IRA in a peculiar way.'[48] According to Crowley, it came into the man's

Two pages from the Auxiliary intelligence diary (courtesy of the Bureau of Military History)

156

possession in early 1922, along with 'a lot of "paper" left behind by the Tans'.[49] There have been some suggestions that the diary was found when the workhouse was repaired in the late 1920s, but as the building was burned to the ground in mid-summer 1922 this seems unlikely. Crowley's 1971 series identified only four named informers: two IRA men who had information beaten out of them, one paid informer and one loyalist. He also states that 'strangely the names of the [previously] known informers are never mentioned'.[50] He did not give the four men's names and this has led to much of the controversy and speculation surrounding the diary, but they are legible in the photographed version. On 27 November Crowley wrote about the loyalist's motives:

> In his case it must have been out of his sense of loyalty on the one hand and his source of resentment against young men of his own locality whom he regarded as his enemies – it must be one or other of those two things that prompted him to turn informer. I knew that man in my young days and I never heard one word of suspicion uttered against him. He was a loyalist, yes, but many others were loyalists as well as he was and they did not do what he did.[51]

The article clearly rules out any of the men shot during the Dunmanway killings being taken from this list, as this loyalist was still alive after 1922 and the other three men are clearly identifiable in the military archives and do not include those killed.

According to Flor Crowley, the diary and the other papers found in the workhouse had been sent to IRA headquarters in Bandon for analysis. As previously stated, Meda Ryan suggests that those shot in Dunmanway were listed as 'helpful citizens' in the Dunmanway 'find'.[52] She claims that all the names of those killed are to be found in documents that were in the possession of Dan Cahalane, or in Tom Barry's private correspondence, or in other documents and evidence in her possession or that she has seen.[53] Such is the controversy surrounding this subject that all source documents should be made publicly available – redacted if necessary. This includes Peter Hart's anonymous interviews.

Two other entries in the diary may be related to the men shot in 1922: the first is '"Rushfield House" Saturday night' (underlined). In the 1911 census in Bengour, William Howe owned Rushfield House in Castletown-Kinneigh. He was likely to have been a cousin of Robert Howe, and Rushfield is only two kilometres from Prospect Cottage in Ballaghanure where Robert was shot. This connection between Rushfield House and the Auxiliary diary may have caused Robert Howe to be targeted in error by individuals who knew a Howe in Castletown-Kinneigh was in the diary, or it may just be a coincidence. It is also possible that John Chinnery was shot because he was William Howe's nephew.

The case of Robert Howe has always been particularly problematic, as there is no evidence to connect him to any anti-Sinn Féin conspiracy. Even Peter Hart's attempt to explain his targeting is unsatisfactory. Hart states that he was 'no stranger to political controversy, having been accused of slander during the 1914 county council elections'.[54] In fact, Howe took out an advertisement to apologise to local national schoolteacher Patrick Galvin for claiming that 'he had sold his vote for a pecuniary consideration'.[55] As there is no mention of any political affiliation, it is hard to see the relevance of this to the later murders.

John Chinnery must be considered in tandem with Robert Howe. The Chinnery household is fifty metres south-east of Prospect Cottage, and the Howes and Chinnerys were most likely distant relations.[56] Given that they lived next door to one another, it is possible that Chinnery and Howe were actually shot for the trivial reason of refusing the 'order' to harness a horse by a couple of trigger-happy gunmen heading west to shoot John Buttimer and James Greenfield at Caher, five kilometres (an hour's walk) to the west. However, Meda Ryan states that a 1949 letter from Risteárd Ó Glaisne, in Tom Barry's private collection, says that John Chinnery had been targeted by the IRA on a number of occasions after the IRA had caught him red-handed when he dropped a letter he was posting to the British Army.[57] Again the reader will have to weigh this information and decide how valuable Ó Glaisne's letter is, given the fact that it was written more than twenty years after the event.

The second entry that may be connected with the 1922 killings says 'Sun Lodge – information Buttimer Manch – by Blackwater Bridge'. Sun Lodge is marked on the 25-inch Ordnance Survey map just off the main Dunmanway–Bandon road at Manch. John Buttimer and James Greenfield lived in Caher, less than two kilometres away up the hill from Sun Lodge, and it is possible that this diary information may have been used to target these victims.

Among modern historians, only Meda Ryan has seen all the available documents that were part of the Dunmanway 'find'. I do not know if the pages in the Military Archives are the complete 'find' but I am certain that they are exactly the same documents covered in the 1971 series by Flor Crowley. As the diary does not identify the 1922 men as spies, and the only loyalist spy it mentions was alive after the killings (according to Flor Crowley in 1971), it is difficult to see – other than for the Rushfield and Sun Lodge entries – what relevance it may have had.

Turning to how the rest of the men were targeted, it must be remembered that Michael O'Neill's brother, Sonny, was the intelligence officer of the Southern Brigade and would have had access to all information in the brigade's possession.[58] If he was asked by the killers, it is possible that he might have provided some of the information that caused the targeting of these men. As there is no openly available verifiable documentary evidence to either confirm or deny this theory, it is impossible to make a proper judgement on it, but nothing suggests that he was involved.

In *Tom Barry: IRA Freedom Fighter* Meda Ryan states that Dunmanway woman Eileen Lynch told her that, as children, they had been warned away from David Gray because his kindness was a mask for gathering information. Ryan says that both David Gray and Francis Fitzmaurice have been 'firmly established' as spies, but presents no reference for this.[59] It is difficult to assess the value of the evidence of someone who was a child in 1922, although Lynch undoubtedly gave an accurate portrayal of what she remembered. She also lists five Protestant families in Dunmanway who she said were either helpful to their Catholic neighbours or actively nationalist: O'Meara, Atkins, Smyth, Cox and Wilson. However, some doubt is cast on her recollection when other facts are considered. For example, one of the three Wilson families in the town was caught up in the Dunmanway killings and fled to England for a month. The other was the rector's family, who remained, and the other Wilsons were Roman Catholic. The only Smiths or Smyths in the town were also Roman Catholic and provided a car for Tom Barry after the Fanlobbus ambush.[60]

There is another possible reason for the killings. An amnesty had been granted to all for the 'wrongs of the past' once the Treaty was signed in December 1921 and was issued on 9 February 1922 by the Provisional Government, but it only went as far as the writ of the Free State ran.[61] Collins may have unintentionally stoked the pot by replying forcefully to Lord Bandon 'that loyalists will be afforded the protection of the government in accordance with the recent amnesty proclamation' in a letter published in the *Southern*

Star on 8 April. The West Cork IRA may well have repudiated any such proclamation, as it did not recognise the Provisional Government, but there is no evidence of this.

It has been suggested that the victims of April 1922 were members of either the Protestant Action Group or the Anti-Sinn Féin Society, which would explain their targeting, but many scholars, including Hart and Murphy, claim that these names were a cover for the Auxiliaries, 'who dressed up as a bunch of old farmers' to go on raids, and evidence of an 'unfailing IRA belief in conspiracy theories', and they dismiss the possibility of a native Anti-Sinn Féin group existing in Bandon.[62] This might be the case, but Meda Ryan argues, with justification, that there is ample evidence of a local Anti-Sinn Féin Society from both published sources and IRA interviews.[63] Ryan states that the 1922 victims were shot because they were known members of this Anti-Sinn Féin Society. Even Thomas J. Bradfield's inadvertent confession provides some evidence of this group's existence. The testimony of Major Neave – the Officer Commanding the Essex Regiment in Bandon – to the Wood-Renton Compensation Committee also supports the existence of such a group. He stated, 'There had been rumours of an Anti-Sinn Féin Organisation.'[64] As he shamelessly lied in much of the rest of his evidence, it is difficult to assess the honesty of this statement.

However, there can be no such doubt about a confidential report by the Bandon RIC Divisional Commissioner for March 1921 that a shed used by Sinn Féin was burned by 'members of the Anti-Sinn Féin Society'. This is conclusive proof of its existence, but not of its membership.[65] Nor is there any doubt that the Divisional Commissioner of the RIC in Cork, Major Moore, told British civil servant Mark Sturgis that an Anti-Sinn Féin Society existed in the city. While Major Moore attempted to minimise the role of the British Army in starting the fires in Cork in December

1920, he was unequivocal about the Anti-Sinn Féin Society: 'The Anti-Sinn Féin League does exist and is not a myth to cover the "Armed Forces of the Crown".' As a result, it defies logic to claim that an Anti-Sinn Féin Society of local unionists did not exist.[66] However, this is not evidence that the victims of April 1922 were members.

The BMH files present the strongest claim for the involvement of the victims of the Dunmanway and Ballygroman killings in an anti-Sinn Féin organisation from inside the anti-Treaty IRA. When Michael O'Donoghue was moved to Bandon, he was intimately involved in the 3rd Brigade's affairs until his transfer to Donegal at the end of March 1922. Along with Michael O'Neill, he certainly saved one love-struck Black and Tan's life in February 1922. Writing in 1952, long before there was any controversy about the motive for the Dunmanway killings, O'Donoghue's analysis is blunt, unemotional and unapologetic:

> Several prominent loyalists – all active members of the anti-Sinn Féin Society in West Cork, and blacklisted as such in I.R.A. Intelligence Records – in Bandon, Clonakilty, Ballineen and Dunmanway, were seized at night by armed men, taken out and killed. Some were hung, most were shot. All were Protestants. This gave the slaughter a sectarian appearance. Religious animosity had nothing whatever to do with it. These people were done to death as a savage, wholesale, murderous reprisal for the murder of Mick O'Neill.[67]

He said that the killings were 'murderous' and that some of the men 'were hung', which agrees with Alice Hodder, who claimed the Hornibrooks were hanged. Writing at a time when there was no controversy, did he have any reason to lie? To put it bluntly, why admit that the anti-Treaty IRA committed these murders if it did not? Why say the men were members of an Anti-Sinn Féin Society if they were not? This is the simplest explanation for the killings, and in the face of O'Donoghue's statement there is no need to build complex theories about what might have happened. Crucially, the leadership of the Cork IRA were out of the county on 27 April 1922 at a final meeting in Dublin to try to avert civil war.[68] If they had been in West Cork, they would have exerted some discipline on the men under their command. The fact that they stopped the killings when they returned proves this.

However, caution is necessary, as only one BMH statement or memoir mentions O'Donoghue. This is from Seumas O'Mahony, who was a member of the UCC IRA Company. According to O'Mahony, along with O'Donoghue, the UCC IRA Company included Mick Crowley, a section leader in Tom Barry's column, and Pete Kearney. These are Mick Crowley of Kilbrittain and Peadar Kearney of Dunmanway, both of whom are central to this story. The press reports noted that O'Donoghue was an 'engineering officer of the West Cork 3rd Brigade' after his election as GAA President in 1952. Given Tom Barry's robust manner and the fact GAA Secretary Pádraig Ó Caoimh had been an officer of the Cork Brigade in the War of Independence, O'Donoghue could not tout his war record during an extremely tight presidential election, which he won by three votes, unless it was true. He also reiterated it in his acceptance speech at the GAA convention.[69]

If we accept O'Donoghue's evidence, then the killings were carried out as a direct, targeted, 'murderous reprisal' for Michael O'Neill's death. During the Civil War, the 4th Brigade in North Cork borrowed the concept of disproportionate reprisals from the Black and Tans when it threatened to kill ten Free Staters for every one of its men who was executed.[70] O'Donoghue's statement is critical in understanding what happened. This was a wildly disproportionate IRA reprisal for Michael O'Neill. Members of the IRA believed that the men they shot were members of the Anti-Sinn Féin Society.[71] O'Donoghue's evidence agrees with evidence from William Jagoe, who was also sought for murder on 26–27 April, and from Mark Sturgis.

On 10 June William Jagoe, who had been attacked in Dunmanway on the night of 26 April, had a letter published on page one of the *Southern Star*. He had been told that his targeting was as a result of being a Freemason and a contributor to the Orange propagandists.[72] Jagoe denied that he was either a Freemason or a contributor to any loyalist cause and stated that his contributions were to the Free State election fund, the White Cross and the Belfast Distress Fund (Roman Catholic). He continued that he had received huge support from the people of the town after the attack, but signed himself W. J., which suggests he was still concerned for his safety. In a letter to the same paper the following week he was supported by Dunmanway-based Free State councillor McCarthy, who claimed the attack on Jagoe was a result of lies and jealousy and confirmed the support Jagoe had given to the pro-Treaty party.[73] He was apparently not concerned about being offside with the electorate in the week of the 1922 general election.[74] The main difficulty with these letters is that they do not explain whether their information was the result of local gossip or was coming from those who did the killing.

This testimony mentions two target groups: Freemasons and Free Staters. It is already known that the target in Clonakilty on 27 April was Tom Nagle, the caretaker of the local Masonic Hall burned down on the night. He was identified as a spy in 1921.[75] Tom's other job was as a process server for the British courts and he would have been an automatic target in the War of Independence. While either of his two jobs on their own would not have been significant enough to have him shot, the fact that he held both may also have attracted the attention of the killers. It must also be remembered that David Gray's assassins called him a Free Stater. The Jagoe letter suggests that individuals were being targeted for what they did rather than their religion, and that the targeting was poor to say the least.[76]

On 25 May 1922 Mark Sturgis, who was one of the last civil servants working in the Irish Office, forwarded Winston Churchill 'a list of the murders e.t.c., of loyalists, including soldiers and police, in Southern Ireland since the Truce' for use in the meeting between the Irish and British Treaty signatories on 26 and 29 May.[77] The list is culled from the newspapers. The person's religion is usually mentioned if the person is Protestant. More importantly for this story, Sturgis also included a representative sample of people who had made an application to the Irish Distress Committee, which was set up in London to help refugees from Ireland. It later became the Irish Grants Committee. The sample includes eight people who had left West Cork as a direct result of incidents that took place at the end of April. It provides evidence of other victims and targets at the end of April and gives a good picture of the situation within a month of the Dunmanway killings. It is raw, unpolished data as close to the event as possible and shows a clear cause and effect between the killings and the flight.

The first person mentioned is 'A. F.' from the south of Ireland whose son was shot in his place at the end of the previous month (April). The seventy-year-old father of eleven sons and one daughter was a civil bill officer. His wife had been warned that he and his sons would be shot once the killers got hold of them. A couple of days later his sons received threatening letters even though they lived in different parts of Ireland. There can be little doubt that this is Thomas Nagle from Clonakilty.

Hewart and James Wilson had been living in Dunmanway. According to their statement in the Sturgis document:

> There were six brothers in the family, four of whom served with His Majesty's forces in the late War in the course of which two were killed. They were Protestants [Methodist actually] and at the end of the previous month [April] their house was attacked ... and they were threatened with death unless they left the country at once.

Sturgis notes that the brothers were returning to Ireland so their names should not be disclosed by Churchill to the Provisional Government, presumably because they might be shot. Two of the Wilson brothers were in the British Army and two in the Australian Army.

Gilbert S. Johnston had served as a member of the Royal Air Force during the war:

> On [Thursday] April 27th, at Bandon, he was brutally assaulted and threatened by six armed men who stated that they were members of the Irish Republican Army. He was told by these men that he was being thrashed because he was a Protestant and an ex-soldier and that if he did not leave the country at once he would be shot.

Robert and James Bennett were Protestants living in Ballineen:

> Early on the morning of [Friday] 28th April a gang of armed men searched their house and intimated to their sister that they were looking for them with the intention of shooting them and a note to this effect was left with the sister.

The Bennetts worked as bakers in the town. As the only bakery in the town was Cotter's, it is logical to assume that the Bennetts worked for it. When the bakery was finally burned in 1922, presumably they both lost their jobs. Once again people working in Cotter's had been attacked. It will be remembered that Alfred Cotter was shot in 1921 for alleged spying and supporting the British. It is also important to note that James was a sailor in the Royal Navy during the Great War and another of his brothers, Walter, had joined the Royal Navy in 1913.[78]

'Mr B. B.' and 'D. Cameron' were also mentioned:

Mr B. B. resided in Southern Ireland in a small community where there were a number of Protestants. He himself having been discharged from the Army ... A short time ago his house was raided by armed men, his brother most brutally murdered and he forced to leave Ireland at a moment's notice.

D. Cameron was a 73-year-old Protestant from Crookstown Co. Cork and he was warned to leave the country.

The others in the sample include Edward Wynne, Cahir, Co. Tipperary; Mr Forsyth, Limerick; Hugh Broderick, Rathkeale; James Doynelain (Donellan?), Limerick; and Fergus Ferris, Milltown, Co. Kerry.

The Sturgis note shows that most of the forty-four killings between the Truce and 21 May 1922 involved Protestant ex-soldiers and Catholic ex-RIC.[79] As the military was overwhelmingly Protestant and the RIC overwhelmingly Roman Catholic, this is not statistically significant. Of the civilian deaths, nine were the Dunmanway killings and there were four others.[80] The Sturgis note lends support to the evidence of the Southern Irish Loyalists Relief Association that anyone with a British connection was being attacked. If this was a representative sample of the cases before the committee, then the IRA committed the beatings and killings.

In many ways Gilbert Johnston's evidence is the kernel of the massacre. He states he was beaten up because he was a Protestant and an ex-soldier. He was not shot. Perceived active unionists were suspected (which is hardly surprising) and targeted (which is indefensible). It must be remembered that 27 April was the night that Michael O'Neill's body was guarded by IRA officers in Bandon church and the night of the killings in Ballineen and Clonakilty. Is it reasonable to surmise that the six men who assaulted Gilbert Johnston could have travelled west on the main roads to both Ballineen and Clonakilty later the same night? Splitting the group of six in two could easily have accomplished all the killings on that night.

The Sturgis briefing note presents compelling evidence of the killings and the flight, and contributes to an understanding of these events. It widens the area of attack, increases the number of actual and potential victims, narrows the target group and provides direct evidence that some West Cork Protestants felt safe enough to return to Cork by 25 May.

We now turn to the story of Richard J. Helen. On the face of it, his case is simple. He had been identified as an enemy agent by the IRA in July 1921. He informed the Irish Grants Committee that he was captured on the night of 27–28 April 1922 in Clonakilty and walked towards to the edge of town, where it was presumed he was going to be shot. He is unique in this: everyone else was shot in their homes. Somehow he escaped from his captors, who apparently did not fire at him as he left. In his statement he said that he was a resolute supporter of the British flag and that he had received £225 compensation for dislocation to England.[81] His claim was supported by an ex-RIC District Inspector Higmaw, who said he had provided valuable information.

But that is not the full story. Richard J. Helen lived with his sister Lissie on Sovereign Street in Clonakilty, according to the 1911 census. He was forty-two and she was forty-eight; both were single. On 20 April 1922 he proposed a motion at the Kilgarriffe (Clonakilty) Select Vestry which testified 'to the extremely good feelings and friendship that always existed between Protestants and Roman Catholics in this parish and district'.[82] The *Southern Star* also records on 20 May 1922 that he attended the Clonakilty race meeting, which presumably means he was in Clonakilty before that date to make it into the weekly newspaper. In 1926 Lissie Helen died and her brother R. J. Helen – chairman of the Urban District Council, member of the Clonakilty Racing Club and the local Farmers' Union – was the chief mourner. Of his brothers and sisters only one lived overseas. The *Southern Star* records that the large funeral was a mark of the 'esteem in which the deceased and the members of her family are held by the people of Clonakilty and surrounding districts'.[83]

Can the Richard Helen who was chairman of Clonakilty Urban District Council in 1926 be the same person who tells the Irish Grants (Wood-Renton 2) Committee that he was attacked in 1922 and dislocated to England? There is no doubt that he is, and this means that even though his period of dislocation was less than a month, his compensation for this was greater than €5,800 in today's money. Four years later his 'enemies' wanted him as first citizen of their town. He died in Clonakilty in 1937.[84] Is it possible that the evidence he gives to the Irish Grants Committee is exaggerated or possibly even fabricated in large part? The committee was very sceptical and it awarded him far less than he was expecting.

How are historians expected to approach the rest of the claims made to the British compensation committees if it can be shown that the first citizen of Clonakilty might not be telling the truth? His solicitor, Jasper Travers Wolfe, an officer of the court and TD, must have known that this evidence was suspect, but appears to have allowed him to proceed. What does this say for the value of other submissions? The reader will have to judge, but it is probably best to be highly sceptical about uncorroborated testimony from witnesses in this story, especially when the evidence is in their own interest.

There is another possible way that the attackers may have identified their victims of late April. Throughout the month of April 1922 the anti-Treaty IRA began to call themselves the Republican Party in West Cork and were organising themselves in Dunmanway. The 'Dunmanway doings' section of the *Southern Star* on 1 April noted that a meeting would take place the following Sunday, to be addressed by Harry Boland and the lord mayor of Cork, among others, and a republican collection would be taken up in the near future. It also noted that there was to be a pro-Treaty meeting addressed by Michael Collins and that the last time Michael Collins addressed a meeting in Dunmanway, it had been broken up by 'the late [RIC] District Inspector Keeney'.[85]

The anti-Treaty meeting took place on 2 April and was presided over by Commandant Peadar Kearney, who apologised for the fact that neither Harry Boland nor the lord mayor of Cork had turned up, but on the platform were Professor Stockley,[86] Mr O'Hanrahan of Dublin, George Ross and P. J. Crowley of Dunmanway.[87] The meeting took place after mass and was regularly interrupted by applause and cheers, which shows that the cause had good support. On 8 April the *Southern Star* reported that a collection in aid of republican funds was being made and the response was 'prompt and generous'. The pro-Treaty party was also collecting money for the election campaign, and on 22 April the *Southern Star* reported that the collectors in Clonakilty had been the victims of an attempted robbery in which the attackers 'had fired some shots over their heads. The collectors had sturdily refused to part with the money and eventually the holders-up withdrew.'[88]

Once again, as had happened with the IRA levy in the War of

Independence, the people of the town were being asked to choose sides, and it is likely that if people refused to support the anti-Treaty party they would have been called Free Staters. As we know from William Jagoe's evidence, the causes that people supported (or did not support) were apparently used to target them. It would be more than surprising, given their known politics, if any of Francis Fitzmaurice, David Gray or James Buttimer had subscribed to the republican collection. Would this have marked them out for death? It would explain the comments about David Gray being a Free Stater.

It has been suggested that all of the Protestants attacked during the War of Independence and Civil War period had little in common. But Colonel Warren Peacocke, Fred Stennings (another 1921 Inishannon Protestant shooting victim) and David Gray knew each other through angling.[89] Another link between the 1921 British spy ring and the later killings is cricket.[90] The *Southern Star* carried reports on cricket matches in the area until the outbreak of the Great War. The Ballineen team consisted mostly of the Cotters and the Bennetts. It has also been established that the Bennetts worked for the Cotters and that Robert and James Bennett fled Ballineen. Another member of the Ballineen team, William Daunt, was also shot at through the window of his bedroom on the night Alexander Gerald McKinley was shot. The Clonakilty team included the Bennetts, the Fitzpatricks, a Fitzmaurice and R. J. Helen, so these men would have known each other well.[91]

There is no doubt that there was a breakdown in discipline by some members of the IRA in Bandon at this time. Michael O'Donoghue returned to Bandon from his home in Lismore, along with Lismore man William Healy, at the end of May 1922, and Tom Hales asked him to take one of the local IRA officers back to the north with him. O'Donoghue stated that Tom Hales:

... asked me, as a great favour and relief, to take Conneen Crowley back along with me to Ulster, away from West Cork altogether.[92] Conneen was a tough little gunman, always in trouble, always fighting. When in drink, he was dangerous, merciless and irresponsible. He was a holy terror when he got going on his mad escapades, and Brigadier Hales was at his wits' end to restrain him. Conneen, a much-wanted man by the R.I.C. and Tans for his deadly shooting prowess, was captured by the Macroom Auxiliaries a few days before the Kilmichael ambush ... Since his return to his West Cork home in Kilbrittain, he had become notorious for quarrelling and brawling and acting the 'Wild West desperado' and now Tom Hales was much perturbed at how to handle such a fierce little warrior. I agreed to bring Conneen along to Donegal, to the Brigadier's great relief.[93]

The Kilbrittain IRA BMH statement shows Crowley had been a neighbour, colleague and very close friend of Michael O'Neill throughout the War of Independence, and in many ways their careers mirrored each other. Crowley guarded O'Neill for three weeks after he was injured at the first raid on Howe's Strand Coastguard Station, and both were arrested and interned at Ballykinlar before Kilmichael. It is noticeable that Con Crowley's name is often next to Michael O'Neill or Jack O'Neill on lists of participant in ambushes and attacks, suggesting they were always associated with each other in the minds of the company.[94] Whether Con Crowley was involved in the spate of killings after O'Neill was killed is a matter of conjecture but the Hales request does show that he had serious worries about losing control. O'Donoghue left Bandon on about 12 June with John Donovan, Jim Lane, Con Crowley and Willie Healy, and they reported to the Four Courts garrison before continuing to Donegal to rejoin Peadar O'Donnell's anti-Treaty forces.

At least thirty individuals, mostly, but not exclusively, Protestant, were attacked over these few days, and it has been possible to discover a likely cause for their targeting in the case of many of the victims. What most likely happened is that a small number of the anti-Treaty IRA decided to take unauthorised retaliation on 'known' loyalists in revenge for the killing of Michael O'Neill. The evidence of the 'trial' of the love-struck Black and Tan shows that strict control was needed in Bandon, and when Tom Hales returned this strict control was put back in place. In some cases it seems that the people attacked had provided information to the police about the IRA during the War of Independence, which should not have been surprising given that they were loyal subjects of the crown.

It is probable that the full details of what happened over these four days will never be confirmed. The most likely scenario has been presented in this chapter, but even this has to base most of its analysis on second-hand sources. As nobody ever came forward to admit guilt, nobody can prove beyond reasonable doubt who committed the killings. However, the weight of circumstantial evidence points in the direction of elements within the Bandon Brigade of the IRA. Michael O'Donoghue's information suggests a motive, but we will never really know unless a direct confession from one of the killers is found. We can all speculate as much as we like, but without a confession it will never be more than speculation. By no stretch of the imagination can it be suggested that these murders were justified. After all, even if these men had been 'hostile' during the War of Independence their side had lost: they were the defeated 'enemy' if they were the enemy at all. The reader will have to decide for themselves.

There is one final event which must be considered in relation to the killings: the execution of three British intelligence officers and their driver in Macroom between 26 and 29 April.

8

THE MACROOM KILLINGS

While evidence has been discovered connecting the events at Ballygroman and the Dunmanway killings, no such connection has yet been made with the Macroom killings which happened at the same time. On the morning of the 26 April 1922 three British Army intelligence officers – Ronald Hendy, George Dove and Kenneth Henderson – and their driver, Private J. Brooks, left Ballincollig Barracks in Cork ostensibly on a fishing expedition. It is likely that they called to an old friend of theirs, Major Thomas Clarke at Farran, halfway to Macroom, for lunch.[1] Later they drove to Macroom, arriving after 4 p.m., where the local IRA became suspicious of the strange car without plates parked outside Dick William's hotel and went to investigate. Apparently, the responses of the driver made them even more suspicious and Hendy, Dove and Henderson were arrested in the snug of the hotel and interrogated. Their cover story was quickly exposed as they had no fishing equipment with them. They were definitely shot, along with Brooks, some time between 26 and 29 April, and were buried at Clondrohid, six kilometres north-west of Macroom.

John Regan, in his examination of the Macroom killings, suggests that the officers may have been sent west in response to the events of the morning, and according to him they called to Farran, which is eight kilometres from Ballygroman. Certainly, if Herbert Woods was a 'British Secret Service agent' as suggested by Michael O'Donoghue, then this would have prompted an immediate investigation by his colleagues in the service; hence the strange decision to go into the heart of enemy territory without permission from either the Free State authorities or the anti-Treaty IRA, which was a clear breach of the Treaty. Regan further speculates that information taken from the officers at Macroom led to the death of those killed in Dunmanway and Ballineen. He makes clear that this is speculation and there is no direct evidence to link the two events.[2]

In his BMH statement, James Murphy, who was a member of the Macroom garrison, states that after the British officers were captured, they were held in the RIC barracks while the garrison asked Brigade headquarters in Cork by telephone for instructions. Headquarters ordered the killing of all four, and this was carried out that night (26 April): 'Two of these officers (Hendy and Dore [*sic*]) were members of the British intelligence who had tortured and shot unarmed prisoners during the fight. They were wanted men and were taken prisoners by our forces ...'.[3]

There are many other BMH statements (including those of Tim Buckley, Michael Brew, Dan Corkery and Nora Cunningham) that include the same information and state that the men were shot the night they were captured, after orders had been received from Cork IRA Brigade headquarters. Given that it was peacetime and that by their actions Hendy, Dove and Henderson clearly had little concern for their own safety, the officers could easily have had a notebook or list with them identifying who they intended to visit, which could have led to the targeting of the people on that list. However, the Mark Sturgis document discussed earlier, along with other unpublished material soon to be published by Andy Bielenberg, appears to show that the incidents in the Bandon Valley were of a more general nature, so it seems unlikely that a link between these Macroom killings and the others between 26 and 29 April can be convincingly established.

Unsurprisingly, on the morning of 27 April, General Strickland sent a senior officer, Major (later Field Marshal) Bernard Montgomery, with an army company to investigate the disappearance of the four soldiers and to rescue them if possible. This resulted a few days later in a tense stand-off between the IRA behind Macroom Castle's walls and a British unit accompanied by at least one armoured car in the middle of the square outside, until a British officer was invited to inspect the IRA headquarters in the castle. As the officer found no evidence that the four soldiers had ever been in the castle, Montgomery retreated.

General Nevil Macready reported to the British cabinet on 6 May that neither side of the IRA was claiming responsibility for the disappearance of the four soldiers:

> Efforts to discover trace of these British soldiers is [*sic*] now being carried out by the leaders of both parties of the I.R.A. who assure me, and I think in good faith, that they know nothing of the incident. This may be true as there are armed bands in existence who admit allegiance to no party. On the other hand it is difficult to believe that the Republican garrison of Macroom can be entirely ignorant.[4]

It is not surprising that the soldiers were not found in the castle if James Murphy is correct, as they were in the RIC barracks, which was 200 metres to the west on the other side of the bridge.

Austen Chamberlain, Lord Privy Seal, was forced to apologise to Captain Henderson's father for suggesting that the men had gone off without leave, and to admit that intelligence officers are always on duty. As General Strickland had recorded their absence in his diary by saying 'they had gone out on I. work and not returned', it is clear that they had been allowed out by him or members of his staff.[5]

IRA officer Frank Busteed claimed that he had killed them after they had been abducted from a pub in Farnanes, ten kilometres to the east of Macroom. Given the wealth of evidence placing them in Macroom, it is most likely that Busteed is confused about this. He may have been involved in the killings, or he may have wanted to claim the killing of Hendy, who it is suggested had caused the death of Frank's mother by throwing her down her stairs.[6]

Even in the Macroom killings, new evidence points to a somewhat more complex story than that currently accepted. Almost as an aside, Daniel McCarthy of Rylane records: 'Early in 1922 I was instructed to take a section of men to Coachford to intercept and hold up some British officers who were expected to pass through. Although we spent two days in the area there was no appearance by the British officers.'[7] This shows that the IRA intelligence service was still keeping an eye on the British and had enough prior information to organise the interception of some British Army officers. Combined with eyewitness testimony referenced by John Regan, that the IRA at Macroom was on alert on the morning of 26 April, it suggests that Hendy, Dove, Henderson and Brooks were expected.

In itself the information has no great significance unless the reader understands the geography of the Lee Valley. If someone was leaving Major Clarke's house in Farran, for example, the journey to Coachford is about eight kilometres, and there are only two main roads through the valley to Macroom. In 1922 the Coachford road was better, and the only bridges across the river were at Coachford and Carrigadrohid a few kilometres to the west. To get to Macroom the officers would most probably have gone via Coachford. So how did the IRA know when these officers were travelling? How much advance warning did the Rylane Company get, or need, to mobilise? Why did the Rylane Company spend two days waiting for British officers who never came? Were these officers regarded as important? And were these the men who were eventually captured in Macroom, which would suggest that their trip may not have been connected to the killings earlier in the day?

Before yet another conspiracy theory is invented, it is necessary to point out that this still provides no link between the Macroom killings and the Dunmanway killings. What it does suggest is that it is still far too early to rule anything in or out in the telling of these stories. Ultimately, we have to keep digging.

9

AFTER THE KILLINGS

The British government was shocked but not particularly concerned by the Dunmanway killings, as can be seen from British cabinet papers for the period.[1] General Macready, Commander-in-Chief of the British forces in Ireland, refers directly to the killings on 29 April 1922, but also says that the situation in the south is improving as the overall rate of violence had dropped dramatically with the Truce. Churchill reported on 16 May that the refugee problem was not large in volume, but if the situation became worse there might be a large stream of refugees. Lloyd George noted at the cabinet meeting of 30 May that there had been thirty-seven murders in the south from 6 December 1921 to 30 May 1922.[2] Churchill told the House of Commons:

> The number of members of the Royal Irish Constabulary murdered since the signing of the Treaty on the 6th December, 1921, is 26, of whom 15 were Roman Catholics and 11 Protestants. The number of ex-members of the force murdered [across the whole of Ireland] since that date is eight, of whom five were Roman Catholics and three Protestants.[3]

Lloyd George felt there was some merit in holding a judicial inquiry into the killings in Belfast, but that one in the south was neither necessary nor appropriate as the IRA had committed those killings, and the Free State was a dominion and so no longer part of the United Kingdom.[4] He had received information on the perpetrators of the southern killings from Michael Collins when they met in Downing Street early on the morning of 30 May. Churchill, who was also at the meeting, had the Mark Sturgis briefing note about the killings and the subsequent exodus with him. Lloyd George reported that Collins said the Dunmanway killings occurred as a result of the Belfast 'pogroms', and that Collins and Griffith were distressed and angry:

> They talked of the extermination of the Catholics. I retorted that that was a great exaggeration, 80 Catholics have been killed, and 168 wounded since December 6th, 1921. They are considerable figures, but they do not justify Mr Collins' description. It just happens that 72 Protestants have been killed, and considerable numbers wounded. We could get Mr Collins to talk of nothing else, and when we were at last able to point out that there had been 37 murders in the South, he replied that this was due to the excited state of feelings provoked by Belfast,[5] and that unless something were done the whole of Ireland would get out of hand.[6]

Collins' comment is significant. He spent the week of the murders talking with Tom Hales in Dublin to prevent civil war. It would be incredible if Tom Hales had not contacted Bandon to find out what was going on and Michael Collins, who was the local TD, did not ask him about it.

When asked why he was not giving protection to the RIC and the unionists, Collins had replied 'he does in fact provide protection and prevents many outrages', and behind 'fanatical republicans who were pure in motive' there were 'desperate elements of the population who pursued rapine for private gain'.[7] There was concern on both sides that the situation could deteriorate, but there is no evidence at British cabinet level that there was any massive flood of refugees into the country from Ireland. There was undoubted political concern that if any such flow developed it could have a negative effect in the United Kingdom. (Churchill's suggestion on 16 May that the British might have to set up a Pale around Dublin would probably have brought a few wry smiles around the cabinet table.)

If British reaction was sanguine, the immediate Irish reaction was of shock and an attempt to assure Protestants of their safety. Meda Ryan provides a wealth of verifiable information about the pro- and anti-Treaty IRA response to the killings across West Cork.[8] It is easy to turn these appalling personal disasters into allegations of increasing sectarian tensions and to claim the IRA was attempting to drive a defenceless minority away, but both the Methodist and Church of Ireland ministers of Dunmanway declared that they had neither been attacked (as reported in early news reports) nor had there ever been sectarian trouble in Dunmanway.[9]

When the first reports had reached Cork on 28 April, Cork Corporation as its first order of business under the Lord Mayor's Privilege declared that, while they condemned Michael O'Neill's killing, they called on 'our men of West Cork to show every conceivable restraint in the present trying circumstances [of Belfast]' and tendered 'our sincerest sympathies for the cruel and unusual murders' of 'Protestant fellow countymen'.[10]

The motion was circulated to all public bodies, including Cork County Council, which objected to 'an insinuation in the Cork Corporation resolution that the shootings of the Protestants were reprisals for Commandant O'Neill's death', but otherwise did not demur. The County Council did split the motion because it did not give sufficient mention to the death of Michael O'Neill, but there is no doubt that it condemned the killings. Most other public bodies, including Macroom and Skibbereen Urban District Councils, adopted the resolution verbatim.[11]

On 8 May the District Council in Bandon declared that:

> ... these cruel shootings were contrary to every conception of justice and liberty and to every sentiment of religious and moral obligation to one another ... many of the men who were most 'wanted' in that strenuous time were sheltered and supported by their Protestant neighbours.[12] There was no more need for fear or alarm. The trouble was at an end, and they hoped to live with their Protestant neighbours in the same friendly spirit as in the past.[13]

Roman Catholic parish priests in Bandon, Castletown Bere and Dunmanway all roundly condemned the killings in the strongest terms.[14] Some of the priests' language is bizarre, especially in Bandon and Dunmanway, where oblique reference is made to the fact that while these men were not true Christians they were still entitled to be left alone.

As part of a direct forceful condemnation of the killings, the Roman Catholic Bishop of Cork, Dr Daniel Cohalan, had telegraphed the parish priest in Enniskean to cancel planned confirmations on Sunday 1 May, stating that celebrating the sacrament would be in 'unseemly and painful contrast with the feelings of insecurity and panic in the Protestant community'. He concluded that while the Roman Catholic bishops could not offer physical protection they could offer moral protection, and he demanded that all such attacks stop immediately.[15] Understandably, the Protestant community might have appreciated his words, but the words were largely ineffectual on the men of the flying column, just as his excommunication of the IRA after Kilmichael was unsuccessful.[16]

More effective was the IRA's own response. Guards were placed on many vulnerable homes across West Cork, starting with Skibbereen and Bantry as soon as the first hint of the killings reached these areas. When Tom Hales and Tom Barry returned, the protection was extended to their areas also.

Tim Pat Coogan also notes that Diarmuid O'Hegarty (the Irish cabinet secretary) accepted liability 'for the large and increasing number of persons who have been driven from their homes by intimidation', and repeated assurances were given to the Church of Ireland by Michael Collins that the government would secure 'the restoration of their homes and property to any persons who have been deprived of them by violence and intimidation'.[17]

Even before the killings, the IRA in Dunmanway issued a notice in the *Southern Star* stating: 'In the case of claims to land from which claimants [*sic*] predecessors have been evicted, the claims must be submitted to the Republican Courts. Claimants will not be permitted to take the law into their own hands.'[18] The Dunmanway anti-Treaty IRA under Peadar Kearney acknowledged that there was a problem – people were evicting alleged 'land-grabbers'. It made it clear that illegal seizure would not be tolerated. Its members were democrats and they understood the need for the rule of law.[19] Inherent in democracy is the right to private property, and this notice explicitly acknowledges this. If the anti-Treaty IRA committed the killings, and there is little doubt it did, it appears that land was not the motive.

Many of those who had 'evicted' Protestant and Catholic 'land-grabbers' in Cork had been arrested, lodged in the county jail and refused bail by 19 May, when *The Irish Times* reported that the police were determined to put a stop to such practices.[20]

The matter had been raised in Dáil Éireann on the same day and Minister for Agriculture Patrick Hogan said, 'There is an attempt being made to deal with the land problem by way of confiscation … It was bad enough when this thing was dictated by mere greed, but when notices like this are served on Protestants–'. He was immediately ruled out of order by the shocked Ceann Comhairle (the speaker), who clearly did not want this allegation pursued. This forced the anti-Treaty side to condemn land confiscations in general, and removed one of its main attractions to the landless who were supporting it. Anti-Treaty TD Art O'Connor replied on behalf of the opposition:

> I do not approve of the confiscation of the lands of any individual. The only parties in this country who have any power to order lands to be dealt with in any particular way for the benefit of any individuals, or of the community in general, are the Government of the Republic and that is Dáil Éireann.[21]

All this suggests that the IRA leadership on both sides had re-gained complete control over the region twenty days after the last of the killings. In West Cork on 27 May the *Southern Star*, under a heading 'Claims to Farms', carried a notice from Dáil Éireann that 'anyone against whom claims are made should immediately send a written report to the registrar of the District Court, to the O.C. Police for the area, or to the local barracks'.[22]

On the same day it reported the removal of 'restored' families from farms they had taken. In Castletown-Kinneigh, the North-ridge farm had been occupied along with parts of the Hosford and Wood farms.[23] The Irish Republican Police had 'compelled Ds. Sullivan to vacate a holding at Manch Bridge to which he was unofficially restored a few weeks ago'. In another case, local

auctioneer Henry Smith had purchased a Mr Salter's farm at
Kilronan for £2,600.[24]

The Irish Times argued throughout 1922 that what was happening in the south and west was not sectarianism but greed, and
agreed with Michael Collins' analysis of 30 May. Its leader on 3
October is a good example:

> We can detect no signs of a 'well organised system' in this campaign
> of destruction. The ex-Unionists have not been the only victims. They
> have been the chief victims, because their local isolation and their
> relatively high standard of prosperity have made them easy marks for
> lawlessness and greed.[25]

The Irish Times continued by pointing out that the vast majority of
ex-unionists had not fled, that they were willing to tough it out,
and that as Irishmen they were willing to serve the new state. In his
analysis, Paul McMahon shows that, despite a wide range of pessimistic reports being fed into the British cabinet (and to Churchill
in particular), neither Alfred Cope (who was in Dublin working
with General Macready on the withdrawal of British troops) nor
Lionel Curtis (who arrived in the country on 17 September 1922
to see for himself) could support the pessimistic view expressed in
the reports above. Cope went as far as to state that 'loyalists were
not especially victimised'.[26]

10

PROTESTANT FLIGHT
FROM CORK

The Protestant population of County Cork declined by 43 per cent between 1911 and 1926. The West Cork figure was 30 per cent. These figures might be read as suggesting that the War of Independence had driven Protestants out of the county. However, my research has shown that most of this decline was a result of the British military withdrawal.[1] According to the Church of Ireland Bishop of Cork, Cloyne and Ross, Charles Dowse, 'We could not have wondered had panic seized our people, and a wholesale exodus followed as a result of these events. But such was not the case. With splendid bravery the vast majority held their ground, and went on quietly with their work.' This was despite the fact that, according to his address to the diocesan synod in 1922, many of the best and brightest had been forced to leave.[2]

There is no doubt that the Dunmanway killings resulted in the flight of some of the Protestant population from the area. On 1 May *The Irish Times* was reporting that 'more than 100 persons left the district and travelled to Cork leaving in most cases female relatives to look after their homes during what, they hope, will only be a temporary absence … so hurried was their flight that some had neither handbag or an overcoat'.[3]

The following day another *Irish Times* article entitled 'Sisters in sorrow' commented on a meeting at Amiens Street (Connolly) Station between a Dunmanway Protestant woman going to Scotland to give her nerves a rest, and a Belfast Catholic woman returning to Belfast a month after her house was burned. Another article on the same date noted that ten Protestant families arrived from Cork into Belfast on Friday 28 April 1922. They had been left to fend for themselves until helped by a member of the Royal Black Preceptory who took in seven families. The writer also notes press reports that large numbers of southern Protestants were in Rosslare, heading for England. *The Irish Times* didn't mince its words in its editorial on the same day: 'Nine innocent persons have been done down – apparently for no other reasons than they were Protestants. The public conscience is shocked by this hideous – and in Southern Ireland – unprecedented outbreak of sectarian violence.'[4] The paper went on to blame the power vacuum for the breakdown of order, and demanded that the Provisional Government take control of the country.

The *Cork Examiner* noted the flight from West Cork on Wednesday 3 May in a brief report,[5] and the *Cork Constitution* reported that the preliminary meeting for the Protestant Convention heard that 'until the recent tragedies in County Cork hostility to Protestants by reason of their religion has been almost, if not wholly, unknown in the twenty-six counties in which Protestants are a minority'.[6] On the same day *The Irish Times* reported:

A certain number of refugees from Southern Ireland has arrived in London driven thence by the reign of terror which prevails in some parts of that area. Many of them are accompanied by their families and all agree in the belief that there is no visible prospect of a safe return to their homes. Tradesmen, farmers and professional classes are included in the arrivals ...[7]

Locally, Con Connolly, leader of the Skibbereen IRA, warned on Friday 5 May: 'it has been brought to our knowledge that threatening notices have been sent to Protestants warning them to leave this district under pain of death … we will do all in our power to protect the lives and property of all citizens irrespective of creed.'[8]

The same report also provides direct evidence from Bantry of cause and effect between the killings and Protestants fleeing the area.[9] Commandant Gibbs Ross, the leader of the local brigade, stated that 'there was no necessity for the wild stampede that took place. Parties that did apply and seek such protection at the barracks did receive it, and ample provision was made and steps taken to ensure that the wave of human destruction did not enter this particular Brigade area.'[10]

On 12 May *The Irish Times* quoted a leading article in the *Morning Post* asking did Lloyd George 'form a mental picture of a crowd of refugees streaming into this country with their harrowing stories of murder, outrage, and arson? … It may at any time reach the dimensions of a flood. We are only at the beginnings of the Irish Trouble.'[11]

The *Morning Post* of the same day had a very pessimistic view of what the future held, stating that 'the true government of Ireland at the present time is a secret society in close touch with our enemies'.[12] On the following day the British government wrote to the Provisional Government of 'a large and increasing number of persons who have been driven from their homes in Ireland by intimidation, or even by actual violence, at the hands of men acting openly in defiance of the authority of the Provisional Government'.[13]

In West Cork this was mostly an urban flight, and it represented approximately 100 to 150 families across the area.[14] Some fled to Cork and Kinsale, some to Bantry (according to the Bantry estate archives in University College Cork), some to Dublin and Belfast, and some to England.[15] The *Cork Constitution* reported: 'Many persons from Dunmanway, Ballineen, and Bandon left their homes and proceeded by the Rosslare Mail [train] to England, others went by Dublin and Holyhead and all together the exodus was a very large scale [*sic*].'[16]

The same paper puts a figure on the number who fled, stating that it was 'upwards of 100', which was 0.8 per cent of the 1911 West Cork population. This was a lot in one weekend but certainly no 'pogrom'. The majority of native West Cork Protestants had returned or remained in place by 1926, and this is especially true in the rural areas.

The *Cork & County Eagle* and *Southern Star* also recorded the effects of this Protestant exodus. On 20 May the 'Dunmanway doings' section of the *Southern Star* noted 'that some of those who had fled in late April had returned but many had sold up and left'. Clarina (Clara) Buttimer, James' wife, had instructed six houses in Dunmanway to be sold on 8 June, while Killowen Cottage – where John Bradfield was shot – was sold on 15 June.[17] In the same month David Gray's Medical Hall in Dunmanway had re-opened under the management of Mr Owen. Later on Miss B. Peyton (who now owned the house where Alexander Gerald McKinley was shot in Ballineen) sold and left on 21 December 1922. However, it must be noted that other Protestant and Roman Catholic houses and farms were for sale before the killings for a variety of reasons – including giving up farming, retiring, moving to better farms in the east of the county – and retired British military were returning to 'the mainland', as can be seen from the sales advertised during the month of April 1922. The number of advertisements doubled in May and June, but this increased them to only eight in the unionist *Cork & County Eagle*, where most Protestant advertisements from the area would be expected to be placed. It is possible that houses were sold without being advertised.

It is clear that by 29 April many of the Protestant males in the area decided that discretion was the better part of valour and fled as a direct result of the killings. In his memoir, William Kingston – who was a friend, cousin and junior partner of Jasper Travers Wolfe, the crown solicitor for West Cork – gave a detailed account of his own departure from the area after the Dunmanway attacks. His own view was that the country was 'sitting on top of a volcano'. As it was 'rumoured that there was to be a general massacre of Protestants' and 'rumoured that the shootings … were that night [28 April] to be carried out in Skibbereen … few men slept in their own beds … or … they had a well planned means of escape'.[18]

On 29 April he joined many other West Cork Protestant males on the train to Dublin, where a few weeks later he witnessed the destruction of the Four Courts from his brother's house in Glasnevin.[19] On 30 June Kingston even managed to pick up some of the papers that had been blown on the wind the three kilometres to Glasnevin from the explosion at the Public Records Office in the Four Courts.

Kingston's often-quoted journey through Ireland bears testimony to the very disturbed nature of the country, as people split into 'Free Staters' and anti-Treaty IRA. He also provides some evidence that local Protestants were emigrating out of the area during 1920 and 1921 to escape the increasing levels of violence, but suggests that there was a strong element of 'wait and see'. He makes it clear that it was only after the killings of April that some people lost confidence in their own safety. Kingston emigrated in 1922. One of his main motivations was to see the world, rather than simply being driven out of West Cork, and he returned to Ireland in 1924. If Kingston's memoir is combined with the evidence from Jasper Travers Wolfe's biography, it gives a much clearer picture of what happened in West Cork during this period.[20] He never implies that this was a large permanent exodus, and all the evidence suggests that the migration flow in West Cork for the entire War of Independence period was less than 10 per cent of the 1911 population.

Possibly a more famous example from another part of Ireland is that of Lady Augusta Gregory – Irish literary icon and founder of the Abbey Theatre – who refused to leave her home at Coole Park in Gort, County Galway. On 10 April she had been threatened with shooting by Malachai Quinn over some of her land on which he was demanding first refusal. She had replied that she sat at her desk in the evenings between 6 and 7 with the blinds drawn up. Quinn's wife had been killed by the Auxiliaries outside Gort on 1 November 1920, which might explain – but does not excuse – the threat.[21] Lady Gregory's journal records sixty-one incidents and rumours between 22 April and 15 May 1922. Understandably the diary shows a terribly disturbed period in which the pro-Treaty and anti-Treaty IRA found it difficult to maintain law as individuals with real grudges, old scores or perceived slights took advantage of the split. However, when her two grandchildren came across armed men, probably anti-Treatyites, in the woods at Coole, it turned out that they were guarding the estate from intruders of any sort. The diary also shows that even at this early stage the anti-Treaty side was melting away. By 1 May she felt brave enough to decline two anti-Treaty offers of help in her land dispute and to 'leave it to the law'. Because her journal is a diary and she is receiving information from all over the country, it creates a graphic day-by-day image of the very real (and the imagined) risk at this time.[22]

Ultimately, much more lethal to her chance of keeping her house at Coole was Lady Gregory's increasing poverty, caused by the loss, through land purchase, of the rents that backed up the great house; the house was sold to the Land Commission in 1927. Lady Gregory passed away in 1932. In what can only be described as an act of vandalism, the house itself was pulled down in 1941.

In her famous letter to her mother, Alice Hodder clearly refers to the targeting of 'Protestant loyalists' and 'loyalists' as opposed to simply Protestants.[23] The examples she gives of people who had fled are the Williamson family from Mallow, who were ordered out in six hours, and the Hayes family of Crosshaven House, whose son went to England as a precaution.[24] In both families the fathers were justices of the peace, which meant a declaration of unionism in the eyes of republicans. The rest of the Hayes family remained in Crosshaven House until 1973, while the Hodder family still live in Fountainstown House. Despite Alice Hodder's graphic account and her obvious revulsion at what happened to Captain Woods, these families decided to stay.

Hodder wrote that Johnny Derant was evicted in Fountains-town, but when he reported the matter to the Irish Republican Police in Carrigaline he was immediately reinstated. Meanwhile, Kingston of Gort, Grennan of Fountainstown, Nicholson of Hoddersfield, McLocklan and Frank Hayes were all visited by the Republican Police, who told them to ignore notices to quit if they got them and to inform the regular IRA, which would presumably provide any necessary protection. Alice Hodder was convinced that the impetus for the evictions came from the Trades Union Council in response to farmers reducing wages because of the post-war recession. She concludes by saying that Noel Furlong (of Riverstown) was ordered out and went.[25] There is an obvious fear in her letter that killings like the Dunmanway killings might happen elsewhere, but it is clear that both sections of the IRA were determined to maintain order from 28 April. When the letter finally made it to the Colonial Office on 29 June it was obsolete, as Lionel Curtis observed, but it is one of few direct eyewitness reports in the file.[26]

When he asked in a House of Lords debate on 11 May 1922 what loyalists were expected to do, Sir Edward Carson summed it up:

> After being faithful to British rule for all these years, and fighting your battles – and these are the men who did fight – surely it is not much to say: 'What do you advise us to do? Do you advise us to stay here till we are shot, or till we die of our nerves as a consequence of this terrible treatment, or do you advise us to emigrate to England? And if we go there, how shall we be supported?' What you are saying to these people really is: 'We do not care what happens to you.'[27]

The picture Carson painted was not supported in *The Irish Times* report of a Protestant convention held in the Mansion House on the same day to discuss the future for Protestants in the Free State.[28] It had been arranged before the murders in West Cork. It states there was little or no sectarianism in the south, but Sergeant Hanna, a British legal officer, noted that while murder would always be immediately condemned, the cruelty of taking a man's livelihood tended to excite less protest among citizens.[29] He said that they had been raised from the depths of despair by 'the prompt and vigorous denunciations of those outrages by individuals through-out the length and breadth of the country'.[30] But he also pointed out that, 'Unless this campaign of murder, exile, confiscation and destruction of property comes to an end in Southern Ireland an exodus of Protestants must ensue.'

The convention sent a delegation to Michael Collins to find out if Protestants would be welcome in the new state. Collins answered yes, and promised to 'restore everyone who had been a victim to their house and property. If that were not feasible – or wanted – Ireland would pay reasonable compensation' via the British government to *bone fide* claimants. The level of compensation was increased on all claims by 10 per cent in 1925.[31]

After a meeting in the House of Commons between a delegation of southern Irish loyalists and eighty Conservative and Unionist Party members, the Irish Loyalist Defence Fund was set up with a central registration bureau in London on 9 May. It was established to help distressed loyalists fleeing from Ireland and the secretary issued a statement outlining the problem. Those being driven out were 'British citizens of all classes and religion' and:

> … everyone who has in the past shown any sympathy or friendship for the British connection. Being 'willing loyally to serve the Provisional Government … made their position worse as the Republicans are exercising terrorism over all those who support the Free State'. Houses had 'been occupied by bodies of strangers, who are said to be Roman Catholic refugees from Ulster, but are, as a matter of fact, Communists. The Red flag is flying over many a country house'.[32]

The secretary was getting his information from those directly affected. Although there have been claims that this was ethnic cleansing, the victims themselves believed that the cause was nationality, class and politics rather than religion.[33] He was writing immediately after the refugees had arrived from southern Ireland, when the raw facts were stuck in their minds, so this is likely to be a truer story than the somewhat more polished and 'lawyered' claims submitted to the grants committees. This same rawness is echoed in the 'Memorial from Southern Loyalists', which had been handed to Churchill, and circulated to the cabinet, two weeks after the meeting on 25 May. It concluded with the lines, 'Ireland is now a country in which there is no restraint on the lawless, and a strong hostility towards the loyalists. A massacre is now only a matter of time.'[34]

The 'Memorial' was not discussed at the cabinet meeting. As has been seen, when discussing British reactions to the Dunmanway killings, the concerns of southern unionists were no longer central to the deliberations of the cabinet. Even though they had great sympathy with the loyalists, they had good reason to be sanguine, and in many ways the 'Memorial' was already obsolete as both factions of the IRA had taken steps to control the situation. In fact, when the 'Memorial' was raised by Churchill with Griffith, Duggan and O'Higgins at their meeting of 26 May, the Irish reply was that the situation had already improved.[35]

The 26 June 1922 House of Commons debate gives a good idea of British reaction to the general situation in Ireland. Coming four days after Henry Wilson's assassination by the IRA, this highly emotional debate examines the situation in Northern Ireland and the South, and the refugee problems, and offers a range of suggestions as to how to proceed, ranging from complete reinvasion, through taking over Donegal for a more defensible border, or attacking the Four Courts with British troops, to hoping that the Irish would see sense before civil war broke out.[36]

There have been various estimates about how many claims for compensation were submitted by both nationalist and loyalist victims to the various British compensation committees. The Shaw Commission dealt with compensation claims up to July 1921, and as these included British Army, nationalists and loyalists, the total figures paid out came to £5,000,000, split 60:40 between the two governments, with the British paying out £3,000,000. The Irish Distress Committee initially dealt with post-Truce claims of loyalist refugees, before it was redesignated the Irish Grants

Committee in 1924 and took on all claims. It was later replaced by a second Wood-Renton Committee after the Dunedin Report in 1926 made clear that some of the cases could not be concluded if the normal rules of evidence were used, not least because many of the records had been destroyed during the Civil War in Ireland. The Irish Grants Committee ceased to exist on 31 March 1925. In an appendix to its final report in January 1925 it stated:

> Total Grants, Loans and Advances made on the Recommendation of the Irish Grants Committee from May 1922 to December 31, 1924.
>
> 1. Total number of applications received: 21,801 [6,000 nationalist].
>
> 2. Grants and loans made to refugees in relief of distress: £73,298 14s. 1d.
>
> 3. Advances on claims under Irish Land Act, 1923: £26,320.
>
> 4. Advances on decrees or claims for compensation in respect of pre-Truce injuries: £117,261 10s.
>
> 5. Advances under the Irish Free State Damage to Property (Compensation) Act and other post-Truce claims: £197,184.[37]

This secret report to the cabinet analyses the various groups of claimants and emphasises that the people who suffered personal injury before the Truce did so for their active opposition to the revolution.[38] There can be no doubt as to the experience, personal integrity and sympathetic attitude of the committee members. Equally significant is a comment from as late as 1925 that 'Loyalists who had remained in the Free State' continued to suffer persecution: this is rarely referred to in any of the histories of the period or in any of the newspapers, so it is difficult to find the source for these claims. It is possible, given the wholesale rejection of post-1925 claims, that some or all of the later claims may have been less than honest.

The 4,000 claims made to the second Wood-Renton Compensation Committee after 1925 included those of Roman Catholics (many ex-RIC) and Protestants. Half were rejected at the first examination.[39] The 25,800 claimants also included English and other loyalists who had been caught up in the rebellion, so the maximum number of native claims (including many who did not leave) is unlikely to be greater than 15,000, which would represent 4.5 per cent of the total Protestant population of the Free State area in 1911.[40]

Overall, the evidence from the period of the Dunmanway massacre points to attacks on loyalists, both Roman Catholic and Protestant, not on any particular religious group. Of course many loyalists were Protestants. If there was large-scale cleansing, or revolutionary dispossession, of loyalists then the motive was political. Even this 'political cleansing' was neither absolute nor particularly targeted. If it had been, then Rev. Ralph Harbord, Rev. John Charles Lord and Richard J. Helen should have been forced to leave as well. Harbord had been shot, and Rev. John Charles Lord had been implicated as the centre of a 'Bandon Anti-Sinn Féin Society'. However, both continued to serve as clergy and leading members of society in West Cork until their deaths many years later. Similarly, Helen remained a leading citizen in West Cork until his death in 1937. This suggests that the events of 1922 were exceptional, rather than part of a systematic attempt to drive out the Protestant minority.[41]

CONCLUSION

It would be impossible for England to restore peace to Ireland without the employment of an army of at least 200,000 and an expendi-
ture of many millions. Even then it would be an armed occupation.
The people would never be sympathetic to English rule. They must
shape their own destinies, and if the task is hard it will at least explain
to them some of the difficulties which have harassed England in its
attempt to govern Ireland.

Major W. E. de B. Whittaker, 19 September 1922[1]

It is important to present as much evidence as possible about the
sequence of events so that the reader can make up their own minds
about what happened during the Ballygroman and Dunmanway
killings. Even though these killings occurred in the same week and
are linked, there is a difference between the Ballygroman events
and those in Dunmanway. Whether the executions of the intelligence agents in Macroom had any bearing must be left to one side
until (if) further evidence of a connection is found.

The evidence of Michael O'Donoghue provides an explanation
as to why the ten Protestants in West Cork were targeted after
Ballygroman. The 3rd Brigade of the IRA had developed powerful
communications and intelligence systems during the War of
Independence, so it is possible that these names were on a list in
the possession of the local IRA and this is why they were killed.
It is also possible, but unlikely, that the killings were sectarian
reprisals dressed up as 'informer' executions. Whether the men
selected were actually spies and informers is not relevant to the

fact that they were suspected by the members of the IRA of being so, according to Michael O'Donoghue. Yet, they were not attacked during the War of Independence, which suggests that there was insufficient evidence against them, or that the men in charge of the IRA refused to take action against them, or that the evidence was found after the Truce. Some of the killings may have been random, some may have been copycat and some may have been personal. Nobody knows for certain.

What does seem to be certain is that the killings were carried out by elements of the IRA and that they were in reaction to the death of Michael O'Neill. It is clear that the individuals at the head of the Bandon IRA had either been shot (Michael O'Neill) or were missing in Dublin at the crucial moment when it was decided to take revenge for O'Neill's death. It is significant that respected local commanders (Connolly in Skibbereen and Ross in Bantry) were able to maintain control of their areas without apparent difficulty and that order was restored once Tom Hales returned to Bandon.

The killings caused understandable panic among Protestants in West Cork, and some locals pursued ancient land grudges against both Catholics and Protestants under cover of the war. However, when push came to shove, those doing the shoving were faced down by both sides in the Civil War and people were restored to their property if they wanted to be.[2]

This was a savage period in Irish history; there is no denying it. Terrible atrocities occurred on all sides. Innocent people were caught up in the events, but suggesting that a main impetus of the War of Independence and the Civil War on the republican side was latent sectarianism effectively misses the point. This was, first and foremost, a struggle for self-determination. The leaders on the Irish side never lost sight of this, no matter in which direction they were dragged by events, or by elements in the movement.

What was conceded by the greatest empire the world has ever known was messy and incomplete but grudgingly accepted. Those who believed in the republic above all else took up arms against the settlement and quickly realised that the Irish people had made up their minds that the settlement would have to do for now. As it turned out, the Treaty was 'a stepping stone' to real freedom, but at the time nobody was certain of this.

This is not the end of this story. Researchers who revisit the killings in future years may uncover more evidence. The IRA pension applications are still unavailable, and Ernie O'Malley's notebooks are a valuable source which are slowly becoming accessible to the general public.[3] Buried – like the Mark Sturgis note – in the British and Irish archives, there are probably other documents that will add to our knowledge.

One thing is very clear – these killings were a direct result of the way the War of Independence ended and the divisions that the Treaty caused within the IRA. Once the IRA lost its discipline and cohesion then anything could happen. One of the tragedies of the War of Independence was that in many ways it was not necessary. If there had been a British willingness to countenance independence within the empire after the 1918 general election, then there would have been no need for Dan Breen and Seán Treacy in Tipperary to force the issue by starting the war in 1919.[4] The war was fought because the British would not even consider allowing the words 'Irish Republic', and the Irish republicans would accept nothing less.[5] It took the creative genius of South African Prime Minister (and ex-Boer 'terrorist') Jan Smuts to find a way out of the impasse when he arrived for the imperial conference in 1921. This republican ideal was also the primary impetus of the Civil War as the 'diehards' rightly recognised that what was conceded in the Treaty was not what they had fought for.

Two years before Ireland's declaration of a republic in 1949, independence within the British Commonwealth was granted to India and Pakistan by the socialist Earl of Listowel, the Secretary of State for India in the Attlee government.[6] However, it is unlikely this would have happened without the example of Ireland to guide the minds of the Labour government.[7] This had been explicitly referred to by the Secretary of State for India, Samuel Hoare, when he had introduced the Government of India Bill in 1935.[8] In 1948 Churchill – who had found it almost impossible to countenance an Irish Republic – called for an orderly retreat from the subcontinent, a call in direct contrast to the seething opposition that he had expressed to Indian demands from 1929 to 1935 and that had led to his resignation from the Conservative Party front bench. Events change all minds.[9]

Only fools would suggest that all the men and women of West Cork who fought the War of Independence were as pure as the driven snow.[10] Tom Barry acknowledged in *Guerilla Days in Ireland* that there was sectarianism among Roman Catholics and among Protestants but the IRA's intention was to fight the British. It concentrated on this and refused to allow itself to be distracted from its course by anyone – including Tom Barry himself, who wanted to hand over the 'ranches' – large dairy farms – to the landless. He was ignored.

However, there is clear evidence that at least two people in 1921 were involved in passing information to the Essex Regiment in Bandon. Others either revealed themselves or were identified as informants. It appears from Michael O'Donoghue's evidence and the July 1921 intelligence report in the Florence O'Donoghue papers in the National Library that the selection process for killing in April 1922 was based on lists in the possession of the IRA. While it seems that the lists were not from the diary left in the workhouse in Dunmanway, there is clear evidence from Flor Crowley's activities that the IRA had sufficient capability to gather any list it wanted.

The events at Ballygroman – and subsequently in Dunmanway, Ballineen, Clonakilty and Bandon – were a dark stain on the reputation of the Bandon IRA. They were shocking because they were so out of character with the conduct of the war before they occurred. There was a genuine fear among Protestants that the motive was a response to the 'pogroms' of Belfast and that no Protestant could be safe as a result. This perception was unwittingly confirmed by nationalist leaders who made a clear linkage between these events. Cork County Council even went as far as denying that Michael O'Neill's death had anything to do with the Dunmanway killings. If it did not, then the only possible reason was Belfast.

As Herbert Woods had clearly broken the law when he killed Michael O'Neill, and the Hornibrooks apparently helped him resist arrest for a time while the house was surrounded, then the family should have been brought before a public court of law and tried to decide if they had a murder charge to answer. On the other hand, there seems to be no justification at all for the Dunmanway killings. Even if each and every one of the men shot was an informer in the War of Independence, the British had signed a treaty of peace and were leaving. While many on the anti-Treaty side were highly sceptical of British intentions, the War of Independence officially ended when the British surrendered Dublin Castle on 16 January 1922. However, if the anti-Treaty side had repudiated Collins, then some members of the local IRA may have decided that the Free State amnesty no longer applied – the full truth may never be known.

It seems that there was an unauthorised and illegal attempt between 26 and 29 April 1922 to punish and drive out mostly

Protestant unionists (a political group) by some members of the IRA for the murder of Michael O'Neill. Overall, however, nationalists and Roman Catholics did not 'close ranks against' local Protestants and divide up the spoils, as Peter Hart claimed.[11] While people may try to downplay or to exaggerate these killings, they are equivalent to events such as the Ballyseedy massacre of 7 April 1923, when nine members of the anti-Treaty IRA were tied to a land mine by Free State soldiers in revenge for a trap mine laid in Knocknagoshel on 16 March. Eight were blown to pieces or murdered by the Free State forces after surviving the initial blast, and the ninth, Stephen Fuller, was blown clear. It is his version of events that is now accepted as correct.[12] The Free Staters lost their moral authority by this action, and the same happened with those members of the Bandon IRA most likely involved in the Dunmanway killings. In neither case were the perpetrators brought to account.[13]

I believe that I have come as close to the truth as I can. The case is unlikely to be proved beyond reasonable doubt at this stage, but these killings have the arrogance of unfettered military power at their centre. There is still the unfinished business of the final resting place of Woods and the two Hornibrooks. Uncovering this must be the next, and final, part of this story.

Appendix 1

1. Francis Fitzmaurice: he and his brother were giving information to the British according to his brother W. J. Fitzmaurice's statement.
2. W. J. Fitzmaurice was allegedly sought but this does not appear to be the case from the inquest evidence.
3. David Gray: Eileen Lynch suggested he was gathering information.
4. James Buttimer: nephew called J. Buttimer identified as a spy in 1921.
5. John Buttimer: lived next door to Sunlodge Manch Bridge where a Buttimer had been identified as a spy in the Dunmanway diary. May be related to the J. Buttimer reference on the 1921 spy list.
6. John Greenwood: shot with John Buttimer.
7. Robert Howe: Robert lived within 2 km of William Howe, Russagh House, Castletown-Kinneigh, who was identified as a likely informant in the Dunmanway diary.
8. John Chinnery: John was William Howe's nephew. Risteard Ó Glaisne claimed after the fact that John was giving information to the British.
9. Alexander Gerald McKinley: there is a suggestion in Hart (1998) that Tom Nagle and Alexander's uncle (Holtsbaum?) were hiding the valuables of the Masonic Lodge in Clonakilty on 28 April 1922. This is the only possible connection other than a suggestion, also in Hart, that he was 'a friend of the police', and Gerard Murphy's tenuous suggestion about a connection to his theory about Freemasons being shot in Cork which he now suggests is more to do with internal church politics.
10. Robert Nagle: shot in place of his father, who appeared on a 1st Southern Command list of informers according to Hart (1998), p. 286.

11. Reverend Ralph Harbord: shot at Murragh Rectory on 27 April; he survived. His brother Alfred died at the Somme.

12. John Bradfield: shot in place of his brother William, who was an ex-military man and allegedly passed information to the military during the War of Independence.

13. James Wilson: from Dunmanway, he was sought and fled to England; his sister was told that he would be shot.

14. Hewart Wilson: sought and fled to England; his sister was told that he would be shot.

15. George 'Appy' Bryan: gun placed to his head on 26 April in Dunmanway, but the gun misfired.

16. William Jagoe: sought on 26 April, but was not at home; windows shot out.

17. John McCarthy: house was shot up on 26 April in Dunmanway.

18. Tom Sullivan: heard voices outside his house and fled, taking refuge in the graveyard.

19. Bank of Ireland was attacked on 26 April in Dunmanway.

20. William Morrison: house was attacked on 26 April in Dunmanway but he was not at home.

21. Gilbert Johnston: beaten up in Bandon by six IRA men because he was a Protestant and an ex-service man.

22. R. J. Helen: claimed he was attacked in Clonakilty and escaped.

23. William Daunt: attacked in Ballineen on 27 April; no reason given.

24. Henry Bradfield: also sought on the night John Bradfield was shot at Killowen.

25. W. J. Bradfield: sought on the night his father was shot in Cahir, Ballineen.

26. Thomas Hornibrook: arrested and shot after a firefight at Ballygroman House following the shooting of Michael O'Neill.

27. Samuel Hornibrook: arrested and shot after a firefight at Ballygroman House following the shooting of Michael O'Neill.

28. Herbert Woods: arrested and probably hanged following the shooting of Michael O'Neill at Ballygroman House.

29. James Bennett: sought on the night of the Ballineen killings; worked for the Cotters who had been boycotted and Alfred Cotter killed in 1921.

30. Robert Bennett: sought on the night of the Ballineen killings; worked for the Cotters who had been boycotted and Alfred Cotter killed in 1921.

31. Jasper Travers Wolfe: apparently sought on the night of 28 April and fled to England; he was at court in Cork the following week according to the *Cork Examiner*.

32. William G. Wood: apparently sought on the night of 28 April and fled to England.

33. Edward Woods: warned to leave Cork after the shooting of Thomas and Samuel Hornibrook and Herbert Woods by the anti-Treaty IRA according to his witness statement to the Irish Grants Committee in 1927.

34. Matilda Woods: warned to leave Cork after the shooting of Thomas and Samuel Hornibrook and Herbert Woods by the anti-Treaty IRA, but she was still in residence in 'Glenbrae', Cross Douglas Road, in June 1922.

35. Family of Tom Nagle: nine brothers written to and warned to leave the country after the shooting of Robert, despite the fact that they lived in other parts of Ireland.

36. D. Cameron: a seventy-three-year-old Protestant from Crookstown, County Cork, he was warned to leave the country; no known reason.

APPENDIX 2

IMMEDIATE AND TERRIBLE WAR

'Immediate and terrible war' was the phrase apparently used by Lloyd George to force a conclusion to the negotiations about the Articles of Agreement for a Treaty between Great Britain and Ireland on 3 and 5 December 1921. What this meant is rarely explained, but a rarely accessed set of documents in the British National Archives outlines exactly what was involved. This is the blueprint for the suppression of Ireland after the Truce and shows that the British did not regard the Truce as the end of the war by any means. It is reproduced here simply as an example of the documents now available free to access online.

From the National Archives, Kew
Current reference CAB 43/2, pp. 74–7[1]

Very Secret.
Memorandum by the Secretary of State for War.

1. In the event of the present Conference failing to reach an agreement and hostilities recommencing, we must be prepared to face the condition that these hostilities may open before the expiration of the 72 hours of grace.

It is essential that the General Officer Commanding-in-Chief should be given a free hand to take the initiative at once, and to assume the offensive wherever possible. It is also essential to increase the forces at his disposal at the earliest possible date.

2. Martial law should be proclaimed in the 26 counties, or in all Ireland

if the Northern Government agrees. A draft has been agreed by the Irish Situation Committee, and is with the Secretariat.

3. Parliament should be called together (if it is not sitting) and speeches made by the Prime Minister calculated to stir the country. This should be followed by intensive propaganda, for, unless a wave of enthusiasm is created, it may not be possible to raise the necessary troops.

4. Recruiting should be commenced on one year's engagement of ex-service men

a. for the Regular Army. About 35,000 men will be required to bring the 67 Infantry battalions in Ireland up to 1,000 strong, and a further 15,000 men can be absorbed in these battalions – say 50,000 Infantry. [total 83,000]

b. for permanent guards and a small mobile reserve will be required in Great Britain for internees and prisoners and for those vulnerable points for which the War Office is responsible – say 25,000 men.

c. for the other arms and the departmental corps which will also be required to be filled up R.E. and Signals, R.A.S[ervice].C., R.A.O[rdnance].C, and R.A.M[edical].C. – say 10,000 men.

When the above have been obtained, new units might be formed from the Yeomanry and Territorial Army and other special sources, but the first effort should be to secure the 85,000 men required for (a), (b) and (c) above.

5. A Proclamation should be issued (following a statement in the House of Commons) that the Irish rebels, whilst not recognised as belligerents, will, as an act of grace, be treated as belligerents if they conduct their operations in accordance with the rules of war as laid down in Article 1 of the Annex to the Hague Convention, subject to the reservation of the right to try and punish for high treason all leaders and organisers of rebellion. ...

6. The women and children of the families of officers and other ranks in Ireland should be moved to this country, and provision made, where

necessary, for their accommodation and maintenance. Preliminary arrangements for this have been made.

7. The present internees, about 4,000, should be moved ... to Great Britain, and provision made ... for, say, 20,000 more. The internees accommodated in English prisons and camps should be guarded and fed by the Army. The preliminary arrangements for this have been made and the guards for this are included in 4(b) above. The Navy should prepare and be responsible for, say 2,500 at Scapa and Osea Island.

8. The General Officer Commanding-in-Chief has framed his plans to carry out an offensive policy ... it is of the utmost importance that General Macready should know now whether he is permitted to carry on, so that he can complete his arrangements and be ready to act without any delay, if and when the occasion arises.

9. Such forces as are available in this country can be despatched to Ireland at short notice ...

10. With reference to the policy to be adopted regarding Ulster ... reform the 36th (Ulster) Division on an Imperial basis.

11. ... Provision has been made in co-operation with the Home Secretary to provide police and military guards for the principal places where arms and explosives are stored in bulk, but there are docks, railways and bridges which are open to attack, and stores of explosives are kept near coal mines unguarded. Military protection for these latter will not be available, and the police should therefore be prepared to supply protection.

12. Censorship of the Press will be carried out in Ireland. Schemes have been worked out and staffs (200) are being selected for enforcing censorship of cables at London, Liverpool, and Glasgow; and of postal communications at London, Chester, and Glasgow. These schemes can be put into force at 48 hours and 5 days notice respectively.

13. The main points on which decisions are required briefly [edited by the author]

(a) Martial Law in all Ireland or in the 26 Counties.

(b) Parliamentary Campaign and intensive Press propaganda.

(c) Raising of special forces.

(d) Treatment of enemy.

(e) Dáil etc. to be declared treasonable organisations.

(f) Possession of arms, ammunition or explosives without a permit punishable by death after Drumhead Court.

(g) Control of the Press, censorship.

(h) Passports to enter Martial Law Area from Great Britain or abroad.

(i) Introduction of a system of identity cards.

(j) Restrictions on export of Irish produce, and if necessary the closing of manufacturing establishments.

(k) Destruction of Government property, animals, etc., to be met by requisition without payment [legal theft] on the area concerned.

(l) Stoppage of all Fairs, Markets, Race Meetings etc., as required.

(m) Closing of all ports except Cork and Dublin.

(n) Closing of all Civil Courts throughout the Martial Law area.

(o) Placing 2 Battalions of Marines on 48 hours notice.

(p) Raising of Ulster Division.

The War Office,
22nd October, 1921.

See also the next two documents in CAB 43/2/Admiralty, 'Naval Defence', pp. 82–7, 22 October 1921, and 'Memorandum by His Majesty's Government', pp. 88–93, 24 October 1921, for the reasoning behind the key British demands in the Treaty negotiations. All of these documents are available to download free online from the National Archives, Kew.

ENDNOTES

ABBREVIATIONS
Bureau of Military History (BMH)
Cork City and County Archives (CCCA)
General Post Office (G.P.O.)
Irish Republican Army (IRA)
Irish Republican Brotherhood (IRB)
Royal Irish Constabulary (RIC)
Witness Statement (WS)

INTRODUCTION

1   For example, RIC Auxiliary Cadet Vernon Hart, who was convicted of killing the parish priest of Dunmanway, is often referred to as 'Harte', but in his census returns for 1901 and 1911 and his marriage certificate his second name is spelled 'Hart'. Therefore, I have used the spelling 'Hart'.

2   The following quotation from the BMH's website – http://www. bureauofmilitaryhistory.ie/about.html (accessed 22 August 2013) – sets out the details of the project: 'The Bureau of Military History Collection, 1913–1921 (BMH) is a collection of 1,773 witness statements; 334 sets of contemporary documents; 42 sets of photographs and 13 voice recordings that were collected by the [Irish] State between 1947 and 1957, in order to gather primary source material for the revolutionary period in Ireland from 1913 to 1921.' Tom Barry observed in his refusal to take part in the project: 'Any individual is entitled to make any claim he likes and defame any officers he likes and it must be recorded by your Bureau. In my opinion no history is a real history unless all statements are subjected to the light of publicity during the lifetime of those who took part in the events being recorded', BMH WS 1734, p. 2.

3   David Fitzpatrick, in his review of Gerard Murphy's *The Year of Disappearances*, flags 'the ubiquity of serious factual errors and self-justifying distortion in much republican testimony such as that collected by the Bureau of Military History', Fitzpatrick, D., 2011, 'History

in a hurry', *Dublin Review of Books* 17, Spring, http://www.drb.ie/more_details/11-03-17/History_In_A_Hurry.aspx (accessed 13 May 2013). While admitting its limitations, Eve Morrison gives a far less dismissive view of the witness statements in an interview on Near FM, 'The History Show', episode three: 'Dr Eve Morrisson on the Bureau of Military History: interview with Cathal Brennan', http://nearfm.ie/podcast/the-history-show-episode-3/ (accessed 21 January 2013).

4   National Library of Ireland, Ms. 33,913 (5) Piaras Béaslaí papers, Dublin. Reports include 3rd Cork Brigade, 1st Southern Command, 2nd Cork Brigade, Belfast Brigade, Antrim Brigade, North Roscommon Brigade and others for May and June 1921.

5   There are difficulties in achieving this. I attempted to access the Manchester Regiment's record of civilian arrests, but was informed that this was closed until 2021. Following discussions with the archivist, this closure period was reduced to eighty-four years and the archive is now open.

6   McDonnell, K. K., 1972, *There is a Bridge at Bandon: a personal account of the Irish War of Independence* (Cork, Mercier Press), pp. 159–61.

7   'The colonisation of Castletown-Kinneigh', *Southern Star*, 10 August 1963, p. 6, col. 3, and 31 August 1963, p. 6, col. 3.

8   House of Lords debate, 27 November 1837, vol. 39, col. 241, Earl of Mulgrave: http://hansard.millbanksystems.com/lords/1837/nov/27/state-of-ireland (accessed 26 July 2013).

9   In early November 1920 the cabinet had noted that 'we were liable at any time to be confronted with a demand for interest now due for the past year and a half, and for the accruing interest': National Archives, Kew, CAB 23/23/1, 'Cabinet conclusion', 3 November 1920.

10   Referring to Gladstone's attempts to answer the 'Irish Question', the famous historical parody *1066 and All That* commented that 'whenever he was getting warm, the Irish secretly changed the Question': Sellar, W. C. and Yeatman, R. J., 1931, *1066 and All That: a memorable history of England, comprising all the parts you can remember including one hundred and three good things, five bad kings and two genuine dates* (New York, E. P. Dutton and Co.), p. 116.

1   PRELUDE TO WAR: 1914–1919

1   In the House of Lords, speaking about the Easter Rising, House of Lords debate, 10 May 1916, vol. 21, col. 970: http://hansard.millbank

systems.com/lords/1916/may/10/the-sinn-fein-rebellion (accessed 7 June 2013).

2   In the House of Commons, speaking in response to Lord Midleton, House of Commons debate, 11 May 1916, vol. 82, col. 941: http://hansard.millbanksystems.com/commons/1916/may/11/continuance-of-martial-law (accessed 7 June 2013).

3   It would be wrong to think that everyone involved in this issue had an intellectual understanding of this: it was an emotional war and all the more dangerous because of that.

4   Curtis, L., 1916, *The Commonwealth of Nations: an inquiry into the nature of citizenship in the British Empire, and into the mutual relations of the several communities thereof* (London, Macmillan and Co.).

5   Karsten, P., 1983, 'Irish soldiers in the British Army, 1792–1922: suborned or subordinate?', *Journal of Social History* 17, pp. 31–64.

6   The support for Home Rule consisted of 274 Liberals, 71 Irish Parliamentary Party and 42 Labour against 272 Conservative and Liberal unionists.

7   The Curragh website, 'The Curragh "Mutiny" 1914': http://www.curragh.info/articles/mutiny.htm (accessed 20 December 2012). See also: Florida Irish Heritage Center, 2011, 'My summer in Maine, a great book and an incident in Ireland that changed world history', http://floridairishheritagecenter.wordpress.com/tag/curragh-mutiny/ (accessed 16 July 2013) for a detailed study of the incident; Beckett, I. F. W., 1986, *The Army and the Curragh Incident, 1914* (London, Bodley Head for Army Records Society); Beckett, I. F. W., 1986, 'A note on government intelligence and surveillance during the Curragh incident, March 1914', *Intelligence and National Security* 1, pp. 435–40.

8   The two offending paragraphs were repudiated in the House of Commons by Sir Edward Grey, House of Commons debate, 'Colonel Seely and the Cabinet', 25 March 1914, vol. 60, col. 454: http://hansard.millbanksystems.com/commons/1914/mar/25/colonel-seely-and-the-cabinet S5CV0060P0_19140325_HOC_410 (accessed 10 February 2013).

9   House of Commons debate, 23 March 1914, vol. 60, col. 122: http://hansard.millbanksystems.com/commons/1914/mar/23/motion-for-adjournment (accessed 13 June 2013).

10   *Ibid.*, col. 135 (accessed 10 February 2013); McLean, I., 2010, *What's Wrong with the British Constitution?* (Oxford, Oxford University Press),

pp. 100–27 argues convincingly that the incident could be considered as a *coup d'état*.

11 Taylor, A., 2006, *Bonar Law* (London, Haus), pp. 53–75, provides an in-depth study of the manoeuvring by the leader of the 'Conservative and Unionist Party' to use the situation to force a general election. See also Smith, J., 1996, 'Paralysing the Arm: The Unionists and the Army Annual Act, 1911–1914', *Parliamentary History* 15, pp. 191–207. Lord Willoughby de Broke said during a House of Lords debate on 10 February 1914, vol. 15, cols 5–48: 'I say that we ought to deal with the Army Annual Act in such a way as to make it impossible for the Army to be used in such a way as noble Lords think. If nobody else will deal with it in this way, I shall in the meantime consider whether it is not possible to amend the Army Act in such a manner as to frustrate the sending over of the Army to Ulster to coerce these Ulstermen': http://hansard.millbanksystems.com/lords/1914/feb/10/address-in-reply-to-his-majestys-most (accessed 1 August 2013).

12 The Ulster Volunteers were formed in 1912 by Edward Carson and James Craig (later first prime minister of Northern Ireland) to pressure the British government into withdrawing the 1912 Irish Home Rule Bill which would give nationalist-dominated but limited self-government to Ireland. History Journal.ie, 2012, 'The Ulster Volunteers': http://www.historyjournal.ie/archives/war-in-ulster/143-the-ulster-volunteers.html (accessed 7 June 2013).

13 History Journal.ie, 2012, 'The Ulster Covenant': http://www.historyjournal.ie/archives/war-in-ulster/142-the-ulster-covenant.html (accessed 7 June 2013).

14 Connolly, S. J., 2007, *The Oxford Companion to Irish History* (Oxford, Oxford University Press), p. 303.

15 The Irish Volunteers were formed in November 1913 in response to the Ulster Volunteers and to promote the implementation of Home Rule.

16 Eyewitness to History, 1998, 'The assassination of Archduke Ferdinand 1914': http://www.eyewitnesstohistory.com/duke.htm (accessed 13 May 2013).

17 'England declares war on Germany', *Manchester Guardian*, 5 August 1914.

18 Liddell Hart, B. H., 1972, *History of the First World War* (London, Pan Books), p. 217.

19 There was much bitterness in the House of Lords that the Ulster opt-out was not included as an amendment.

20   University College Cork, 'Multitext project in Irish History: Movements for Political & Social Reform, 1870–1914': http://multitext.ucc.ie/d/John_Redmond (accessed 17 December 2012). See also MacDonagh, M., 1917, *The Irish on the Somme: being the second series of 'The Irish at the Front'* (London, Hodder and Stoughton).

21   At Verdun the French casualties were estimated at around 377,000 with 162,000 killed. The battle failed because the Germans were also bled white with around 337,000 casualties, including 100,000 killed. The British casualties at the Somme were 419,000 with 95,000 killed.

22   Lyons, J. B., 1983, *The Enigma of Tom Kettle: Irish patriot, essayist, poet, British soldier, 1880–1916* (Dublin, Glendale Press), p. 293. His wife was the sister of Francis Sheehy Skeffington, Irish journalist, pacifist and anti-war protestor.

23   Easter 1916: http://www.easter1916.net/ (accessed 18 December 2012).

24   History Empire, 'Easter Rising': http://historyempire.com/ireland/easter-rising/ (accessed 13 May 2013). This is unfair to Maxwell, who was asked to resign in October more for changing his view about conscription than anything else, according to George Dangerfield: see Dangerfield, G., 1966, *The Damnable Question: a study in Anglo-Irish relations* (London, Constable), p. 247.

25   Mac Giolla Choille, B. (ed.), 1966, *Intelligence Notes, 1913–1916, preserved in the State Paper Office* (Dublin, Stationery Office).

26   House of Commons debate, 'Continuance of Martial Law', 11 May 1916, vol. 82, col. 945: http://hansard.millbanksystems.com/commons/1916/may/11/continuance-of-martial-law (accessed 26 July 2013).

27   Morrissey, J., 2006, 'A Lost Heritage: the Connaught Rangers and Multivocal Irishness', in McCarthy, M. (ed.), *Ireland's Heritages: critical perspectives on memory and identity* (Ashgate, Aldershot), pp. 71–87. Available at http://www.nuigalway.ie/geography/documents/Heritage-Chapter.pdf (accessed 18 December 2012).

28   Mansergh, N., 1991, *The Unresolved Question: the Anglo-Irish settlement and its undoing, 1912–72* (New Haven, Yale University Press), p. 119.

29   Lloyd George, D., 1933, *War Memoirs of David Lloyd George* (Boston, Little, Brown, and Co.), p. 323.

30   Cassar, G. H., 2009, *Lloyd George at War, 1916–1918* (London, Anthem Press).

31   Jeffery, K., 2008, *Field Marshal Sir Henry Wilson: a political soldier* (Oxford, Oxford University Press).

32   Woodward, D. R., 1983, *Lloyd George and the Generals* (Newark, University of Delaware Press); Hankey, M., 1961, *The Supreme Command, 1914–1918*, 2 vols (London, Allen and Unwin); Liddell Hart (1972), pp. 327–36; Lloyd George, D., 1938, *War Memoirs* (London, Odhams Press), p. 323.

2   THE POLITICS OF WAR

1   Of course there had been incidents before this but this is the accepted start date.

2   See Kautt, W. H., 1999, *The Anglo-Irish War, 1916–1921: a people's war* (Westport, Conn., Praeger), for a more detailed analysis of the war than presented here. See Hittle, J. B. E., 2011, *Michael Collins and the Anglo-Irish War: Britain's counterinsurgency failure* (Washington, D.C., Potomac Books), for an up-to-date treatment of this subject. See also Fitzpatrick, D., 1977, *Politics and Irish Life 1913–1921: provincial experience of war and revolution* (Dublin, Gill & Macmillan) and Fitzpatrick, D., 2012a, *Terror in Ireland: 1916–1923* (Dublin, Lilliput Press).

3   Simson, H. J., 1937, *British Rule, and Rebellion* (Edinburgh, Blackwood and Sons), analysed the Irish and Palestinian conflicts as failures to win hearts and minds.

4   See Ramakrishna, K., n.d., 'The Role of Propaganda in the Malayan Emergency: lessons for countering terrorism today', p. 8. Available at: http://www.rsis.edu.sg/cens/publications/others/ProfKumarPresenta-tion.pdf (accessed 22 August 2013). See also Hack, K., 2009, 'The Malayan Emergency as counter-insurgency paradigm', *Journal of Strategic Studies* 32, no. 3, pp. 383–414.

5   Charters, D., 2009, 'The development of British counter-insurgency intelligence', *Journal of Conflict Studies* 29, pp. 55–74. Available at: http://journals.hil.unb.ca/index.php/JCS/article/view/15233/19650 (accessed 18 December 2012). See also Walton, C., 2013, *Empire of Secrets: British intelligence, the Cold War and the twilight of empire* (London, Harper Press).

6   Gray, C. S., 2012, 'Concept failure? COIN, counterinsurgency, and strategic theory', *Prism: a Journal of the Centre for Complex Operations* 3, no. 3, June, pp. 17–32. Gray argues that the recent debate among military strategists about its value is a misunderstanding of the concept.

7   Callwell, C. E., 1906, *Small Wars. Their Principles and Practice* (London, printed for HMSO by Harrison and Sons); Combined Arms Research Library Digital Library: http://cgsc.cdmhost.com/cdm/

compoundobject/collection/p4013coll11/id/394 (accessed 8 December 2012). See Davies, C. C., 1975, *The Problem of the North-west Frontier, 1890–1908, with a Survey of Policy since 1849* (London, Curzon Press), for the punitive system in India from 1849. Available at: http://oudl. osmania.ac.in/bitstream/handle/OUDL/1934/218382_The_Problem_ Of_The_North-West_Frontier_1890–1908.pdf?sequence=2 (accessed 15 February 2013). See also Ion, A. H. and Errington, E. J., 1993, *Great Powers and Little Wars: the limits of power* (Westport, Conn., Praeger).

8   Kautt (1999) suggests that the misbehaviour by British soldiers, the Auxiliaries and new recruits to the RIC occurred because they were inexperienced at counter-insurgency, but Callwell (1906) shows that expeditions to punish local communities for attacks against their forces were part of normal British imperial policy; see also Davies (1975).

9   The current version of the *British Army Field Manual* (2009) says that Callwell also omits many factors which would be considered important, such as intelligence, but he states that in guerrilla wars intelligence is essential. Available at: *news.bbc.co.uk/2/shared/bsp/hi/pdfs/16_11_09_ army_manual.pdf.*

10   MacDonagh, O. and Mandle, W. F., 1986, *Ireland and Irish-Australia: studies in cultural and political history* (London, Croom Helm), p. 89.

11   National Archives, Kew, CAB 24/139, 'Situation in Ireland: report by Major Whittaker', 19 September 1922.

12   British Houses of Parliament Archives, Lloyd George papers, LG/F/48/6/8 and LG/F/48/6/10, Lord French to Lloyd George; Holmes, R., 1981, *The Little Field-Marshal, Sir John French* (London, J. Cape), pp. 351–3. French in 1920 suggested that the civilian population would need to be removed from areas to concentration camps before aircraft could be used.

13   Walsh, M., 2008, *The News from Ireland: foreign correspondents and the Irish Revolution* (London, I. B. Tauris), p. 124.

14   *Daily Sketch*, 3 December 1920. See the Royal Irish Constabulary Forum, The Auxiliary Division, C Company: http://irishgenealogyqueries. yuku.com/topic/762/t/C-Company.html.UR1UVB13a_g (accessed 13 February 2013).

15   At the time of this burning it was illegal but was tolerated to avoid having to investigate the Auxiliaries. In 1901 the British legal position had been explained in the House of Commons: 'Article XXIII. (g) of the Hague Convention lays down that the destruction of an enemy's

property is permissible when imperatively demanded by the necessities of war', House of Commons debate, 'Farm burnings', 20 May 1901, vol. 94, cols 579–80, http://hansard.millbanksystems.com/commons/1901/may/20/farm-burning (accessed 26 July 2013) in reply to J. Flynn, Cork North; the Hague Convention 1899 Article 23, http://avalon.law.yale.edu/19th_century/hague02.asp (accessed 18 December 2012). As the British did not declare war during the Irish fight, neither the protections nor the rules applied until martial law was declared in late 1920, though arguments can also be made against this.

16 House of Commons adjournment debate, 13 December 1920, as reported in 'Rebels burned Cork', *The New York Times*, 14 December 1920. (Greenwood had been created a baronet in 1915, and from then on was thus referred to as Sir Hamar Greenwood.)

17 White, G. and O'Shea, B., 2006, *The Burning of Cork* (Cork, Mercier Press), pp. 146–61. There is plenty of evidence in that book that the burning was a planned reprisal that got out of hand. See also 'The burning of Cork', *Southern Star*, 18 June 1921, p. 2, and the discussion of K Company of the Auxiliaries in Chapter 3 of this book.

18 Secretary for India M. Montagu: 'I have not received final figures, but I understand that the total number of deaths in the Punjab, Delhi, Ahmedabad, and Calcutta, is estimated at about 400, and the number of injured at about the same number. Eight or nine Europeans were murdered. The damage done by rioters in the Punjab may amount to something not far short of £1,000,000', House of Commons debate, 28 May 1919, vol. 116, col. 1184: http://hansard.millbanksystems.com/commons/1919/may/28/recent-riots-total-civilian-casualties (accessed 26 July 2013).

19 'Black Hand in Ireland', *Auckland Star*, 13 March 1920, p. 17. Available at National Library of New Zealand past papers: http://paperspast.natlib.govt.nz/cgi-bin/paperspast (accessed 18 December 2012).

20 BMH WS 400, Richard Walsh, pp. 64–6.

21 Office of Public Works, Dublin Castle, 'The end of British Rule': http://www.dublincastle.ie/HistoryEducation/History/Chapter16The EndofBritishRule/ (accessed 8 February 2013). For Alan Bell, see BMH WS 1099, George C. Duggan, assistant to Under Secretary for Ireland, Dublin Castle, 1919–1922, p. 31.

22 James Craig had been made a baronet in 1918 and became Sir James Craig after this. Wylie and Craig had different motives for looking for

Dominion Status with partition, but their analysis of the likely eventual outcome is striking in its similarity.

23 National Archives, Kew, CAB 24/109, 'Notes of a conference with the officers of the Irish Government held at 10 Downing Street, S.W. on Friday, 23rd. July 1920, at 11.30 a.m. and 3.30 p.m.'; Mansergh (1991), pp. 151–3.

24 The GAA Archive, 'Bloody Sunday': http://www.crokepark.ie/gaa-museum/gaa-archive/gaa-museum-irish-times-articles/bloody-sunday, –1920 (accessed 18 December 2012).

25 See comments by Michael Collins dismissing Dominion Home Rule in *Southern Star*, 25 September 1920, at a time when peace feelers had already been put out by both sides. Collins was TD for Cork South in the first Dáil of 1919 and Director of Intelligence for the IRA. In 1919 he had become President of the secret Irish Republican (Fenian) Brotherhood (IRB). During this period he was also acting President of the Irish Republic following the arrest of President Arthur Griffith. In 1921 he would be a member of the Irish delegation during the Treaty negotiations. In 1922 he would be Chairman of the Provisional Government and would command the National Army until his assassination by anti-Treaty forces in August of that year. See also Lloyd George's Guildhall speech on 9 November, when he said, 'We have murder by the throat.' Earlier that afternoon he had opened discussions on a truce with Sinn Féin. British Houses of Parliament Archives, Bonar Law papers, BL/102/7/4 and BL/102/7/5.

26 Collins, M. and Talbot, H., 1923, *Michael Collins' Own Story* (London, Hutchinson and Co.), p. 123.

27 BMH WS 767, Patrick Moylett; Hittle (2011), p. 182. See Smith, R. N., 1997, *The Colonel: the life and legend of Robert R. McCormick, 1880–1955* (Boston, Houghton Mifflin Company), for the involvement of John Steele of the *Chicago Tribune* in the negotiations, pp. 232–3. Both Smith and Hittle confuse the sequence of events, which is unsurprising as this is not central to their research.

28 British Houses of Parliament Archives, Bonar Law papers, BL/102/7/6, 'Memo by C. J. Phillips, Foreign Office', 19 November 1920; LG/F/91/7/7-24, 'Correspondence about C. J. Phillip's interviews with Moylett', October–November 1920; see also Robert Dudley Edwards Archives, University College Dublin, for a second Moylett statement. Moylett makes it clear that Collins, Éamon de Valera (President of the

Irish Republic and senior surviving commandant of the 1916 Rising) and Griffith (the Deputy President) were speaking with one voice.

29 National Archives, Kew, CAB 23/23/13, 9 December 1920.

30 House of Commons debate, 10 December 1920, vol. 135, cols 2601–16: http://hansard.millbanksystems.com/commons/1920/dec/10/prime-ministers-announcement (accessed 26 July 2013).

31 In a September 1922 report to the cabinet, Major Whittaker estimated that 200,000 troops and millions of pounds would be needed to hold southern Ireland against a hostile population. National Archives, Kew, CAB 24/139.

32 National Archives, Kew, CAB 23/38, p. 21. See also I. O. (Street, C. J. C.), 1921, *The Administration of Ireland, 1920* (London, Philip Allan), pp. 160–1, which shows that the British could not understand why the Government of Ireland Act providing Dominion Home Rule without taxes was unacceptable to the Irish.

33 BMH WS 1413, Tadhg Kennedy, pp. 111–12. The British intelligence officer arrived in Tralee by plane and Kennedy 'welcomed' his visitor by organising the column to fire on the plane once it touched down just to get his point across.

34 Kostal, D., 2007, 'British military intelligence-law enforcement integration in the Irish War of Independence, 1919–1921', in *Can't We All Just Get Along? Improving the law enforcement–intelligence community relationship* (Washington, D.C., NDIC Press), p. 138.

35 National Archives, Kew, CAB 24/122/83, 'Irish Situation. Deputation to the Right Hon. the Lord Chancellor', Friday, 15 April 1921; see the first part of this meeting on 28 March. Birkenhead was Frederick Edwin Smith, whose fervent support of armed resistance by Ulster unionists gave way to authoring the 'Articles of Agreement for a Treaty between Great Britain and Ireland', which formally ended the Irish War of Independence.

36 BMH WS 883, Lieut.-Col. John M. MacCarthy, Appendix N, 'Single original copy of captured British intelligence summary'; see also p. 91 of this witness statement, where he discusses how the document came into his possession and its contents.

37 There is a copy of the report in O'Donoghue, F., 1986, *No Other Law* (Dublin, Anvil), Appendix 1. Extracts in the text are from BMH WS 883, Appendix N.

38 Searches by the military, police and Auxiliaries had increased to 6,311

between 1 October 1920 and July 1921 from 1,500 the previous year, according to Jeffery, K., 1987, 'British military intelligence following World War I', in Robertson, K. G. (ed.), *British and American Approaches to Intelligence* (Basingstoke, Macmillan), pp. 55–84.

39 The drought ended in mid July; Shaw, N., 1923, *The Air & Its Ways: the Rede Lecture in the University of Cambridge* (Cambridge, Cambridge University Press).

40 See also the unsuccessful Millstreet British round-up of IRA suspects in June 1921, according to BMH WS 838, Seán Moylan, p. 235. In that case the IRA had sufficient intelligence at Millstreet that the British were coming so waited for lunchtime and slipped through the net.

41 Flor Begley, who became known as the 'Piper of Crossbarry' after he played the bagpipes to raise Irish morale during the fighting, dismisses Barry's claims that there were 1,300 troops and, basing his figure on the number of lorries that converged on the area, puts the figure at 350, which was far better odds for the 100-strong flying column. He also confirms that the Auxiliaries from Macroom arrived late, thus allowing the flying column to escape, in BMH WS 1771, p. 3. In cases like this, where we are relying on the protagonists' memories, it is hard to know who is right in their estimation.

42 BMH WS 832, William Desmond, p. 38. He also states that he attended a funeral for eighteen British soldiers in Bandon Barracks after Crossbarry, p. 48.

43 BMH WS 348, Captain E. Gerrard, A. D. C. 5th Division British Forces in Ireland 1916–1921, p. 8. Gerrard also mentions that Lloyd George had asked for and received a copy of Prendergast, J. P., 1922, *The Cromwellian Settlement of Ireland* (Dublin, Mellifont Press).

44 Jeffery, K., 1984, *The British Army and the Crisis of Empire: 1918–1922* (Manchester, Manchester University Press), pp. 89–92. See also Callwell, C. E., 1927, *Field-Marshall Sir Henry Wilson*, vol. 2 (London, Cassell), p. 299, which shows that there was difficulty getting officers to go to Ireland when sent, which was tantamount to mutiny.

45 While the Black and Tans were not significant in West Cork, these paramilitary police, who were inserted into the ranks of the RIC to stem the flood of resignations, had such a poor reputation in the rest of Ireland that the War of Independence is often named after them.

46 National Archives, Kew, CAB 24/126, 'Weekly survey of the state of Ireland', 13 July 1921.

47 Three companies was about 500 men. National Archives, Kew, CAB 23/25, 'Conclusions of a conference of Ministers held in Mr. Chamberlain's room, House of Commons, S.W., on Friday, 8th April, 1921, at 3.30 p.m.', 15 April 1921, Appendix VII, p. 62.

48 On 16 March 1921 there were fifty infantry and seven cavalry battalions, thirty-three artillery batteries, four Royal Engineer companies and three Signal companies in Ireland, *The Irish Times*, 16 May 1921, p. 5, col. 5. McKenna, J., 2011, *Guerrilla Warfare in the Irish War of Independence, 1919–1921* (Jefferson, N.C., McFarland and Co.), p. 252, suggests the total was 57,000 plus support staff, which is greater than David Fitzpatrick's estimate of 15,000 effective troops in Bartlett, T. and Jeffery, K., 1996, *A Military History of Ireland* (Cambridge, Cambridge University Press), p. 406. Once the strike was called off on 17 April the troops were returned to Ireland. Evidence presented by General Macready in October 1921 says the sixty-seven battalions in Ireland were under strength by 15,000, suggesting that the number of troops in June 1921 was approximately 46,000.

49 Wilson's military solution was to concentrate forces in India, Egypt, Ireland and Germany, but that would have meant giving up on large parts of the British Empire so it was politically impossible.

50 Sloan, G. R., 1997, *The Geopolitics of Anglo-Irish Relations in the Twentieth Century* (London, Leicester University Press), pp. 134–96; National Archives, Kew, CAB 43/2/Admiralty, 'Naval Defence', pp. 82–7, 22 October 1921.

51 Pattison, G., 2010, 'The British Army's Effectiveness in the Irish Campaign 1919–1921 and the Lessons for Modern Counterinsurgency Operations, with Special Reference to C3I Aspects', *The Cornwallis Group XIV: Analysis of Societal Conflict and Counter-Insurgency*, pp. 88–103.

52 National Archives, Kew, CAB 24/124; *The Irish Times*, 23 May 1921; de Valera, É., 1921, *The Struggle of the Irish People: address to the Congress of the United States adopted at the January session of Dáil Éireann, 1921* (Washington, D.C., U.S. G.P.O.) gave a civilian figure (including IRA members not shot in battle) of 270 between 1 January 1920 and 28 February 1921. Sir Hamar Greenwood, House of Commons debate, 'Oral answers: Ireland: kidnapping', 16 February 1922, vol. 150, cols 1196–7: 'The number of persons kidnapped during the period in question is 170, of whom 34 were police, 5 military and 131 civilians. Of the police, 17 have since been released, 15 are believed to have been murdered,

and 2 are believed to have left the country. All the military kidnapped have since been released. Of the civilians, 115 have been released, 8 are believed to have been murdered, and 8 are still unaccounted for [from 1 August 1920 to Truce July 1921]'. http://hansard.millbanksystems.com/commons/1922/feb/16/kidnapping (accessed 26 July 2013).

53 Donnelly Jr, J. S., 2012, 'Big House burnings in County Cork during the Irish Revolution, 1920–21', *Éire-Ireland* 47, pp. 141–97, provides an excellent overview of this topic.

54 BMH WS 1607, Charlie O'Donoghue, pp. 8–9. In contrast, each British soldier carried 150 rounds of ammunition as part of his standard uniform.

55 BMH WS 792, Tadg O'Sullivan, p. 9.

56 Broom, J. T., 2002, 'The Anglo-Irish War of 1919–1921: "Britain's Troubles–Ireland's Opportunities" ', in Huber, T. M. (ed.), *Compound Warfare: that fatal knot* (Fort Leavenworth, Kan., U.S. Army Command and General Staff College Press). Available at: http://norwich.academia. edu/JohnBroom/Papers/998074/The_Anglo-Irish_War_1919–1921_ Englands_Troubles--Irelands_Opportunities_ (accessed 9 September 2012). For a similar conclusion from a very different perspective see Mitchell, A., 1995, *Revolutionary Government in Ireland: Dáil Éireann, 1919–22* (Dublin, Gill & Macmillan), p. 399.

57 Roger Casement was hanged for treason in 1916 by the British government after he was captured in County Kerry during a failed attempt to land German weapons in the days before the Easter Rising. He was a renowned human rights activist and exposed genocide in the Congo and South America in the early years of the twentieth century.

58 'Tom Casement to J. C. Smuts', 30 May 1921, in Van der Poel, J. (ed.), *Selections from the Smuts Papers* (Cambridge, 1973), vol. 5, pp. 83–5, quoted in Shaw, G., 2012, 'The Casement brothers, Ireland and South Africa', *Southern African-Irish Studies* 4, series 2, no. 1, pp. 15–24. Van der Poel suggests that the communication was at the request of de Valera.

59 See BMH WS 994, George Berkley, p. 131 footnote, and BMH WS 1769, P. J. Little, pp. 64–5, for Moore's contacts with Smuts.

60 National Archives, Kew, CAB 23/22/15, 'Cabinet conclusion', 30 September 1920.

61 For an example of the anti-war view in Britain it is hard to beat Martin, H., 1921, *Ireland in Insurrection, an Englishman's Record of Fact* (London, D. O'Connor). Asquith had good cause to 'dig the knife into'

Lloyd George, whom he believed had manoeuvred him out of the prime ministry in 1915.

62   Chamberlain, A. and Self, R. C., 1995, *The Austen Chamberlain Diary Letters: the correspondence of Sir Austen Chamberlain with his sisters Hilda and Ida, 1916–1937* (London, Cambridge University Press), p. 170.

63   *Ibid.*, pp. 166, 170.

64   *Southern Star*, 18 June 1920, p. 2, col. 2, where Smuts outlines his aims at the dock in Southampton.

65   The 1926 Balfour Declaration states, 'They are autonomous Communities within the British Empire, equal in status, in no way subordinate one to another in any aspect of their domestic or external affairs, though united by a common allegiance to the Crown, and freely associated as members of the British Commonwealth of Nations.' It is regarded as one of the founding documents of Australia and it was given force in Great Britain by the Statute of Westminster (1931). Available at: http://foundingdocs.gov.au/resources/transcripts/cth11_doc_1926.pdf (accessed 18 July 2013).

66   See Jeffery (1984), p. 93. For the original cabinet discussions surrounding the Treaty, see National Archives, Kew, 'The Cabinet Papers 1915–1981', 'Irish independence: Truce': http://www.nationalarchives.gov.uk/cabinetpapers/themes/irish-independence.htm (accessed 19 December 2012).

67   National Archives, Kew, CAB 23/27, 'Cabinet conclusions', 6 December 1921. 'Irish independence: Truce': http://www.nationalarchives.gov.uk/cabinetpapers/themes/irish-independence.htm (accessed 19 December 2012). This is a little unfair to Lloyd George, whose basically sound reason for fighting on through the winter of 1920 regarded the retention of taxation inside the imperial parliament; National Archives, Kew, CAB 23/38/1, 'Ministerial conference on Government of Ireland Bill, 1920', 13 October 1920.

68   Collins and Talbot (1923).

69   Washington Naval Conference, or International Conference on Naval Limitation, November 1921.

70   Collins and Talbot (1923), pp. 139–41 for all three quotations. As Collins was dead by the time Talbot published the book, there is no way of knowing how much of it is true. However, a brief cross-check suggests that he is broadly accurate, even if he is suffering from obvious hero-worship.

71 BMH WS 764, Pat O'Brien, p. 63; BMH WS 1619, Daniel Canty; Lord Chancellor Birkenhead speaking in the House of Lords on 21 June 1921, vol. 45, col. 690 'The Government of Ireland' says: 'It is a small war that is going on in Ireland. Week by week, month by month, its true character has developed, ... I think that the history of the last three months is a history of the failure of our military measures to keep pace with, and to overcome, the military measures which have been taken by our opponents.' http://hansard.millbanksystems.com/lords/1921/jun/21/the-government-of-ireland (accessed 30 July 2013).

72 For a good overview of the entire period, see Michael Laffin's series of lectures on the Irish revolution: University College Dublin, Historyhub.ie, 'The Irish Revolution': http://www.historyhub.ie/pages/irishrev.html (accessed 18 December 2012).

73 Terence MacSwiney was elected Sinn Féin Lord Mayor of Cork in May 1921 and explained better than most its aim of a fully independent Ireland. He devised the strategy of indirect war to make the British day-to-day regime redundant rather than confronting its army directly. He was arrested in Cork City Hall on 12 August 1920 and died in Brixton Prison after seventy-six days on hunger strike, having garnered huge international support and attention for the Irish cause.

74 Economic and Social History Society of Ireland, 'Northern Ireland opts': http://www.eshsi.net/Northern_Ireland_opts.htm (accessed 13 May 2013).

75 Walsh, P. V., 1998, 'The Irish Civil War, 1922–1923: a military study of the conventional phase, 28 June–11 August, 1922', paper delivered to The New York Military Affairs Symposium, 11 December. Available at: http://bobrowen.com/nymas/irishcivilwar.html (accessed 13 May 2013). This document is useful for the wealth of force dispositions of the British, the Free State and the anti-Treaty IRA it gives.

76 The start of the Civil War in Cork can be precisely dated to an order issued by Óglaigh na hÉireann on 3 April 1922: 'To OC 5th Batt Cork No. 4 Brigade "It is essential that the proclamation repudiating the Minister of Defence and Chief of Staff be read to all ranks."' On the back of another document, 'Agenda for the Army Convention', dated 12 April, five names were ticked. All were believed to be anti-Treaty at this time. Four others, including Florrie O'Donoghue, were not ticked, suggesting that the split occurred at this time. Cork City and County Archives, Siobhán Langford papers, CCCAU169/31.

77   As the British would not agree to the words 'Irish Republic' under any circumstances, or to anything less than an oath of allegiance to the king, 'Free State' was concocted to give the new, practically independent, entity a name. Those Irish republicans who could countenance nothing but a republic went to war to overthrow it.

78   Gregory, Lady and Murphy, D. J., 1978, *Lady Gregory's Journals*, vol. 1, books 1–29, 10 October 1916–24 February 1925 (Gerrards Cross, Smythe), pp. 353–5. From an old aristocratic, Protestant and unionist family, playwright Lady Augusta Gregory co-founded Ireland's national Abbey Theatre in 1904 to revive Gaelic (Irish) culture, which was being lost. She was revered by nationalists, and Sinn Féin in particular. MacEoin captured the Galway city barracks on 8 July 1922.

79   Dáil Éireann, 'The National Situation – Army Officers' Deputation', 3 May 1922: http://www.oireachtas-debates.gov.ie/D/DT/D.S.192205030007. html (accessed 12 June 2013).

80   Churchill's volatility had the potential to cause disaster. At the start of June 1922 he ordered two battalions of British troops with artillery to attack sixty IRA men at Pettigo in Free State territory, which ran the risk of destabilising the situation in Northern Ireland. Then on 26 June he ordered British troops to attack the Four Courts in Dublin, which would have been military and political insanity. General Macready, who was in Dublin, was not impressed, and went to London to change the cabinet's mind. For the details of the attack on the courts, see Dwyer, T. Ryle, 2012, 'British Army fire did not spark Civil War', *Irish Examiner*, 1 November. Available at: http://www.irishexaminer.com/analysis/ british-army-fire-did-not-spark-civil-war-212534.html (accessed 8 December 2012).

81   House of Commons debate, 'Easter recess (adjournment), Ireland', vol. 153, col. 529, 12 April 1922: http://hansard.millbanksystems.com/ commons/1922/apr/12/ireland-1 (accessed 26 July 2013).

82   This government was formed to cover legally the period between 16 January 1922 and 6 December 1922 when the Free State came into formal existence. See Chambers, I., 2006, *The Chamberlains, the Churchills and Ireland, 1874–1922* (New York, Cambria Press), pp. 227–60 for the pressure that Churchill exerted on the Provisional Government.

83   Quotations from a report of a famous speech in Cork, 21 January 1885, by Charles Stewart Parnell, *Cork Examiner*, 22 January 1885.

84   'Mr Churchill speaks', *Southern Star*, 15 April 1922, p. 1, col. 6.

85 'The History Show', episode eleven: 'Dr. John M. Regan of the University of Dundee about revisionism, Peter Hart and the history wars in Ireland', podcast radio programme, Near FM, Dublin, 14 January 2013: http://nearfm.ie/podcast/the-history-show-episode-eleven/Dr. Regan (accessed 21 January 2013) emphasises the explicit nature of the British threat of re-conquest throughout 1922 and its effect during the Civil War.

86 National Museum of Ireland, 2013, 'Limerick tax roll, Four Courts explosion, 1922': http://thecricketbatthatdiedforireland.com/2013/02/15/limerick-tax-roll-four-courts-explosion-1922-4/ (accessed 12 June 2013).

87 'An Oath of Allegiance was taken by all ranks of the Army to the Irish Republic and the Dáil. When the majority of the Dáil abandoned carrying into effect of ment [*sic*] the disestablishment of the Republic', Irish Republican Army Convention, 12 April 1922. The same document rejects the Free State *casus belli* by dismissing the refusal of Richard Mulcahy, Chief of Staff, to hold an Army Convention, using this logic: 'There is no analogy between the demand made by the Irish Army for a convention and such a demand if made by the armies of other countries. The Irish Army is a volunteer army with full citizen rights. Their opposition to the Treaty is not a matter of interference with politics.' Cork City and County Archives, Siobhán Langford papers, CCCAU169/31.

88 'Letter to Mallow IRA', Siobhán Langford papers, U169/B/(iv), 27 January 1922. Baker later became vicar of St Paul's in Cork and passed away in Limerick in 1962.

3   WEST CORK'S WAR

1 Ellis, P. B., 2004, *Eyewitness to Irish History* (Hoboken, N.J., John Wiley and Sons), p. 242. The Auxiliary police were former British officers who were initially recruited in July 1920 as an elite police corps to seek out members of the IRA. They were first deployed in September 1920. The force eventually grew to a strength of 1,500. Cadet Guthrie, who managed to escape from the ambush itself, was shot later in the day.

2 National Library of Ireland, Ms. 27,458. Alice Stopford's niece recalls: 'After tea, with great stealth and secrecy, the coronet was produced for our admiration and placed on my head. I was glad to get rid of it – it weighed a ton, all gilt and red velvet. I suppose Lord Bandon had to get another one for the next coronation.'

3 For example, in 1911, including the 19 military in barracks, 65 of Bandon's Protestant population of 641 had been born in England.

4 The English-born population of Cork county increased from 8,451 in 1861 to 13,861 (+64 per cent) in 1911 before dropping to 6,258 (-55 per cent) in 1926. The Cork-born population declined by 152,157 (-37 per cent) from 1861 to 1926. Census of Ireland, 1926, vol. 3, part. 2, p. 163: http://www.cso.ie/en/census/historicalreports/census1926reports/census1926volume3-religionandbirthplaces/ (accessed 18 July 2013).

5 For example, Thomas Murphy literally walked off with 5,000 rounds of .303 ammunition after a train loaded with military supplies stopped in Blackpool in Cork city and he opened an unguarded carriage: BMH WS 109, Thomas Murphy, p. 2. Edmond Twomey was a major supplier of British ammunition and gelignite according to his statement, BMH WS 44.

6 Pattison (2010). Patrols raided these areas and IRA members were captured, but the areas became impassable in wet weather. Part of the truculence in de Valera's correspondence with Lloyd George was to draw it out until the autumn to benefit the IRA in the event of a breakdown in negotiations; see BMH WS 873, Charles Brown, pp. 14–15.

7 The phrase was long used by both the British and Irish to suggest that the Irish were ungovernable.

8 This may appear silly, but according to BMH WS 1297, Michael O'Driscoll, p. 10, it worked between Bantry and Coomhola, eleven kilometres away, where the IRA flying column was headquartered just before the Truce. See Borgonovo, J., 2010, 'The guerrilla infrastructure: I.R.A. Special Services in the Cork Number One Brigade, 1917–1921', *The Irish Sword* XXVII, no. 108, p. 208 (the BMH reference is incorrectly transposed as WS 1279). See also BMH WS 505, Seán Moylan.

9 BMH WS 832, William Desmond, p. 33; Deasy, L., 1973, *Towards Ireland Free: the West Cork Brigade in the War of Independence, 1917–1921* (Cork, Mercier Press). Deasy notes that these raids increased after the Kilmichael ambush and had such a demoralising effect on the Manch Bridge and Dunmanway IRA companies that Tom Barry had to meet with them to restore morale.

10 University College Cork, Boole Library and Archives, CO 904/114 'Confidential monthly reports Bandon/Cork West Riding, Cork City-East Riding and Mallow/Cork North'. He was unstinting in his praise

of the Auxiliaries in the January report and wanted more units sent to West Cork.

11   Mulcahy, R., 1921, *Dáil Debates*, vol. T. 9, col. 143, 22 December. This famous quote is taken out of context. http://oireachtasdebates. oireachtas.ie/debates%20authoring/DebatesWebPack.nsf/takes/ dail1921122200003?opendocument (accessed 13 June 2013).

12   BMH WS 1275, Timothy Warren, p. 8; BMH WS 1255, William McCarthy, p. 14; BMH WS 1640, James Doyle, p. 24; BMH WS 1234, Jack Hennessy, p. 13.

13   *British Army Field Manual* (2009); Kardahji, M., 2007, 'A Measure of Restraint: the Palestinian Police and the end of the British Mandate', MPhil thesis, Oxford University. Available at: http://users.ox.ac. uk/~metheses/KardahjiThesis.pdf (accessed 13 June 2013). See also Khalidi, R., 2001, 'The Palestinians and 1948: the Root Causes of Failure', in Rogan, E. L. and Shlaim, A. (eds), *The War for Palestine: rewriting the history of 1948* (New York, Cambridge University Press), pp. 12–36; Cahill, R.A., 2009, '"Going Berserk": "Black and Tans" in Palestine', *Jerusalem Quarterly* 38, pp. 59–68.

14   BMH WS 400, Richard Walsh, pp. 65–7.

15   Ainsworth, J. S., 2001, 'The Black & Tans and Auxiliaries in Ireland, 1920–1921: their origins, roles and legacy': http://eprints.qut.edu. au/9/ (accessed 22 August 2013); Leeson, D., 2011, *The Black and Tans: British Police and Auxiliaries in the Irish War of Independence, 1920–1921* (Oxford, Oxford University Press).

16   According to the Tom Barry papers in the Cork City and County Archive, Barry was the third choice for commandant as Charlie Hurley and Ted O'Sullivan had both turned it down, CCCAU016/1/1, pp. 39–40.

17   The phrase appears regularly in the BMH statements. 'Sometimes they were posted in R.I.C. barracks with the remnant of the old R.I.C. But they never got on well with these "allies" of theirs', BMH WS 1770, Kevin R. O'Sheil, p. 1099.

18   BMH WS 1532, Daniel Harrington, p. 5.

19   Ainsworth, J. S., 2000, *British Security Policy in Ireland, 1920–1921: a desperate attempt by the Crown to maintain Anglo-Irish unity by force* (Perth, Centre for Irish Studies, Murdoch University), pp. 2–3. Available at: http://eprints.qut.edu.au/6/ (accessed 17 July 2013).

20   There were occasional convictions. Two Auxiliaries from Beggar's Bush

Barracks in Dublin were convicted of stealing twenty watches from a jeweller in Balbriggan, eight bottles of spirits from a pub in 'Cloughran' (Cloghran), and a brooch and £4 from a lady in Swords, during raids on 10 and 11 March 1921: *The Irish Times,* 9 June 1921.

21   See Rast, M., 2011, 'Tactics, Politics, and Propaganda in the Irish War of Independence, 1917–1921', PhD thesis, Georgia State University, p. 93; 'Blame Cork Fires on Military Alone', *The New York Times,* 19 January 1921. Available at: http://query.nytimes.com/mem/archive-free/pdf?res =9C04E5D9153CE533A25753C2A9679C946095D6CF (accessed 12 December 2012). See also National Library of Australia, Trove Archive, 1920, 'Chaos in Cork', *Recorder* (Port Pirie, South Australia: 1919–1954), 15 December, p. 1: http://nla.gov.au/nla.news-article95394972 (accessed 21 February 2013).

22   To simplify matters in this book Auxiliaries also include the Black and Tans, but they were two separate forces; Kautt, W. H., 2003, 'Militarising Policemen: the various members of the RIC and their response to IRA violence in Ireland, 1919–21'. Available at: http://www.academia. edu/1686881/The_Auxies_Black_and_Tans_and_the_RIC_and_their_ response_to_IRA_violence_in_Ireland_1919-21 (accessed 18 July 2013), which is part of an extensive and well-argued series of books and articles published by him on the War of Independence.

23   *Limerick Leader,* 20 April 1921.

24   Lord Parmoor's brother had gone to Ireland with his wife on their annual fishing holiday as if there was no risk. The BMH statements are littered with British officers and establishment figures being captured while fishing, which suggests a degree of innocence, arrogance or perceived invincibility.

25   House of Lords debate, 26 April 1921, vol. 45, cols 15–41, Castleconnell Shooting, http://hansard.millbanksystems.com/lords/1921/apr/26/ castleconnell-shooting (accessed 18 July 2013).

26   National Archives, Kew, CAB 24/139, 'Situation in Ireland, report by Major Whittaker', 19 September 1922.

27   Irish Labour Party and Trade Union Congress, 1921, *Who Burnt Cork City? A tale of arson, loot, and murder: the evidence of over seventy witnesses* (Dublin, Irish Labour Party and Trade Union Congress). Available at http://archive.org/details/whoburntcorkcity00dubl (accessed 20 December 2012). This is an essential primary source for many of the incidents covered in this book, including the shooting of Canon Magner,

the Delaney Brothers, the Dillon's Cross ambush, and of course the burning of Cork.

28 See National Archives, Kew, CAB 23/24, 'Cabinet conclusions', 14 February 1921; also meeting about the burning of Cork, 15 February 1921, in the same document, which places the blame on seven ringleaders in K Company who were under arrest for incidents in Dunmanway. Six of the seven were: Baster, charged with passing forged cheques; Coates, Carr, Fitzgerald and Quinn, charged with attempted bank robbery; and Hart, charged with double murder. See also the House of Commons debate, 'King's speech for the opening of Parliament', 15 February 1921, vol. 138, col. 44, where Lloyd George blamed the poor of the city for some of the fires: http://hansard.millbanksystems.com/commons/1921/feb/15/debate-on-the-address (accessed 26 July 2013).

29 See H. A. Robinson's report, which states, 'It has been acknowledged by the Government that in a few cases such as Balbriggan and Cork, the Government Forces ... got out of hand, and the property of loyal subjects, who had no sympathy with Sinn Féin was destroyed in the confusion and excitement of the reprisals', National Archives, Kew, CAB 24/120/37; other evidence suggests that it was intended that Cork be burned in retaliation for the kidnapping of British spy Gerard Horgan; 'Irish Incidents', *The Mail* (Adelaide, South Australia), 11 December 1920: http://trove.nla.gov.au/ndp/del/page/5314316?zoomLevel=1 (accessed 16 December 2012).

30 Tadg was a member of the IRA. Hart's name has been spelled Harte by many commentators (including me), but both the 1901 and the 1911 census show that he spelled it Hart. National Archives, Kew, WO 339/69178, Vernon Anwyl Hart; Auxiliary Service no. 500; born in Lancashire; emigrated to Canada and then Tasmania but returned to the UK; recorded in the 1911 census in St German's, Cornwall, with his wife and family. After release from the asylum he moved to South Africa, where he died in the late 1930s. 'The Auxiliary Division of the RIC' (online), http://theauxiliaries.com/men-alphabetical/men-h/hart/hart.html (accessed 18 March 2012), provides an enormous amount of information about his life. It is usually suggested that the Auxiliaries were on their way to the funeral of those shot at Kilmichael, but this took place on 2 December.

31 Brady had motor transport difficulties throughout 1920. In September he was held up by three masked men and his motor cycle stolen. He was

not best pleased and warned all and sundry that he would deal with the thieves, *Southern Star*, 11 September 1920.

32   There are many versions of the sequence of events; O'Mahony, N., 2010, 'The life & death of Canon Magner', *Times Past: Journal of the Muskerry Local History Society* 9 (2010–11), pp. 59–61.

33   Hart was found guilty but insane. The case would never have got to trial without Mr Brady's insistence on making a statement. The Auxiliaries travelled to Cork in two lorries. Hart had been arrested by his commanding officer, who had turned back once the second lorry was missed and before anyone else arrived on the scene.

34   House of Commons debate, 17 February 1921, 'Ireland: Murder, Courtmartial', vol. 138, cols 244–6: http://hansard.millbanksystems.com/commons/1921/feb/17/murder-court-martial (accessed 26 July 2013).

35   BMH WS 1741, Michael V. O'Donoghue, Part 2, p. 209.

36   BMH WS 444, Peter (Peadar) Kearney, p. 16.

37   A detachment of the Essex Regiment occupied Glengarriff from December 1920, and there is a small amount of evidence that the Beara Peninsula suffered from some Essex excess.

38   For a brief history of the regiment see 'Army Careers' at http://freepages.military.rootsweb.ancestry.com/~cfgamblesresearch/ (accessed 22 August 2013).

39   Callwell (1906), p. 148. See also Davies (1975).

40   These included intelligence officers Captain C. J. Kelly and Lieutenants Green and Keogh. The source is Tom Hales' statement to the Wood Renton Commission sworn at Bandon in July 1924, quoted in McDonnell (1972), p. 161. See also *Torture & Terror*, Pamphlet no. 3 (Chicago, Benjamin Franklin Bureau).

41   Many BMH witness statements mention this incident: BMH WS 1738, Jeremiah Deasy, p. 8; BMH WS 908, Laurence Nugent Athy; BMH WS 1479, Seán Healy; BMH WS 540, Mrs Anna Hurley-O'Mahony.

42   McDonnell (1972), pp. 159–61; BMH WS 682, Vincent Ellis, p. 2; National Library of Ireland, Collection List No. 150, Art Ó Briain papers (Mss 2141, 2154–2157, 5105, 8417-61) Accession No. 1410, six different items; Ms. 8428/25 is the most comprehensive direct testimony of their treatment.

43   BMH WS 682, Vincent Ellis, p. 2.

44   *Southern Star*, 9 February 1924, p. 3, col. 5 for report of Harte's funeral;

Southern Star, 2 February 1924, p. 7, col. 3 for details of Harte's death and of their imprisonment.

45   BMH WS 832, William Desmond (Newcestown), pp. 43–4. For his full account of his capture and imprisonment see pp. 38–50.

46   BMH WS 443, Frank Neville, p. 8.

47   *Ibid.* There is no proof that Jagoe was a spy other than that he left the area.

48   McDonnell (1972).

49   See Hughes, M., 2010, 'From law and order to pacification: Britain's suppression of the Arab revolt in Palestine, 1936–39', *Journal of Palestine Studies* 39, no. 2, pp. 6–22, 'Pacification', pp. 6–9, 'Illegal acts of violence', pp. 9–13. See also Duff, D. V., 1953, *Bailing with a Teaspoon* (London, J. Long), for his time in both the Auxiliaries and the Palestinian police.

50   McDonnell (1972), p. 193. She states that the date was 29 October, but that is clearly a mistake.

51   Her husband, John Annan Bryce, was the former chairman of the Midland Bank and a former member of the House of Commons. The case made the House of Commons in January 1921. For one perspective, see Dyas, E., 2006, 'The Crown campaign against Protestant neutrality in Cork during the Irish War of Independence', *Church & State* 86, Autumn. Available at: http://www.atholbooks.org/archives/cands/cs_articles/articles.php (accessed 18 December 2012).

52   McDonnell (1972), pp. 193–5.

53   Steel or chain mail vests seem to have been standard issue for intelligence officers; BMH WS 380, David Neligan, p. 14; BMH WS 663, p. 12; BMH WS 1337, p. 8; BMH WS 496, p. 13. While such vests would not stop a rifle bullet, they would easily stop a shotgun blast or revolver shot.

54   BMH WS 827, Denis Collins, p. 17.

55   Hughes (2010), 'Pacification', pp. 6–9, 'Illegal acts of violence', pp. 9–13. 750 ex-RIC left Ireland in February 1922 to join the Palestinian police.

56   Callwell (1906); Davies (1975), p. 25.

57   Kipling R., 1898, 'Fuzzy Wuzzy', http://allpoetry.com/poem/8445285-Fuzzy-Wuzzy-by-Rudyard_Kipling (accessed 18 December 2012).

58   BMH WS 1478, Ted O'Sullivan, p. 30.

59   Colonel Hudson wrote to Barry from the Curragh Camp on 28 August 1921 to make sure that he had got the coat back. His letter is in the Tom Barry papers in the Cork City and County Archive with a note from Barry saying that he had. Hudson expresses a wish that he

could have met Barry when he was recently in Cork after the Truce: CCCAUI6/1/5.

60 The hotel was leased to the British War Office from 1918 to 1920. During this time it was known as the Queen Alexandria Home of Rest for Officers and was occupied by soldiers recuperating from the trauma of the Great War. It cost one guinea (€30) per week for full board with fishing and shooting rights. From 1920 to 1921 the hotel was occupied by troops of the Essex Regiment, 'Eccles Hotel History' (online), http://eccleshotel.com/history (accessed 12 December 2012). *The Irish Times* reported on 30 December that the hotel had been commandeered by the Auxiliaries on Christmas Eve. This was clear retaliation, as the commandeering of the hotel would mean the paying guests were evicted. Mrs Annan Bryce's main interest at the time was designing her famous Italian gardens on Garnish Island (which are now cared for by the Irish state).

61 The Auxiliaries.com, 'The Eccles Hotel': http://theauxiliaries.com/companies/j-coy/eccles-hotel/eccles-hotel.html (accessed 28 June 2013).

62 'The Sack of Bantry', *Southern Star*, 25 October 1920, p. 3; 'Stirring times recalled', *Southern Star*, 18 October 1930, p. 10; *Southern Star*, 22 January 1927, p. 5, shows that the Biggs' premises was only starting to be rebuilt.

63 Museum of Liverpool Life (Maritime Archives and Library Information Sheet 40), http://www.liverpoolmuseums.org.uk/maritime/archive/pdf/kings%20regiment%20no40.pdf (accessed 13 May 2013). It must also be remembered that Liverpool was a very Irish city and the territorial battalion of the regiment was known as the Liverpool Irish, so there may have been a personal element in this.

64 Barry, T., 1949, *Guerilla Days in Ireland* (Dublin, Irish Press), p. 116.

65 BMH WS 444, Peter (Peadar) Kearney, pp. 15–16.

66 Barry, T., 1974, *The Reality of the Anglo-Irish War, 1920–21 in West Cork: refutations, corrections, and comments on Liam Deasy's Towards Ireland Free* (Tralee, Anvil Books).

67 BMH WS 1402, Edward (Ned) Young, p. 17.

68 BMH WS 1234, Jack Hennessy, p. 12.

69 BMH WS 1741, Michael V. O'Donoghue, Part 2, p. 225.

70 *The Irish Times*, 16 December 1920, p. 5.

71 *Cork & County Eagle*, 29 January 1921.

72 BMH WS 470, Denis Lordan, p. 20; Dr Crowley is the doctor (Roman

Catholic), but Dr Welply (Protestant) did attend to Charlie Hurley; BMH WS 1771, Florence Begley, p. 5, observed that Welply was medical officer to the British troops stationed in Bandon.

73   BMH WS 792, Tadg O'Sullivan, p. 9; the £12,000 O'Sullivan was carrying is the equivalent of €326,193 today.

74   See Mitchell (1995), pp. 268–70 for examples of the difficulty of collecting money from nationalist farmers.

75   *Cork & County Eagle*, 29 January 1921; see the compensation claim for Sam Shannon on same page. Sweetnam was seeking compensation and made his suffering as dramatic as possible. County Court Judge Hynes was notorious for accepting without question 'loyal' compensation claims and granting huge sums to the victims (John W. Hynes, KC, is better known as an Irish international cricketer – he won 174 caps between 1883 and 1896).

76   For further information about the Sweetnam family see Census of Ireland 1911, http://www.census.nationalarchives.ie/pages/1911/Cork/ Killeenleagh/Lissangle/440679/ (accessed 20 September 2012).

77   *Cork & County Eagle*, 5 February 1921; McCarthy was Roman Catholic and Townshend was Church of Ireland.

78   BMH WS 1740, Cornelius O'Sullivan, p. 12.

79   BMH WS 710, Patrick Cronin, p. 5. The valuation was the British Poor Law Valuation. Cronin also identifies an IRA prison in Aherla where three British soldiers and three spies were shot (pp. 1–2). The spies were Nagle from Waterfall, another named McCarthy and Jimmy Devoy; Cronin states Nagle informed on Leo Murphy but BMH WS 1524, Michael O'Regan, p. 9 suggests a different local man as culprit.

80   National Library of Ireland, Ms. 31,325, Florence O'Donoghue papers, http://www.nli.ie/pdfs/mss%20lists/A18_%20FlorODonoghue.pdf (accessed 30 May 2013).

81   BMH WS 1542, Richard Collins, p. 9; see also BMH WS 1529, Patrick Wilcox, p. 8.

82   Barry (1949), p. 114.

83   Sheehan, W., 2005, *British Voices from the Irish War of Independence 1918–1921: the words of British servicemen who were there* (Cork, Collins Press), p. 113.

84   BMH WS 1603, Michael J. Crowley, p. 3. One raid in Ahiohill went disastrously wrong for Michael: 'On bursting in the door I was shot by the occupant receiving a full charge of shot in left lung from a range

of approx. five yards. The occupant was driven back to the rear of the house by revolver fire and I was removed.' The house was Thomas Bradfield's.

85 Donal Hales states that Seán Hales burned Castle Bernard in reprisal for the burning of the Hales house at Knocknacurra by the Auxiliaries, BMH WS 292. See *Cork & County Eagle*, 12 March 1921, for a report of the Hales burning.

86 She died in 1925. For more information on her life see Ó Loinsigh, P., 1997, *Gobnait Ní Bhruadair: the Hon. Albinia Lucy Brodrick: beathaisnéis* (Baile Átha Cliath, Coiscéim). See also Hochschild, A., 2011, 'John French and Charlotte Despard: the odd couple', *History Today* 61, no. 6, pp. 30–40; Despard is buried in the Republican Plot in Glasnevin Cemetery, Dublin.

87 Morrissey, C. J., 2011, 'The Earl of Bandon and the burning of Castle Bernard, 1921', *Bandon Historical Journal* 27, pp. 32–43. For further detail on this story see Morrissey, C. J., 2012, 'The Bernards of Bandon: a County Cork landed family and their estate, 1639–1921', *Bandon Historical Journal* 28, pp. 49–65.

88 Sheehan (2005), p. 131.

89 BMH WS 540, Mrs Anna-Hurley O'Mahony (née Walsh), pp. 4–5.

90 The actual date was 14 June and this is correctly identified by Richard Russell, BMH WS 1591, p. 23.

91 BMH WS 470, Denis Lordan, pp. 28–9; the telegraph office in Mallow was also infiltrated by the IRA, BMH WS 1133. Annie Barrett's statement gives a detailed description of how British Army codes were broken, and how messages got out to the IRA.

92 BMH WS 1422, Thomas Reidy, p. 6.

93 BMH WS 1575, Ted Hayes, p. 4.

94 BMH WS 873, Charles Browne, pp. 46–7.

95 BMH WS 812, Patrick O'Brien.

96 BMH WS 810, Tim Herlihy and seven others, p. 13.

97 It must be noted that a majority of those who were shot as spies in West Cork were Roman Catholic.

98 In British military parlance, a spy was one of its members sent out to find out information about the enemy. An informer was someone who gave information for money, and an informant was someone who gave information willingly or had it extracted from them.

99 In a secret meeting in April 1921 Birkenhead stated that the British

sources of information had increased and this had brought an inevitable response from the IRA: National Archives, Kew, CAB 24/122/83.

100 Reference in an essay by Thomas Earls Fitzgerald: http://www.scribd. com/doc/104308089/Who-were-the-people-killed-as-'spies'-and-'informers'-by-the-I-R-A-in-west-Cork-in-early–1921-and-why-were-they-targeted (accessed 22 August 2013); 'County Inspector for Bandon's Confidential Monthly report for January 1921', No. 2.2.1921 in Townshend, C. (ed.), *The British in Ireland. Part 4, Police Reports, 1914–1921* (Brighton: Harvester Press Microform Publications). Copy held on microfilm in the Berkeley Library, Trinity College, Dublin.

101 This includes the Civil War.

102 See Ryan, M., 2005, *Tom Barry: IRA freedom fighter* (Cork, Mercier Press), pp. 122–9.

103 See Barry (1949); 'Memories of Childhood and the Old IRA: Burned homes of Knockavilla', *Southern Star*, 18 October 1986, p. 7, for a detailed and sympathetic account of the effect of the burnings on both sides.

104 See BMH WS 1603, Michael J. Crowley; BMH WS 1643, Seán Healy, p. 18.

105 Ó Broin, L., 1985, *Protestant Nationalists in Revolutionary Ireland: the Stopford connection* (Dublin, Gill & Macmillan), pp. 176–7. This story also appears in Hart, P., 1998, *The I.R.A. and Its Enemies: violence and community in Cork 1916–1923* (Oxford, Clarendon Press), p. 305. See also BMH WS 470, Denis Lordan, p. 14, where he also discusses this event.

106 *Cork Constitution*, 27 January 1921, p. 5.

107 Rev. Lord remained as rector of Kilbrogan long after the War of Independence as shown by the *Bandon Postal Directory* of 1933: http://www.bandon-genealogy.com/local-postal-directory–1933.htm (accessed 12 January 2013).

108 BMH WS 1684, James Murphy, pp. 12–13.

109 BMH WS 470, Denis Lordan, p. 16, tells this story. Thomas Kingston, the owner of Burgatia, and his staff were held under house arrest while the IRA engineers produced a mine for the attack on Rosscarbery barracks. The local postman happened on the scene and was told he would be shot if he warned the RIC two kilometres away in Rosscarbery. However, once released, he went straight to the barracks and the column was lucky to escape as the house was quickly approached by British forces.

110 *Cork Constitution*, 27 January 1921.

111 *Cork Constitution,* 15 February 1921; *Cork & County Eagle,* 16 April 1921.

112 *Cork & County Eagle,* 16 April 1921. The only type of bullet that could inflict this type of wound was a dum-dum or soft-tip bullet. *Vide* means see.

113 *Southern Star,* 25 June 1921, p. 7. It also deals with the Good shootings discussed in the next paragraph.

114 *Southern Star,* 29 May 1926, p. 4. At the time of the 1926 case Elizabeth was living, the court report stated, in 'Upper Copcourt, Tetworth [*sic*], Oxford'. Another report in the *Southern Star,* 8 May 1926, deals with the case of Thomas J. Bradfield, whose widow had to pay rates on his farm even though it was still unused five years after his death.

115 Irish Medals.com: http://irishmedals.org/gpage49.html (accessed 18 December 2012); *Cork & County Eagle,* 29 January 1921.

116 The Sweetnam family resettled in Chew Magna, Somerset, where the youngest daughter, Agusta, was married in 1924; *Southern Star,* 3 May 1924, p. 4. The Skibbereen farm was sold in October 1923.

117 Kingston, W., 'From Victorian Boyhood to the Troubles: a Skibbereen Memoir'. Available at: http://durrushistory.files.wordpress.com/2012/09/memoir-of-willie-kingston-1885-1975-skibbereen-solicitor-and-historian1.pdf (accessed 28 September 2012). He states that Connell had been given a warning to leave, but had not taken it. He also says that before their shooting, George Jennings came to him with information that the IRA were at Lug, and that the two men were in danger. Local JP E. A. Swanton had laughed at the idea when Kingston asked his advice, suggesting it was an attempted land-grab. That night the two men were shot, p. 32.

118 *The Irish Times,* 28 February 1921. Aged thirty-five, he was shot at 9.15 p.m.

119 BMH WS 1234, Jack Hennessy, p. 12.

120 BMH WS 1275, Timothy Warren, pp. 6–7.

121 *Southern Star,* 16 October 1920, p. 2; O'Leary, D., 1975, *Kilmeen and Castleventry Parish, Co. Cork* (self published), p. 89: 'A Ballineen baker supplied bread to the British soldiers stationed [at Oak-mount], and one of the bread van drivers was believed to be supplying information on the volunteers ... two members of the Kilmeen Company shot the unfortunate horse ... This served as a warning to the driver who was allowed to depart alive.' We know, from BMH WS 1275 and WS 812,

p. 9, that this was Cotter, who was boycotted throughout 1920 and was protected by the eighty members of the Essex Regiment, *Southern Star*, 16 October 1920, p. 2.

122 House of Commons debate, 2 June 1921, vol. 142, cols 1221–3, http://hansard.millbanksystems.com/commons/1921/jun/02/murder-colonel-peacocke (accessed 31 January 2012).

123 The Irish Unionist Alliance was the Southern unionist party. It was hardline in the sense that it was not willing to countenance Home Rule in any circumstance and had split with the Anti-Partition League led by Lord Midleton on this issue.

124 Barry (1949), p. 110.

125 The news reports and the British records state that one RIC officer was guarding him.

126 This litany included her son's murder, the burning of her home at Skevanish, the theft of livestock and the auctioning by the IRA of her machinery after the Truce without interference from the British government. Ethel Peacocke had been rewarded in the 1920 New Year's Honours List for her work as Honorary Secretary, Cork Women's Association for Prisoners of War Fund, *London Gazette*, 26 March 1920: http://www.london-gazette.co.uk/issues/31840/supplements/3853 (accessed 18 December 2012). The Peacocke estate was offered for sale on 18 July 1931 by the owner, who is not identified.

127 BMH WS 1591, Richard Russell, pp. 22–3 for the investigation and pp. 25–6 for the shooting of Colonel Peacocke.

128 The IRA confiscation of his crops and those of Mathew Sweetnam of Skibbereen in August 1921 were regarded as Truce violations by the British Secretary of State for War, who said that 'this sort of thing would lead to a collision', *Southern Star*, 12 November 1921, p. 1, col. 2.

129 On 7 June 1921 a circular was issued for use with a 'person associating with the military'. Final Notice – Part (4): 'You are hereby warned that if after this final notice has been served on you it is found that you continue this association you will be regarded as a spy and dealt with accordingly.' From the file it appears that three previous warnings would have been issued, CCCAU169 21–30.

130 See Sheehan (2005), pp. 133–6 and p. 140, where Percival explains, 'On one occasion the secretary of the Demobilised Soldiers and Sailors Federation asked for an interview with me.' After several interviews it was discovered that this man was the battalion commandant of the

IRA. If these interviews were conducted in Percival's office then the commandant would have seen the map.

131 *Record of the Rebellion in Ireland in 1920–1*, vol. 2, 1922, Jeudwine papers 72/82/1, Imperial War Museum. Hart (1998), p. 305, claimed that loyalists had little information to give and so argued that the Dunmanway killings were sectarian, but he omitted to mention the second part of the quotation. For some reason Peter Hart never explained why he omitted this crucial qualification, which is undoubtedly damaging to his theory, up to the time of his death in 2010, despite being challenged to do so on more than one occasion.

132 Tadhg Kennedy states that Captain Kelly spent the last months of the War of Independence with his son in Dublin Castle and left Ireland at the Truce. His statement gives great detail about Kelly's origins and career; BMH WS 1413, Tadhg Kennedy, pp. 33–5; as Captain C. J. O'Kelly was still the intelligence officer for the British 6th Division in Cork when he wrote a highly recommended (by Macready) report that was circulated by the War Office called *Sinn Féin. Internal Dissension* to the British delegates negotiating the Treaty on 10 October 1921, this is unlikely to be true: National Archives, Kew, CAB 43/2, 'Truce violations', October 1921, p. 49.

133 John Regan says, 'It is difficult to identify any event other than the April massacre for which the Record's description applies but it could equally apply to the murder of the Protestant spies in early in 1921': http://www.academia.edu/1710059/_The_Bandon_Valley_Massacre_revisited_TCD (accessed 1 June 2013). It was Peter Hart who initially linked the document to the April killings.

134 BMH WS 810, Tim Herlihy and seven others, pp. 10–11.

135 Barry (1949), p. 112. Percival states that such was the danger that he only approached loyalist houses after dark: Sheehan (2005), p. 134.

136 Valiulus, M. G., 1992, *Portrait of a Revolutionary: General Richard Mulcahy and the founding of the Irish Free State* (Lexington, University Press of Kentucky), p. 68 for the official procedure of how to try a spy.

137 General Order 20 issued on 20 April 1921: 'All executions of spies to be ratified by brigade commandant.' An explanation and summary had to be sent to GHQ in all cases, but this order gave the brigade commandant the power of life and death: Cork City and County Archives, Siobhán Langford papers, CCCAU169/21–30.

138 Ernie O'Malley observed that Seán O'Hegarty had a reputation for

not being scrupulous about evidence, but dismissed this as talk, adding that all killings of spies had to be cleared by GHQ: Dungan, M., 1997, *They Shall Not Grow Old: Irish soldiers and the Great War* (Dublin, Four Courts Press), p. 39. Whether this was actually done every time is another question.

139 O'Hegarty, P. S., 1998, *The Victory of Sinn Féin: how it won it and how it used it* (Dublin, University College Dublin Press), p. 38; the other side in the Civil War would regard acceptance of the Treaty as a moral collapse, given that the Free State had broken the republican oath. Both sides were correct.

140 *Ibid.*, p. 98.

141 *Ibid.*, p. 84.

142 BMH WS 1741, Michael V. O'Donoghue, Part 2, pp. 284–5; O'Donoghue was on the anti-Treaty side during the Civil War.

143 A Bandon RIC man who warned the IRA that the man had 'given the game away' is quoted in BMH WS 1771, Florence Begley, p. 4. See also Sheehan (2005), p. 126, where Major Percival confirms this.

144 National Archives, Kew, CAB 43/2, 'Breaches of the Truce. Week ending Nov. 19th 1921', pp. 180–90. Other parts of the country also recorded none.

145 General Macready reported that Tom Barry was being difficult in July 1921 around the issue of getting the British to acknowledge the IRA as an army, and went on to comment: 'Thomas Barry, a student who appears to be about 23 years of age, with an exaggerated opinion of his own importance was not likely to be any assistance in making matters run smoothly', National Archives, Kew, CAB 24/126.

146 This discipline extended to Cork city, as a document in the Ristéard Langford papers, U156/3/ Period 7, April 1921–11 July 1921 (xviii) L, Cork City and County Archives, shows: 'Lt. Keo (of Roche and Hales fame) … together with 4 other IOs [British Military intelligence officers] traced to Grosvenor Hotel [Cork] and thence to Palace [Theatre] … Owing to Truce nothing could be done in the matter.' Keo was a prime target for the Cork No. 1 Brigade and this suggests that the city IRA maintained strong discipline after the Truce.

4   THE BACKGROUND TO BALLYGROMAN

1   Bandon, 'Irish compensation – Loyalist claimants plight', *The Times*,

London, 3 March, p. 8, col. 5. Lord Bandon gives his address as 25, Victoria Street, SW 1.

2   *Southern Star*, 8 April 1922.

3   This is how Michael O'Neill is described in his mortuary card.

4   Martin Midgley Reeve, who penned the foreword to this book, is his cousin.

5   His military record in the National Archives, Kew, WO 339/86747, states that he was born in 1884, but his birth certificate shows that he was born in 1892 in Skibbereen.

6   Hart (1998), p. 282; this is from a letter written by Hodder to her mother that famously ended up as part of the British cabinet papers.

7   See Findmypast.ie (online), court records. There is no evidence of the sentence.

8   He joined at Fermoy. He was transferred to the 2nd Battalion on 29 August 1917, *Supplement to the London Gazette*, 3 December 1917, p. 12649.

9   *London Gazette*, 16 September 1916, issue 29749, p. 9006, simply mentions that he was awarded the medal.

10   This is in the possession of Martin Midgley Reeve.

11   http://www.dnw.co.uk/medals/auctionarchive/searchcataloguearchive/itemdetail.lasso?itemid=21167 (accessed 12 May 2012).

12   Mental breakdown was usually a cover name for shell-shock.

13   Why it was hoped that a man with shell-shock or mental breakdown might do well in returning to a Trench Mortar Battery is another question. Hitchcock, F. C., 1988, *'Stand to': a diary of the trenches 1915–1918* (Norwich, Gliddon), p. 276, footnote 1, says he was shot in Ireland.

14   *London Gazette*, 16 July 1918, p. 8478: http://www.london-gazette.co.uk/issues/30801/supplements/8478 (accessed 2 May 2013).

15   Hitchcock (1988), p. 295.

16   National Archives, Kew, WO 372/22/62091, WO 339/86747.

17   'Temp. Capt. H. Woods, Gen. List, relinquishes the temp, rank of Col. on ceasing to be spec, empld', 1 September 1921, *Supplement to the London Gazette*, 15 November 1921, p. 9115: http://www.london gazette.co.uk/issues/32519/supplements/9115/page.pdf (accessed 18 July 2013).

18   Census of Ireland 1911: http://www.census.nationalarchives.ie/pages/1901/Cork/Rathclarin/Clooncalabeg/1090312/ (accessed 2 July 2013).

19   BMH WS 556, Mary Walsh.

20 BMH WS 812, Patrick O'Brien, p. 19.

21 BMH WS 1607, Charles O'Donoghue, p. 9.

22 *Evening Echo*, 10 April 1971; Lordan, D., 2006, 'The Gallant Volunteers of Kilbrittain', *Bandon Historical Journal* 22.

23 BMH WS 560, James (J. J.) O'Mahony, Denis Crowley, John (Jack) Fitzgerald.

24 *Ibid.*, p. 5.

25 *Ibid.*, p. 7. Hunger strike documents from John O'Driscoll of the Irish Volunteers Commemorative Society: http://irishvolunteers.org/ (accessed 26 August 2013).

26 BMH WS 560, James (J. J.) O'Mahony, Denis Crowley, John (Jack) Fitzgerald, p. 13; 'Ballykinlar' refers to the internment camp of that name in County Down.

27 *Cork Constitution* and *Cork Examiner*, 5 May 1922.

28 BMH WS 1741, Michael V. O'Donoghue, Part 2, pp. 224–6.

5 **THE HORNIBROOKS AND THE WAR OF INDEPENDENCE**

1 National Archives, Kew, CO 762/133/5, 'Matilda Warburton [*sic*] Woods, County Cork, No. 2254'.

2 Murphy, G., 2010, *The Year of Disappearances: political killings in Cork 1921–1922* (Dublin, Gill & Macmillan), p. 186; Hart (1998), p. 280.

3 This claim is made in his submission to the Irish Grants Commission in 1927. The O'Flynn, Exham and Company documents in the Cork City and County Archive show that a Mr Warren took the Woods family to the High Court in 1884 and the distillery was sold by Marsh and Company auctioneers under duress as Warren needed his investment back in a hurry. This was probably connected with the collapse of the Munster Bank. See Stratten's (1892) *Dublin, Cork and South of Ireland: a literary, commercial, and social review*: http://www.corkpastandpresent. ie/places/strattensdublincorkandsouthofireland (accessed 18 July 2013) for a history of the distillery, which shows that the Sugrue family owned it.

4 National Archives, Kew, CO 762/133/4, 'Edward Woods County Cork, No. 2253'. The *Cork Examiner* and *The Freeman's Journal* reported on 23 October 1922 that the distillery was raided. It ceased trading and was offered for sale to Woodford Bourne & Co. in 1925, University College Cork, Boole Library and Archives, UCC BL/BC/WB B/3(54). Prohibition had been introduced in the United States, and many small

Irish distilleries geared towards the US market closed. Allman's in Bandon suffered the same fate, closing in 1925.

5   Hart (1998), pp. 1–18.

6   Cork City and County Archives, CCAPR4/4/92, Terence MacSwiney papers; when the Irish government attempted to pay the promised pensions for those who resigned for 'nationalist' reasons, the British government wouldn't give them the addresses. This mess of conflicting loyalties again points to the complexity of the break-up between the two countries: Brennan, N., 1995, 'Compensating the Royal Irish Constabulary 1922–1932', PhD thesis, University College Dublin. Available at: http://www.ucd.ie/pages/95/Brennan.html (accessed 3 July 2013). See also Brennan, N., 1997, 'A Political Minefield: Southern Loyalists, the Irish Grants Committee and the British Government, 1922–31', *Irish Historical Studies* 30, pp. 406–19.

7   Cork City and County Archives, Terence MacSwiney papers, PR4/4/ (FILE 4): http://www.corkarchives.ie/media/PR4web.pdf (accessed 18 July 2013).

8   See Stafford, T. A., 2005, 'The Collapse of the Royal Irish Constabulary: policing insurgency in Ireland, 1914–1921', MA thesis, University of New Brunswick, Canada, for a good analysis of what brought about the demise of the RIC, even if it downplays Michael Collins' national leadership role and the IRA policy of systematically and personally targeting the RIC for the first time. Available at: http://hdl.handle. net/1882/43501 (accessed 18 December 2012). For another balanced view, see Charters (2009).

9   BMH WS 1639, Laurence Morrough Neville, p. 10.

10   BMH WS 1714, Leo Buckley, p. 5.

11   BMH WS 1630, George Hurley, p. 4.

12   BMH WS 1714, Leo Buckley, p. 7.

13   O'Callaghan, S., 1974, *Execution* (London, Muller), p. 60–2; Hart (1998).

14   O'Callaghan (1974), p. 63. The YMCA was the Church of Ireland youth organisation suspected by the Cork City IRA of having been recruited by members of the Freemasons spying for the British during the War of Independence.

15   BMH WS 1708, William Barry, pp. 6–7.

16   BMH WS 1657, Jeremiah Keating; BMH WS 1708, Patrick Collins; BMH WS 1547, Michael Murphy. Sarah was Fred Blemens' daughter.

17 BMH WS 1707, Patrick Collins, p. 8.

18 In *Guy's Directory* (another name by which *Guy's Almanac* is known) for 1921 his name has been removed from the list of county JPs, but he remains a JP in the Ovens list. The latter is probably an oversight.

19 In BMH WS 1706, pp. 5–6, Seán O'Connell also mentions this raid, recalling that Captain Clarke was shot in the hand.

20 BMH WS 810, Tim Herlihy and seven others, p. 4. He was not the only loyalist to take defensive action – see BMH WS 1518, Seán O'Driscoll, p. 5.

21 Interview with Nora Lynch, Coolroe, Ballincollig, 17 May 2012.

22 Manchester Regiment Archive, Tameside Local Studies and Archives Centre, Central Library, Old Street, Ashton-under-Lyne, UK, Item MR1/11/2, Record of Civil Arrests of 1st Battalion in Ireland, 1920–1921, 1 vol.; email: localstudies.library@tameside.gov.uk. Thanks to Larysa Bolton, archivist, for her professionalism, courtesy and helpfulness in sourcing this reference.

23 O'Donovan, D., 2012, 'Some Ballincollig petty session reports', *Times Past: Journal of Muskerry Local History Society* 10, pp. 72–81.

24 *Southern Star*, 18 February 1922, p. 7.

25 *Southern Star*, 22 April 1922, p. 5, col. 4.

26 *Record of the Rebellion in Ireland in 1920–1*, vol. 2, 1922, Jeudwine papers 72/82/1, Imperial War Museum.

27 Ryan, M., 2003, *Tom Barry: IRA freedom fighter* (Cork, Mercier Press), p. 158.

6   26 APRIL 1922: THE SHOOTING ON THE STAIRS

1   'Brutally Murdered: Inquest of Commandant', *Southern Star*, 29 April 1922, p. 1, col. 5.

2   *Cork & County Eagle*, 6 May 1922; *Cork Examiner*, 27 April 1922.

3   'Civil War claims: applications in Cork Circuit Court', *Cork Examiner*, 10 November 1925. Margaret was living in Macloneigh, Macroom, in 1925, Census of Ireland 1911, http://www.census.nationalarchives.ie/pages/1911/Cork/Ballygroman/Ballygroman_Upper/374008/ (accessed 24 June 2013).

4   *Cork Examiner*, 27 April 1922.

5   'Commandant shot dead', *Southern Star*, 29 April, p. 2, col. 5.

6   'Ovens tragedy', *Cork Examiner*, 29 April 1922.

7   Hart (1998), pp. 279–81.

8   *Ibid.*, p. 279; it is not clear who called Leo Murphy 'bad boy'; a number of the BMH statements tell precisely what happened to Leo Murphy and there is no suggestion whatsoever that his body was dragged behind a car.

9   Kearney, R. D., 2002, 'A time of revenge, a time of tragedy', *Cork Hollybough*, p. 64; R. D. Kearney is a former owner of Ballygroman House.

10 Among the evidence for this is an article about Edward's death in the local paper in Essex, which states that the family were not living in Ballygroman at the time.

11 Conversation with me, 25 November 2012.

12 1911 census return for O'Halloran family at Scartnamuck, Templemartin, CensusofIreland1911:http://www.census.nationalarchives.ie/pages/1911/Cork/Templemartin/Scartnamuck/374530/ (accessed 2 June 2012).

13 1911 census return for O'Connell/Lynch family in Scartnamuck, Templemartin, Census of Ireland 1911: http://www.census.national archives.ie/pages/1911/Cork/Templemartin (accessed 2 June 2012).

14 1911 census return for the Horgan family in Templemartin, Census of Ireland 1911: http://www.census.nationalarchives.ie/pages/1911/Cork/Templemartin (accessed 2 June 2012). Seán Crowley points out that as Lynch's Forge was not built in 1922, the Hornibrooks could not have been held there. However, during the same interview it was pointed out that there could have been confusion on the location as O'Connell was the father-in-law of Lynch, who opened a forge in Scarriff.

15 Later the same year, on 22 August, a priest at Cloughduv was asked to give absolution to Michael Collins and went back to get his anointing oils. Emmet Dalton, thinking he had refused to give absolution, almost shot him in the back.

16 Census of Ireland 1911: http://www.census.nationalarchives.ie/pages/1911/Cork/Ballygroman/Grange/373989/ (accessed 13 March 2013).

17 Crowley S., 2005, *From Newce to Truce: a story of Newcestown and its hinterland* (Newcestown, self-published), pp. 464–5. Thanks to Dr Andy Bielenberg for coming across this reference. Dr Bielenberg, Dr John Borgonovo and I met with Seán Crowley in Newcestown on 17 October 2012. We also visited Quinlan's boreen in Farranthomas bog, Newcestown, with archaeologist Damien Shiels, who concluded that it would take massive resources to search the bog. The tape of this interview is in my possession.

18 Julia lived next door to Mary Horgan, who was Daniel's mother. Daniel and Mary Horgan were living in house six in Scarriff in 1911, and Good's house was house two. House five was owned by the Lynch family. The Horgans later bought back their original farm, doubling their landholding in the process.

19 BMH WS 1524, Michael O'Regan. The BMH statements were supposed to stop at the Truce in July 1921 to avoid people talking about incidents in the Civil War, but more than 400 witnesses ignored this and continued into 1922.

20 See also O'Flynn, D., 2010, 'They missed the train and lost their lives', *Times Past: Journal of the Muskerry Local History Society* 9 (2010–11), pp. 63–4. My thanks to Liam Hayes for lending me his copy.

21 Tadg O'Sullivan identifies two spies: Crowley, who was shot at Crosspound, and Dwyer, who was tried after the Brinny ambush, but the location of the trial is not given: BMH WS 792.

22 The source for this information was John Lucey, and Donal O'Flynn is a second source for the fact that John Lucey was an eyewitness.

23 Interview with Donal O'Flynn, 14 December 2012. The tape of this interview is in my possession.

24 *Ibid.*

25 Nora Lynch was told it was the dinner service.

26 All of the BMH statements speak of incidents where the witness is reporting facts that were told to them by other members of the company, and it is the combination of different sources that builds their credibility. In the Scarriff case the number of witnesses is too great to be ignored.

27 Unedited copies of the O'Flynn (restricted access) and Crowley interviews have been lodged, along with Herbert Woods' military papers, Matilda Warmington Woods' Irish Distress Committee statement and the administration papers for Thomas Hornibrook's estate, with the Cork City and County Archives as of January 2013.

28 Hart (1998), p. 291.

29 National Archives, Kew, CO 739/14/15/16, 'Colonial Office, correspondence, 1922, individuals'.

30 The *Morning Post* was a right-wing paper in Britain that was vehemently opposed to Ireland leaving the UK. *Morning Post*, 1 June 1922, quoted in Hart (1998), p. 279, footnote 37; *Southern Star*, 3 June 1922, p. 3; House of Commons debate, 'West Cork Arrests, statements in Commons', 31 May 1922, vol. 154, cols 2084–6: http://hansard.millbanksystems.com/

commons/1922/may/31/murders S5CV0154P0_19220531_HOC_81 (accessed 30 December 2012).

31 The only place that Edward Woods says he had to leave Ireland in 1921 is his Irish Grants Committee statement. All the other evidence suggests he left in 1922.

32 BMH WS 1741, Michael V. O'Donoghue, Part 2, p. 227.

33 'Officer shot dead', *The Irish Times*, 27 April 1922, p. 6.

34 All references for correspondence in this section are taken from Military Archives, Cathal Brugha Barracks, Dublin, File A908. A copy was supplied to me by Dr Andy Bielenberg of University College Cork.

35 'Letter from Dan Breen, Tom Hales, H. Murphy, S. O'Hegarty, Seán Mullan, R. A. Mulcahy, Owen O'Duffy, Gearóid O'Sullivan, Michael Collins to Four Courts garrison to end occupation and allow a plebiscite on the Treaty', *The Irish Times*, 2 May 1922.

36 'West Cork arrests statements in the Commons', *Southern Star*, 3 June 1922, p. 3.

37 House of Commons debate, 'Irish Office questions', 26 June 1922, vol. 155, cols 1693–811, l. 1767: http://hansard.millbanksystems.com/commons/1922/jun/26/irish-office-etc (accessed 3 July 2013).

38 Thomas Henry Hornibrook Jnr.

39 This letter does not appear to survive as it cannot be traced.

40 National Archives of Ireland, TSCH/S2059, 'The murder of Thomas Henry Hornibrook J.P.'

41 National Archives, Kew, CAB 24/140/18, '"The Murders at Cork and Macroom" memorandum from the Secretary of State for the Colonies: Devonshire': http://discovery.nationalarchives.gov.uk/SearchUI/Details?uri=D7732097 (accessed 18 July 2013).

42 'Three men taken from home: never heard of again', *The Irish Times*, 14 April 1923, p. 6, col. 5.

43 A copy of the cutting from the paper was supplied to me by Martin Midgley Reeve.

44 *London Gazette*, 1 May 1934, p. 2819: http://www.london-gazette.co.uk/issues/34046/pages/2819/page.pdf (accessed 20 January 2013).

45 'Mrs Matilda Warmington Woods of Burlescombe House, Burlescombe-road [*sic*], Thorpe Bay, Essex, who left £17,437 gave her property to her four daughters in equal shares, directing that the share of each should be held in trust for her for life, or until she joined the Roman Catholic church, or intermarried with a member of that church', newspaper

cutting in the possession of Martin Midgley Reeve. In today's money, the estate's value is €516,590.

46 The house and lands had been valued at £1,000 in 1927, and Matilda had received compensation of more than £5,000 for the family's losses at that time, as well as retaining the house and lands. Andy Bielenberg explains (in correspondence with the author) that by 1949 property prices in Ireland had collapsed under the strain of massive emigration, so this was a bad time to sell. The house was rented to Daniel Corkery in 1931 and the land was fallow until it was bought by Mr Murphy, whose family still own the farm. A copy of the deed is in my possession.

47 Hart (1998), p. 279. If they were seized, they were in Matilda's possession a week later. Matilda also complained to the Grants Committee that the Irish government appealed a malicious injuries award as she wanted to use it for other property and the Department of Finance demanded it be used to repair Ballygroman House as the rules stated it must. After this the property could be sold.

48 Only Matilda is mentioned as beneficiary in either of the court reports, but she acknowledges her half-brother's interest in the Grants Committee submission.

49 'Cork Circuit Court', *Cork Examiner*, 29 July 1926, p. 12, cols 6, 7.

50 'Ballygroman House', *Cork Examiner*, 31 July 1926, p. 5, col. 3.

51 National Archives, Kew, CO 762/133/5. Edward also submitted his own claim. This was the closing date for submissions to the second Wood-Renton Commission, which had been established to 'tidy up' any outstanding claims by southern Irish loyalists.

52 This amount is €372,600 in today's money, plus the house and lands at Ballygroman, and Thomas and Samuel Hornibrook's effects. The quote is from the handwritten report of the hearing.

53 *Irish Weekly Times*, 12 May 1928. According to the index of wills in the National Archives of Ireland, he left a tiny estate of £49 so there was presumably a legal reason to extinguish his claim to the property.

7   THE DUNMANWAY KILLINGS

1 On the sack of Verulamium (St Albans) by Queen Boudicca in Churchill, W. and Woods, F., 1975, *A History of the English-speaking Peoples. Vol. 1: the Birth of Britain* (London, Library of Imperial History), p. 27.

2   The *Morning Post* quoted in *The Freeman's Journal*, 5 May 1922, p. 6.

3   These were a solicitor, a chemist, a retired draper, five farmers, a farm labourer, an ex-soldier, a postal worker, an invalid, an unemployed youth and four soldiers. The retired draper, James Buttimer, was an 'ex-naval man', according to the *Cork Examiner*, but as yet there is no other evidence for this: *Cork Examiner*, 28 April 1922, p. 3, col. 2. For accuracy, one of the soldiers killed in Macroom was Roman Catholic.

4   Hart (1998), p. 274.

5   According to the *Cork Constitution*, there were three raiders, one of whom put her out of the house.

6   'Four victims', *The Irish Times*, 2 May 1922, p. 5; the *Cork Examiner* report is more detailed and also mentions a third raider.

7   According to the *Cork Constitution*, 1 May 1922, p. 5, the three Roman Catholic clergy in Clonakilty made a point of attending the funeral, which was extraordinary as Roman Catholics were banned by their own church from attending services in Protestant churches.

8   *Southern Star*, 29 April 1922, p. 5, cols 2, 3.

9   'West Cork tragedies', *Southern Star*, 6 May 1922, p. 6.

10 Linge, J., 1994, 'British Forces and Irish Freedom: Anglo Irish defence relations 1922–1931', PhD thesis, University of Stirling.

11 Moore, H. K., 1930, *Reminiscences and Reflections from Some Sixty Years of Life in Ireland* (London, Longmans, Green and Co.), pp. 275, 278–9. Moore also says that besides the Dunmanway killings there was little sectarianism in the south.

12 Macardle, D., 1968, *The Irish Republic* (London, Corgi), p. 705.

13 In 1908 the Roman Catholic Church issued a decree stating that if a Roman Catholic married someone of another religion, then all the children had to be raised as Roman Catholics. A 1910 Belfast case decided this was a contractual obligation for the non-Roman Catholic.

14 'An Irishman's diary', *The Irish Times*, 9 January 1990. To add to the confusion, there were two people called Sonny Crowley: Sonny Dave, who fought at Kilmichael, and Denis 'Sonny' Crowley of Kilbrittain. Lest there be any doubt: see Deasy (1973), p. 66.

15 Coogan, T. P., 1992, *The Man who Made Ireland: the life and death of Michael Collins* (Niwot, Colo, Roberts Rinehart), p. 391.

16 In the preface of *The IRA and Its Enemies*, Hart acknowledges the assistance of, among others, Kevin Myers.

17 The thesis on the Dunmanway killings is best summarised in Hart

(1998), pp. 290–1. Much of the evidence used to support the argument on those pages is not accurate.

18 See the *Southern Star*, 13 September 1920, for a discussion of how some Roman Catholics viewed their Protestant neighbours. A Labour Party meeting had been called to set up a Belfast Distress Fund, and as no Protestant had attended there were a few veiled threats as to what might happen if they were not seen to take part in the 'revolution against the usurper'.

19 Hart (1998), p. 288.

20 *Ibid.*, p. 314.

21 I myself dismissed the early criticism of Hart, as I assumed it was exaggerated.

22 Murphy mentioned this in his first review of *The IRA and Its Enemies*, but because it was published in the somewhat obscure *Month: Review of Christian Thought and World Affairs* this did not get the reaction it should have: Murphy, B., 1998, '*The I.R.A and Its Enemies*: a review article', *Month: Review of Christian Thought and World Affairs* 31, pp. 381–3. See also Murphy, B., 2005, 'Peter Hart: the issue of sources', *Irish Political Review* 20, no. 7, July, pp. 10–11. Available at: http://www.indymedia.ie/attachments/aug2005/brianmurphyiprarticle.pdf (accessed 18 July 2013).

23 Hart (1998), pp. 285, 305. Hart also stated in a 1993 publication: 'It might be suggested that Protestants and ex-soldiers were naturally hostile to the IRA and more likely to be working with the police or military, and to be shot. This was not so. The authorities obtained little information from either group [Protestants and ex-soldiers] and, in fact, by far the greatest damage was done by people within the organisation or their relatives'; Hart, P., 1993, 'Class, Community and the Irish Republican Army, 1917–1923', in O'Flanagan, P., Buttimer, C. G. and O'Brien, G. (eds), *Cork: history and society* (Dublin, Geography Publications), p. 979. 'It is a satisfactory feature that information is being increasingly given by well disposed persons – who see a hope of escape from the Sinn Féin terrorization.' National Archives, Kew, CAB/24/118, General Nevil Macready, 15 January 1921.

24 In addition to Brian Murphy and Meda Ryan, whom the main text has mentioned, John Regan, Niall Meehan, Pádraig Óg Ó Ruairc, John Borgonovo, Joost Augusteijn and John Dorney are listed on Indymedia: http://www.indymedia.ie/openwire?search_text=Peter+Hart&x=-1235&y= (accessed 18 July 2013) and there are more.

25   National Archives, Kew, WO 141/93, 'Record of the rebellion in Ireland 1920–1921'.

26   Hart (1998), p. 305.

27   Ryan, M., 2007, 'The Kilmichael Ambush: exploring the "Provocative Chapters"', *History* 92, no. 306, pp. 235–49.

28   Murphy, B. and Meehan, N., 2008, *Troubled History: a 10th anniversary critique of Peter Hart's The IRA and Its Enemies* (Millstreet: Aubane Historical Society), pp. 21–8. Available at http://gcd.academia.edu/NiallMeehan/Books/75341/Troubled_History-a_tenth_anniversary_Critique_of_Peter_Harts_The_IRA_and_its_Enemies (accessed 5 July 2013).

29   At least I found them difficult to follow.

30   See Regan, J. M., 2012, 'The "Bandon Valley massacre" as a historical problem', *History* 97, no. 325, pp. 70–98.

31   The entire debate, including David Fitzpatrick's (2012b) article in *History Ireland*, has been placed on academica.edu by John Regan: http://dundee.academia.edu/johnregan/Papers/1622199/_Dr_Regan_and_Mr_Snide_Professor_David_Fitzpatricks_response_to_Regans_The_Two_Histories_Dr_Jeykl_and_Mr_Hyde_plus_other_letters_re_Peter_Hart_Bandon (accessed 18 July 2013).

32   Fitzpatrick, D., 2012b, 'Dr. Regan and Mr. Snide', *History Ireland* 20, no. 3, May/June, pp. 12–13.

33   Keane, B., 2013a, 'The Dunmanway killings – murder, myths and misinformation – Protestant decline in Cork 1911–1926 in context': http://www.academia.edu/1862050/The_Dunmanway_killings-_murders_myths_and_misinformation-_Protestant_decline_in_Cork_1911-1926_in_context; Keane, B., 2013b, 'Protestant Cork decline 1911–1926: murders, mistakes, myths, and misinformation, updated 14 April 2013': https://sites.google.com/site/protestantcork191136/home/protestant-cork-decline-1911-1926-murders-mistakes-myths-and-misinformation-updated-25th-july-2012. Both articles cover the same ground but have slight differences.

34   Hart (1998), pp. 290–1.

35   All oral history is expected to be deposited in a repository to be accepted as historical documents. I do not know which institution is the holder of the Peter Hart archive.

36   Murphy (2010), pp. 192–4. He spells Jagoe without the e.

37   'Cork Cloyne and Ross report', *Church of Ireland Gazette*, 24 February 1922, p. 110, col. 3; Murphy (2010), p. 193, mentions a similar report in the *Cork Constitution*; correspondence with Gerard Murphy.

38 *Cork Examiner*, 1 May 1922, p. 3; *Southern Star*, 6 May 1922. See Lane J., 2012, *The Dunmanway Killings Curiouser and Curiouser* ... (Millstreet, Aubane Historical Society). To declare my interest: in its role as the local history society, Aubane published *The Bard* (2012), my biography of my great-grandfather who was one of Millstreet's heroes in the Land War between 1881 and 1891.

39 BMH WS 812, Patrick O'Brien, p. 19; Piers de Havilland was a member of the Leinster Regiment (Royal Canadians), so was a brother officer of Herbert Woods: National Archives, Kew, WO 339/13124, 'Major Piers de Havilland. The Prince of Wales's Leinster Regiment (Royal Canadians)'.

40 'The third battalion – inheriting the spirit of Fenianism', *Southern Star*, 27 November 1971, p. 6, cols 5–6.

41 There were many lists. See also Cork City and County Archives, Siobhán Langford papers, CCCAU169/B/(iv) 31/10/21, 'To OC 5th Batt. From O/C Intelligence 5th Batt (6): "Urgent Please furnish not later than 3rd Nov. a complete list of all loyalists in your district male and female with addresses distinguishing those prepared to remove to England for a time should hostilities be renewed."'

42 Cork City and County Archives, Siobhán Langford papers, CCCAU 169/21-30 2/6/1921.

43 National Library of Ireland, Florence O'Donoghue papers, Ms. 31,215 intelligence officer report, 3rd Cork Brigade No. 7/21 enemy agents, 1) Mrs Beamish, Main Street, Dunmanway; 2) R. J. Helen, Sovereign Street, Clonakilty; 3) Buttimer J., [Sovereign St.]; 4) J. Cullinane, 5) Annie O'Mahony, Lamb Street, Clonakilty; Hart (1998), p. 304, references a July 1921 West Cork intelligence report in the Mulcahy papers but does not discuss it; Hamel, P., 2004, 'The Buttimers of Dereen': http://home.alphalink.com.au/~datatree/wolf%2034.htm (accessed 1 June 2013); National Archives of Ireland, Census of Ireland 1901 & 1911 for Sovereign Street, Clonakilty: http://www.census.nationalarchives.ie/pages/1901/Cork/Clonakilty_Urban/Sovereign_Street/1096242/ (accessed 1 June 2013).

44 See also Meehan, N., 2011, 'Distorting Irish History 2, the road from Dunmanway: Peter Hart's treatment of the 1922 "April killings" in West Cork', *Spinwatch*, 24 May. Available at http://gcd.academia.edu/NiallMeehan/Papers/618347 (accessed 31 January 2013), where this is discussed and the references footnoted; also upcoming research (as of May 2013) by Dr Andy Bielenberg on the Dunmanway murders.

45 Ryan (2003), pp. 156–63; Ryan (2005), pp. 211–15.

46 Despite some suggestions to the contrary as part of the ongoing 'Peter Hart' controversy, there is no doubt about the existence of the diary. Its provenance is recorded in the BMH's *Index of Contemporary Documents* as 'Accession No. 31', which is accessible online at the BMH website, and photographs of each page of the diary (including the list of informers referenced by Flor Crowley in the *Southern Star* series) are in the Military Archives.

47 'The Black and Tan diary', *Southern Star*, 23 October to 27 November 1971.

48 'Lot picked up', *Southern Star*, 23 October 1971, p. 4, col. 1.

49 Crowley does not identify the person who loaned him the diary, Flor Begley, who was an intelligence officer for the West Cork Brigade and had possession of the document in 1947. See the *Southern Star*, 21 January 1922, p. 3, for evacuation by Auxiliaries, and the *Southern Star*, 1 September 1922, p. 1, for the burning of the workhouse by the anti-Treaty IRA.

50 As the 1922 men were not 'known informers' this does not refer to them.

51 'The informers', *Southern Star*, 27 November 1971, p. 6, col. 8. In a different article in the *Southern Star*, 27 November 1971, p. 5, col. 7, Crowley states that he knows some of the people listed by the writer of the diary: James Crowley, James Cronin, John Lynch, Patrick Murphy, Michael Cronin, Sam Jennings, George Chambers, Tim Crowley, Jerry Collins, C. McCarthy, C. Hurley and Jack — (illegible). However, this is not a list of informers as far as we know.

52 Ryan (2005), pp. 209–29.

53 *Ibid.*, p. 213. It is not explained which documents in the possession of Dan Cahalane are part of the 'Dunmanway find' and which are other documents. Neither is it explained whether Mr Cahalane got the documents from Flor Crowley or it was the other way around.

54 Hart (1998), p. 287. The reference is to the *Cork & County Eagle* (West Cork), which is available only in the National Library of Ireland and the Cork County Library, so it is particularly difficult to access.

55 'Apology', *Cork & County Eagle*, 1 August 1914, p. 4.

56 See census 1901 and 1911, Howe (Rushfield), Howe (Ballaghanure) and Chinnery (Castletown), which shows that Rushfield House was owned by the Howes; William Howe, Rushfield, and Rebecca Chinnery, Castletown, were brother and sister. See also Keane (2012) for 'Picture

of Chinnery Headstone'; http://www.flyingphotons.com/gen/fuller.html (accessed 22 August 2013) for details of Prospect Cottage; Ordnance Survey of Ireland map view for location of Prospect Cottage. 650 metres to the west of Castletown; 1911 census for outbuilding returns for Chinnery house in Castletown townland. Only one house in the townland beside Castletown House (still Hosfords) fits this description and is fifty metres from Robert Howe's house. William Howe sold Rushfield House in 1929, according to the *Southern Star*, 9 February 1929.

57   Ryan (2005), pp. 226, 450 note 72. Other information, not as yet in the public domain, apparently suggests that he was a member of the All for Ireland League and supportive of the local IRA. As I have not seen this information, I cannot comment on it other than to note its existence. Philip Chambers, the Officer Commanding the local IRA company, lived next door to Robert Howe. He never suggests that either victim was in any way suspect. He comments that he was ordered to tie two locals to the gates of the Roman Catholic church (much to his disgust at the method) for attacking the rectory in Castletown-Kinneigh, which suggests that the IRA stamped down hard on any sectarian abuse, BMH WS 738, Philip Chambers, p. 10.

58   *Southern Star*, 10 June 1950; however, the list of divisional officers in the Siobhán Langford papers does not mention him, Cork City and County Archives, U 169/B/(iii).

59   In the Irish Grants Committee statement of William Fitzmaurice he says he and his brother Francis, who was shot in Dunmanway, were providing information to the British; Bielenberg, A., 2013, 'Exodus: the emigration of Southern Irish Protestants during the Irish War of Independence and the Civil War', *Past and Present* 218, pp. 199–233.

60   BMH WS 812, Patrick O'Brien, p. 12.

61   'General amnesty', *Southern Star*, 18 February 1922, p. 2, col. 2; a copy also in a list of post-Treaty murders in Ireland prepared by British civil servant Mark Sturgis for cabinet.

62   Hart (1998), p. 302. In fact, McIvor's 'old farmers' comment (Brewer, J. D., 1990, *The Royal Irish Constabulary: an oral history* (Belfast, Institute of Irish Studies, Queen's University, Belfast) p. 115) is ambiguous and may not refer to Bandon.

63   Ryan provides a comprehensive list of sources for the existence of an Anti-Sinn Féin League in Ryan (2007), p. 244, footnote 28; Regan, J., 2012, 'The History of the Last Atrocity', *Dublin Review of Books*:

http://archive-ie.com/page/90903/2012-07-08/http://drb.ie/more_
details/12-06-22/The_History_of_the_Last_Atrocity.aspx   (accessed
18 July 2013); Borgonovo, J., 2007, *Spies, Informers and the 'Anti-Sinn
Féin Society': the intelligence war in Cork city, 1920–1921* (Dublin, Irish
Academic Press).

64   McDonnell (1972), p. 185.

65   University College Cork, Boole Library and Archive, CO 904/114, p.
839. See also BMH WS 1741, Michael V. O'Donoghue, Part 1, p. 85,
who provides further evidence of the city Anti-Sinn Féin Society.

66   Hart (1998), p. 303, note 81; National Archives, Kew, PRO 30/59/3,
'Sir Mark Beresford Russell Grant-Sturgis: diary part 3', 14 December
1920; Sturgis, M. and Hopkinson, M., 1999, *The Last Days of Dublin
Castle: the Mark Sturgis diaries* (Dublin, Irish Academic Press), pp. 90–1.

67   BMH WS 1741, Michael V. O'Donoghue, Part 2, p. 227. I am grateful
to Henry O'Keeffe for finding this reference. As everyone who is known
to have died was shot, only the Hornibrooks and Woods could have
been hanged.

68   'Letter from Dan Breen, Tom Hales, H. Murphy, S. O'Hegarty, Seán
Mullan, R. A. Mulcahy, Owen O'Duffy, Gearóid O'Sullivan, Michael
Collins to Four Courts garrison to end occupation and allow a plebiscite
on the Treaty', *The Irish Times*, 2 May 1922.

69   BMH WS 730, Seumas O'Mahony, p. 3; O'Donoghue accompanied
Mick Crowley to his brother Patrick's funeral in February 1921;
Pádraig Ó Caoimh's capture by the British is accurately described by
O'Donoghue, BMH WS 1741, Part 1, pp. 86–8; *Irish Press*, 14 April
1952, p. 1, col. 3; *Dungarvan Leader & Southern Democrat*, 19 April
1952, p. 1; Dáil Éireann, 25 October 1956, vol. 160, no. 2, p. 31, col. 213,
File Number D.1531. O'Donoghue records a supernatural experience
while in Kinsale Barracks in early 1922 and the men who interviewed
him for the BMH were sceptical of the detail recorded in his enormous
377-page statement.

70   'An area of twelve miles be declared and that 10 Free Staters be executed
in that area for every one of our men executed', cited in Harrington, M.,
2009, *The Munster Republic: the Civil War in North Cork* (Cork, Mercier
Press), p. 105.

71   Hart (1998), p. 291.

72   The Grand Orange Lodge of Ireland was founded in 1798 to defend
Protestants against attacks on them. Its members came to dominate

politics in what is now Northern Ireland and it was central to the partition of Ireland in 1921; http://www.grandorangelodge.co.uk/what-is-the-orange-order (accessed 22 August 2013).

73 *Southern Star*, 10 June 1922, p. 1; *Southern Star*, 17 June 1922, p. 3. Cllr McCarthy identifies W. J. as William Jagoe. It should be remembered that Jagoe had been warned the previous August that truce or no truce seven men would be shot in Dunmanway including himself.

74 The election was a triumph for the pro-Treaty party in the combined constituency of North, Mid and West Cork, with Michael Collins getting 17,000 votes; Pro-Treaty Sinn Féin 25,403, anti-Treaty Sinn Féin 12,587, Labour 10,737 and the Farmers 6,372. Pro-Treaty Sinn Féin took 3 seats, Labour 2, anti-Treaty 2 and Farmers 1, giving a 6:2 majority for the pro-Treaty parties. While the West Cork IRA was anti-Treaty, 77 per cent of the electorate voted the other way.

75 Hart (1998), p. 286.

76 In the case of Robert Nagle and John Bradfield, the original targets were not available so Nagle and Bradfield were shot instead.

77 British Houses of Parliament Archives, Lloyd George papers, LG/F/10/2/72, 'Mark Sturgis, Irish Office, to Mr. Churchill, Enclosure: (a) List of outrages committed since the Truce (b) List of cases which have been brought to the notice of the Irish Distress Committee', 25 May 1922.

78 National Archives, Kew, ADM 188/806/424, 'James Bennett Birthplace Ballineen Date of Birth 20-01-1899 J79924'; National Archives, Kew, ADM 188/684/327, 'Walter Bennett'.

79 Churchill updates these figures on 26 June in reply to a parliamentary question. Serving members of the Royal Irish Constabulary 15, Ex-members of the Royal Irish Constabulary 8, Soldiers 8 (these figures do not include the three officers and the soldier kidnapped at Macroom, or the soldier kidnapped at Rathdawney in January), Ex-soldiers 3, Civilians 15; House of Commons debate, 26 June 1922, vol. 155, cols 1664–6: http://hansard.millbanksystems.com/commons/1922/jun/26/murders (accessed 26 July 2013).

80 One was political/agrarian. The second was a raid in which the victim ignored an order to put his hands up and was shot; he had a revolver in his pocket and this was the purpose of the raid. A third was a blacksmith who took up tongs to attack IRA raiders at his forge. In the last case the killers were unknown.

81   Helen's statement to the Irish Grants Committee, quoted in Meehan (2011). See also National Archives, Kew, CO 762/33, 'Richard Helen'; Hart (1998), p. 286, *passim*.

82   'Clonakilty-Kilgariffe union', *Southern Star*, 29 April 1922, p. 7, col. 3.

83   *Southern Star*, 20 May 1922, p. 3, col. 2; funeral quotation from 'Miss L. Helen', *Southern Star*, 23 January 1926, p. 4.

84   *Southern Star*, 27 June 1925, p. 4, for his election to the Urban District Council; his term as chairman ended in June 1928. The *Southern Star*, 23 October 1937, p. 12, col. 2, reports that the will of Richard James Helen (bachelor) was probated and that he lived on Pearse Street (formerly Sovereign Street). He died on 19 January 1937. His obituary confirms that Richard James is R. J., *Southern Star*, 30 January 1937, p. 9, col. 4.

85   *Southern Star*, 1 April 1922.

86   Professor Stockley was a Protestant nationalist and had been shot at on the night that Lord Mayor of Cork, Tomás MacCurtain, was killed.

87   *Southern Star*, 8 April 1922, p. 2.

88   'Clonakilty notes', *Southern Star,* 22 April, p. 2, col. 4.

89   'At the end of March, 1921, it had been established that Fred C. Stennings … was acting as a spy. A party … was assembled to arrest him on the night of March 30th 1921. As Stennings dashed away, he drew a revolver and opened fire on his pursuers, who … shot him dead.' BMH WS 1591, Richard Russell, p. 21. See also *Southern Star*, 3 April 1915, p. 5, and 21 June 1913, p. 7.

90   BMH WS 1234, Jack Hennessy, p. 12.

91   For example, see *Southern Star*, 10 August 1912 and 23 August 1913. Given the miserable scores by the teams, the matches would not have lasted that long.

92   Con Crowley from Kilbrittain is also known as Conny, Connie, Cornelius and Conneen.

93   BMH WS 1741, Michael V. O'Donoghue, Part 2, pp. 290–1.

94   BMH WS 560, James O'Mahony, Denis Crowley, John Fitzgerald.

8   THE MACROOM KILLINGS

1   It has also been suggested that they had lunch at the Hornibrooks, three kilometres up the hill to the south, or the Tonson-Ryes at Cloughduv, just to the south of the Thady Inn, where Frank Busteed claims he

captured the officers. Neither claim is supported by the evidence. For information on Farran House, see http://www.farranhouse.com/location (accessed 22 August 2013).

2   Regan, J. M., 2011, 'The Bandon Valley massacre revisited', paper presented at Trinity College, Dublin. Available at: http://www.academia.edu/1710059/_The_Bandon_Valley_Massacre_revisited_TCD (accessed 8 December 2012).

3   BMH WS 1633, James Murphy, p. 15. Two of these men are mentioned in BMH WS 1521, Michael Walsh, p. 17: 'I was interrogated by three British intelligence officers named Henderson, Hendy and Hammond (these were later shot by the Cork I.R.A.) ... One of the officers (a one-armed man) then attacked me. While the two others held me he tried to force a small grenade into my mouth.' For a detailed account of the Macroom murders, see http://www.cairogang.com/other-people/british/castle-intelligence/incidents/kilgobnet%201922/kilgobnet-1922.html (accessed 9 July 2012).

4   National Archives, Kew, CAB 24/136. The case is covered in each of Macready's reports to cabinet up to 30 May, when Michael Collins confirmed their deaths to the Prime Minister. They were exhumed and received a full military funeral at Aldershot in December 1923.

5   General Sir Peter Strickland, 26 April 1922, Strickland papers, Imperial War Museum, London.

6   O'Callaghan (1974), pp. 189–91.

7   BMH WS 1457, Daniel McCarthy, Rylane, Co. Cork, p. 9.

9   AFTER THE KILLINGS

1   National Archives, Kew, CAB 23/30, 'Cabinet conclusions', 30 May 1922; National Archives Kew, CAB 24/136/56, 'Report by the General Officer Commanding-in-Chief on the situation in Ireland for the week ending 29 April 1922'.

2   As this was based on the Sturgis briefing note of newspaper reports, he was referring to military, police and loyalist deaths. The actual figure is forty-four, but seven are not attributed.

3   House of Commons debate, 'Written answers "murders"', 29 May 1922, vol. 154, cols 1717–8: http://hansard.millbanksystems.com/written_answers/1922/may/29/murders#S5CV0154P0_19220529_CWA_43 (accessed 18 July 2013).

4   'The Prime Minister said that in the south there was no dispute about the responsibility; it was the IRA.' National Archives, Kew, CAB 23/30/8, p. 15, Cabinet, 30 May 1922.

5   The Belfast 'pogroms' peaked in February 1922, so why retaliation occurred at the end of April 1922 would need to be reconsidered as a cause.

6   National Archives, Kew, CAB 24/136/56, 'Report by the General Officer Commanding-in-Chief on the situation in Ireland for the week ending 20 May 1922'.

7   National Archives, Kew, CAB 43/6, 'Conference on Ireland between ministers of the British government and members of the Provisional Government of Ireland', 1 Jan. 1922–30 June 1922.

8   Ryan (2005), p. 215. On this issue see also the report from the Dublin Peace Conference between pro- and anti-Treaty sides, which failed to agree on anything but 'its horror at the terrible events that have taken place in Dunmanway, Ballineen and Clonakilty', *Cork Examiner*, 1 May 1922, p. 4; the comments about Dunmanway of Arthur Griffith, Seán McEntee and Éamon de Valera in a Dáil Éireann debate, Friday 28 April 1922, vol. S2, no. 6 – though in de Valera's case the comments are ambiguous: http://debates.oireachtas.ie/dail/1922/04/28/printall.asp (accessed 22 August 2013); the report of a speech in Mullingar which contains no ambiguity where de Valera condemns the killings outright: *Cork Examiner*, 2 May 1922; 'A Warning' for de Valera Mullingar report, *Southern Star*, 6 May 1922, p. 7, col. 2; and Doherty, G. and Keogh, D., 1998, *Michael Collins and the Making of the Irish State* (Cork, Mercier Press), p. 176 for the relevant quote.

9   *The Irish Times*, 1, 2 May 1922. One of the best sources for both what happened and the consequences is *The Irish Times*, 1 May 1922, p. 6.

10 It was stated by Peter Hart that only the killing of Michael O'Neill was condemned and that local councils passed two separate motions to ensure that the Protestant deaths were not condemned. This is not true. The Cork Corporation minute book shows that only one was composed extempore at the start of the meeting and passed unanimously. 'Of Belfast' is inserted into the original motion showing that it was being composed in the meeting and not beforehand, as is normal: Cork City and County Archives, 'Minutes of Cork Corporation 1921–1923', p. 246; *Southern Star*, 29 April 1922, p. 5 carried a report of the motion from the night before.

11 'Corporation resolution: endorsed by Bandon Town Commissioners', *Cork Examiner*, 5 May 1922, p. 5.

12 O'Leary (1975), p. 92, shows that the Hawkins family of Geragh, who were still in residence in 1975, had provided a pony and cart for injured IRA volunteer Jim Hurley to escape an Essex Regiment raid on 14 May 1921. The 1911 census shows that the Hawkins family were Cork-born native Church of Ireland. Many of the other local histories for Cork have similar stories.

13 *The Irish Times*, 9 May 1922, p. 5.

14 See *Cork Examiner*, 2 May, pp. 5–6 and *Cork & County Eagle*, 6 May.

15 *Cork & County Eagle*, 6 May 1922, p. 2, beneath the Tom Hales warning of capital punishment for any further attacks.

16 Many members of the IRA outside the column did want to end the campaign on foot of the Bishop's pronouncement. The leadership put many of these men on charge, and they were put doing 'hard labour' for this lapse of discipline. The officers of the Schull company resigned as a result of the Bishop's decree, BMH WS 1519, Charlie Cotter, p. 6; the decree annoyed Tom Barry so much he was still fuming about it in 1974, Cork City and County Archives, U16/1/3.

17 Coogan (1992), p. 361.

18 *Southern Star*, 1 April 1922, p. 5, col. 2.

19 They could justifiably argue that as the Free State was an illegal entity created by British diktat, opposition to it was legal and did not go against the rule of law.

20 *The Irish Times*, 19 May 1922, p. 5. This was in complete contrast to what Tom Barry had in mind for the large estates when he ordered that those which had been abandoned should be broken up without being sold or compensated, Barry (1949), p. 116.

21 'Report of the Minister for Agriculture, Wednesday, 10 May 1922': http://debates.oireachtas.ie/dail/1922/05/10/00008.asp (accessed 12 July 2012).

22 *Southern Star*, 27 May 1922, p. 4, col. 4.

23 William Wood's wife, Rebecca, was John Chinnery's first cousin.

24 'Dunmanway doings', *Southern Star*, 27 May 1922, p. 5, col. 1; this was regarded as a very good price in the locality. Smith later sold it at a loss.

25 'Editorial', *The Irish Times*, 3 October 1922, p. 4. This was in direct response to the Southern Irish Loyalists Relief Association statement of September that year that there was such a well-organised system.

26 McMahon, P., 2008, *British Spies and Irish Rebels* (Woodbridge, Boydell and Brewer), p. 91. Both were dismissed as pro-Irish by the British

'diehards' and Cope was slandered in the House of Lords as being an Irish spy.

10 PROTESTANT FLIGHT FROM CORK

1   Keane, B., 2012, 'Ethnic cleansing? Protestant decline in West Cork between 1911 and 1926', *History Ireland* 20, no. 2, March.

2   'Cork diocesan report', *Cork Examiner*, 26 October 1922, p. 7; Dowse put the native Church of Ireland decline at 8 per cent.

3   *The Irish Times*, 1 May 1922. The figures in this report have been described as 'trainloads' by some researchers, which is an obvious exaggeration.

4   'Editorial', *The Irish Times*, 2 May 1922, p. 4, col. 4. The other articles are on the same page.

5   *Cork Examiner*, 3 May 1922, p. 3.

6   *Cork Constitution*, 3 May 1922, p. 3.

7   *The Irish Times*, 3 May 1922, p. 4.

8   *Cork Examiner*, 6 May 1922, p. 4. Con Connolly's specific reference to his allegiance to Michael Collins and maintenance of the amnesty may suggest that once certain members of the IRA had renounced Collins they felt that they were no longer bound by the Truce and 'cleaned up unfinished business'.

9   *Cork & County Eagle*, 6 May 1922.

10   It was suggested by Hart (1998), p. 283, that Ross was being petulant, which is unfair to his statement, as it was concerned to assure Protestants that they would be safe. A few months later, on 30 August, Ross was killed in a gun battle in Bantry while leading anti-Treaty IRA members who were occupying the post office.

11   *The Irish Times*, 12 May 1922, p. 5. The Irish government replied on 31 May, acknowledging the problem, and committed to restoring to their homes anyone driven out.

12   *Morning Post*, 12 May 1922.

13   'Letter to Provisional Government 13 May 1922': eppi.dippam.ac.uk/ documents/22816 (accessed 16 July 2013).

14   As the Protestant population was much more urbanised than the Roman Catholic population, this is not surprising. See O'Flanagan, P., 1988, 'Urban minorities and majorities: Catholics and Protestants in Munster towns *c.*1659–1850', in Smyth, W. J. and Whelan, K. (eds),

Common Ground: essays on the historical geography of Ireland (Cork, Cork University Press), pp. 124–48; Keane, B., 1986, 'The Church of Ireland decline in County Cork 1911–1926', *Chimera: the UCC Geographical Society Journal* 2, pp. 53–9. O'Flanagan makes the point that Bandon as a Devonshire estate town remained semi-segregated up to the end of the nineteenth century. Evidence from 1911 confirms this. On South Main Street Protestants were head of the family in 31 houses (44 per cent) and Roman Catholics in 39 houses. Protestants made up 31 per cent of the 357 people living on the street and this seeming discrepancy is made up of Roman Catholic servants in Protestant houses and smaller Protestant families. If the town was unsegregated, the figure should have been 22 per cent, Census of Ireland 1911.

15   University College Cork, Boole Library and Archive, Bantry Estate Archive no. 1618 (25 November 1922–13 December 1922): http://booleweb.ucc.ie/documents/Bantryhouse.pdf (accessed 12 June 2012).

16   'The recent horrors', *Cork Constitution*, 1 May 1922, p. 5, col. 3.

17   *Cork & County Eagle*, 20 and 27 May 1922. Clarina sold five other houses on Castle Street at the same time, *Southern Star*, 27 May 1922, p. 8, col. 5.

18   There have been suggestions that he was visited during this night by men intending to kill him, but his memoir makes clear that the only person to knock on his door was a terrified neighbour; Kingston, W., 'From Victorian boyhood to the Troubles: a Skibbereen memoir'.

19   *Ibid.* His journey to Dublin was fraught with danger and his account suggests a group of very frightened people travelling through a very unsettled country riddled with random violence. The train being 'bombed' at the tunnel at Glanmire Station in Cork and shots being fired at Limerick Junction by armed men on the platform are terrifying, but William does not suggest that the people on the train were attacked.

20   Ungoed-Thomas, J., 2008, *Jasper Wolfe of Skibbereen* (Cork, Collins Press).

21   A British Military Court of Inquiry found that she had been killed by the Auxiliaries; BMH WS 1652, Chief Supt. Henry O'Mara, p. 2.

22   Gregory and Murphy (1978), pp. 348–55. The incidents include threats, attacks at her home, the ongoing dispute over her land, the requisitioning of her family home at Roxboro, the departure of her brother and his family to England, the attack on the Talbots (which resulted in the death of Mrs Talbot, and Mr Talbot ending up in a Dublin nursing

home), the poor attendance at de Valera's Gort and Galway meetings, the capture of Galway by MacEoin, the killing of more Protestants in Cork, an untrue rumour that two Protestant gamekeepers had been asked to leave and the theft of the dentist's car.

23   National Archives, Kew, CO 739/14/15/16 (16); Hodder refers in her letter to the fact that the Woods family are Protestants and suggests both class and sectarian elements in the killings and the local response; Coogan, T. P., 1990, *Michael Collins: the man who made Ireland* (Niwot, Colo, Roberts Rinehart), p. 359.

24   Peter Hart says that Mabel Williamson had written a letter which was intercepted by the IRA and as a result she was ordered out of the country: Hart (1998), p. 297. Alice Hodder makes much of the fact that Mrs Williamson (who was seventy-five) was a Cork native, but she was in fact born in India, as was her daughter according to the 1901 census. She was visiting Alton in England for the 1911 census. Her husband, Colonel Robert Williamson, was at home in Mallow.

25   Major Noel Furlong moved to Skeffington Hall in Leicestershire. His horse, ridden by his son Frank, won the Aintree Grand National in 1935 and 1936. His wife, Rosemary, was a member of the Murphy brewing family and was a Roman Catholic, which meant that the children would be Roman Catholic if they complied with the *Ne Temere* decree. Furlong had been a member of the South Irish Horse, but this had not stopped him trying to get out of Grand Jury duty along with Henry Longfield in 1913; *Southern Star*, 6 December 1913, p. 1. For evidence of Furlong at Riverstown: http://www.census.nationalarchives.ie/pages/1911/Cork/Riverstown/Hermitage/407830/ (accessed 18 July 2013).

26   Many of the letters in the National Archives, Kew, CO 739 14/15/16, are from a series of well-attended public meetings held in England by the Truth about Ireland League throughout the year, in support of compensation claims from refugees and condemnation of British government policy. Churchill understandably rejects the condemnation and declines to reinvade, which is one of the proposals of the league.

27   http://hansard.millbanksystems.com/lords/1922/may/11/situation-in-ireland#S5LV0050P0_19220511_HOL_40 (accessed 4 May 2012).

28   *The Irish Times*, 12 May 1922.

29   It was suggested that this lack of interest in lesser crimes was more by omission than a deliberate stance on the part of the public, in that

these events tended to get overlooked in troubled times rather than any suggestion of support according to the speaker Sergeant Hanna, *The Irish Times*, 12 May 1922, p. 5.

30   The Catholic hierarchy, the Irish government and the Dáil were specifically mentioned to applause.

31   http://www.irishstatutebook.ie/1926/en/act/pub/0019/print.html sec2 (accessed 8 July 2013); House of Lords debates, 22 August 1922 and 15 July 1922, in which the people most affected by the burning of the 'Big Houses', including Lord Mayo, teased out the extent and effects of the Irish revolution. See also Keane (2013b).

32   *The Irish Times*, 10 May 1922.

33   The term 'ethnic cleansing' is inappropriate. If there was any group targeted, it was Protestant unionists whose loyalty to Britain was the issue. Hart states that, 'In their view Protestant Unionists were traitors' but does not address the logic of his own comment that it was justifiable for the unionist sub-set of the Protestant community to be seen by republicans as traitors: Hart (1998), p. 291.

34   National Archives, Kew, CAB 43/2, p. 275. The opening lines of the 'Memorial' point out that the 'Sinn Féiners are armed, the loyalists are not' and it goes on to observe: 'It seems almost miraculous that up to this all the Protestants and loyalists have not been massacred. It is a moral certainty that they will in the near future.'

35   National Archives, Kew, CAB 43/6, p. 90. Churchill states, 'Their fears may be exaggerated, but they are real.'

36   Wilson, the former Chief of the General Staff, had retired in February 1922. He refused to talk to Lloyd George over the Truce and Treaty until just before he became both a Conservative member of parliament and military advisor to the Ulster government. He had just returned from unveiling the Great Eastern War Memorial at Liverpool Street Station when he was shot outside his home in London's Eaton Square on 22 June 1922; House of Commons debate, 26 June 1922, vol. 155, cols 1693–1811: http://hansard.millbanksystems.com/commons/1922/jun/26/irish-office-etc (accessed 26 July 2013).

37   National Archives, Kew, CAB 24/173, 'The position of loyalists in the Irish Free State'. 'It also reported that the *Southern Irish Loyalists Relief Association* have recently [1925] brought to our notice a large number of cases of continued persecution and suffering among loyalists who have remained in the Free State.'

38   *Ibid.*, Appendix 1, p. 7, Conclusion 16: 'We have been impressed with the severe hardship suffered by Crown supporters prior to the Truce where the losses did not give rise to a claim for compensation. These cases, the majority of which have already been brought to your notice, are distinguished by reason of the fact that the losses arose mainly as the result of assistance given to Crown forces.'

39   House of Commons debate, 19 February 1929, vol. 225, cols 967–1020: http://hansard.millbanksystems.com/commons/1929/feb/19/dominion-services#S5CV0225P0_19290219_HOC_275 (accessed 26 July 2013). Churchill explains that £2,188,459 was paid out to 4,030 claimants to this second committee. The total paid out to loyalists was £10 million.

40   Bielenberg (2013), pp. 199–233.

41   While there was a general prohibition on killing clergy, there was no prohibition on ordering them out. In the cases of Harbord and Lord this did not happen. Harbord died in 1966 and Lord died in 1936.

CONCLUSION

1   National Archives, Kew, CAB 24/139, 'Situation in Ireland report by Major Whittaker (circulated by the secretary of state for the colonies)'. Whittaker was sent to Ireland specifically to assess the possibility of reinvasion.

2   There was an ugly postscript to these events in July 1935, when attacks on Roman Catholics in Belfast led to retaliation on southern Protestants, church buildings and social halls. The Church of Ireland in Kilmallock was burned, and in Dunmanway tar was painted in the road with the words 'Remember 21', which was taken as a reference to the 1922 killings. While these sectarian attacks caused considerable panic within the Protestant community, the police intervened quickly, protecting Protestant institutions and securing convictions for the culprits in Kilmallock: *The Irish Times*, 22 and 23 July 1935.

3   Mercier Press is publishing a series of these by county under the series title, *The Men Will Talk To Me*. So far Galway and Kerry are available and Mayo will be available in 2014.

4   BMH WS 849, James Brendan Connolly, p. 19: 'Mr Connolly, England cannot afford to have a republic on her flank,' General Nevil Macready replied to Mr Connolly who was 'appointed American Relief Commissioner to go to Ireland and look into the truth or falsity' of the

charge 'that American Relief money was being used to buy arms'.

5   This was recognised as the central unsolvable problem by the British Lord Chancellor in the April 1921 meeting, National Archives, Kew, CAB 24/122/83. The *Southern Star*, 25 September 1920, p. 7, reported that Michael Collins had commented that Dominion Home Rule was being offered by Lloyd George to get rid of the republican movement, and that 'the same effort that would get us Home Rule would get us a Republic'. In the same article, Éamon de Valera said that the Irish would only meet the British as equals. The compromise was a treaty between equals that granted Dominion Status.

6   One of the earl's family homes, at Convamore outside Mallow, was burned by the IRA in 1921. His grandfather, the 3rd Earl, complained bitterly to the House of Lords until his death in 1924 about the 'miserable' compensation he was getting for the restoration. The family had to retire to their other residence at Kingston House in Knightsbridge, London, which was demolished in 1937.

7   What had been unimaginable in 1922 was dispensed with in a five-page top secret cabinet annex circulated on 28 October 1948, which dealt with the new Indian republican constitution, National Archives, Kew, CAB 128/14/3.

8   Hoare was not suggesting that India be allowed independence any time soon, but not giving Home Rule would inevitably result in a disaster along the lines of Ireland. The nationalism, racism and paternalism that permeated the Irish debates through the nineteenth century were evident in the Indian debates of the twentieth century.

9   Among the myths about Churchill is that it is generally assumed that he resigned over appeasement, but it was the Conservative Party leader's endorsement of the Prime Minister's proposal of a round table conference on India in 1930 that led to his resignation from the shadow cabinet. This gave rise, in February 1931, to one of his most famous insults: 'It is alarming and also nauseating to see Mr Gandhi, a seditious middle temple lawyer, now posing as a fakir of a type well known in the east, striding half-naked up the steps of the viceregal palace, while he is still organising and conducting a defiant campaign of civil disobedience, to parley on equal terms with the representative of the king-emperor.'

10   There was a high incidence of abstinence from alcohol among members of the IRA. They were also noted for mass-going, and British forces

held up and interrogated people leaving Sunday services on more than one occasion.

11 Hart (1998), pp. 290–1. Of course, some did as some will always do.
12 The Dáil debate, 10 April 1923, gives the official version and this makes it clear that if anyone was going to be blown up by a trap mine it was going to be 'irregular' prisoners: http://historical-debates.oireachtas. ie/D/0003/D.0003.192304170017.html (accessed 12 June 2012).
13 This interpretation of Ballyseedy was disputed by the Free State at the time, but is now generally accepted.

APPENDIX 2

1 All spelling and punctuation (except ellipses which denote omitted text) within this *Memorandum by the Secretary of State for War* are as they appear in CAB 43/2, pp. 74–7, excluding the details of point 13, which have been edited for brevity by the author.

Bibliography

Anon., *Torture & Terror*, Pamphlet No. 3 (Chicago, Benjamin Franklin Bureau)

Ainsworth, J. S., 2000, *British Security Policy in Ireland, 1920–1921: a desperate attempt by the Crown to maintain Anglo-Irish unity by force* (Perth, Centre for Irish Studies, Murdoch University)

Ainsworth, J. S., 2001, 'The Black & Tans and Auxiliaries in Ireland, 1920–1921: their origins, roles and legacy', paper presented to the Annual Conference of the Queensland History Teachers' Association in Brisbane, 12 May 2001 (available online)

Barry, T., 1949, *Guerilla Days in Ireland* (Dublin, Irish Press)

Barry, T., 1974, *The Reality of the Anglo-Irish War, 1920–21 in West Cork: refutations, corrections, and comments on Liam Deasy's Towards Ireland Free* (Tralee, Anvil Books)

Bartlett, T. and Jeffery, K., 1996, *A Military History of Ireland* (Cambridge, Cambridge University Press)

Beckett, I. F. W., 1986a, 'A note on government intelligence and surveillance during the Curragh incident, March 1914', *Intelligence and National Security* 1, pp. 435–40

Beckett, I. F. W., 1986b, *The Army and the Curragh Incident, 1914* (London, Bodley Head for Army Records Society)

Bielenberg, A., 2013, 'Exodus: the emigration of Southern Irish Protestants during the Irish War of Independence and the Civil War', *Past and Present* 218, pp. 199–233

Borgonovo, J., 2007, *Spies, Informers and the 'Anti-Sinn Féin Society': the intelligence war in Cork city, 1920–1921* (Dublin, Irish Academic Press)

Borgonovo, J., 2010, 'The guerrilla infrastructure: I.R.A. Special Services in the Cork Number One Brigade, 1917–1921', *The Irish Sword* XXVII, no. 108, pp. 205–16

Brennan, N., 1995, 'Compensating the Royal Irish Constabulary 1922–1932', PhD thesis, University College Dublin (available online)

Brennan, N., 1997, 'A Political Minefield: Southern Loyalists, the Irish Grants Committee and the British Government, 1922–31', *Irish Historical Studies* 30, pp. 406–19

Brewer, J. D., 1990, *The Royal Irish Constabulary: an oral history* (Belfast, Institute of Irish Studies, Queen's University, Belfast)

Broom, J. T., 2002, 'The Anglo-Irish War of 1919–1921: "Britain's Troubles–Ireland's Opportunities"', in Huber, T. M. (ed.), *Compound Warfare: that fatal knot* (Fort Leavenworth, Kan., U.S. Army Command and General Staff College Press)

Cahill, R. A., 2009, '"Going Berserk": "Black and Tans" in Palestine', *Jerusalem Quarterly* 38, pp. 59–68

Callwell, C. E., 1906, *Small Wars. Their Principles and Practice* (London, printed for HMSO by Harrison and Sons)

Callwell, C. E., 1927, *Field-Marshall Sir Henry Wilson*, vol. 2 (London, Cassell)

Cassar, G. H., 2009, *Lloyd George at War, 1916–1918* (London, Anthem Press)

Chamberlain, A. and Self, R. C., 1995, *The Austen Chamberlain Diary Letters: the correspondence of Sir Austen Chamberlain with his sisters Hilda and Ida, 1916–1937* (London, Cambridge University Press)

Chambers, I., 2006, *The Chamberlains, the Churchills and Ireland, 1874–1922* (New York, Cambria Press)

Charters, D., 2009, 'The development of British counter-insurgency intelligence', *Journal of Conflict Studies* 29, April, pp. 55–74

Churchill, W. and Woods, F., 1975, *A History of the English-speaking Peoples. Vol. 1: the Birth of Britain* (London, Library of Imperial History)

Collins, M. and Talbot, H., 1923, *Michael Collins' Own Story* (London, Hutchinson and Co.)

Connolly, S. J., 2007, *The Oxford Companion to Irish History* (Oxford, Oxford University Press)

Coogan, T. P., 1990, *Michael Collins: the man who made Ireland* (Niwot, Colo, Roberts Rinehart)

Coogan, T. P., 1992, *The Man who Made Ireland: the life and death of Michael Collins* (Niwot, Colo, Roberts Rinehart)

Crowley S., 2005, *From Newce to Truce: a story of Newcestown and its hinterland* (Newcestown, self-published)

Curtis, L., 1916, *The Commonwealth of Nations: an inquiry into the nature of citizenship in the British Empire, and into the mutual relations of the several communities thereof* (London, Macmillan and Co.)

Dangerfield G., 1966, *The Damnable Question: a study in Anglo-Irish relations* (London, Constable)

Davies, C. C., 1975, *The Problem of the North-west Frontier, 1890–1908, with a Survey of Policy since 1849* (London, Curzon Press)

De Valera, É., 1921, *The Struggle of the Irish People: address to the Congress of the United States adopted at the January session of Dáil Éireann, 1921* (Washington, D.C., U.S. G.P.O.)

Deasy, L., 1973, *Towards Ireland Free: the West Cork Brigade in the War of Independence, 1917–1921* (Cork, Mercier Press)

Doherty, G. and Keogh, D., 1998, *Michael Collins and the Making of the Irish State* (Dublin & Cork, Mercier Press)

Donnelly Jr, J. S., 2012, 'Big House burnings in County Cork during the Irish Revolution, 1920–21', *Éire-Ireland* 47, pp. 141–97

Duff, D. V., 1953, *Bailing with a Teaspoon* (London, J. Long)

Dungan, M., 1997, *They Shall Not Grow Old: Irish soldiers and the Great War* (Dublin, Four Courts Press)

Dyas, E., 2006, 'The Crown campaign against Protestant neutrality in Cork during the Irish War of Independence', *Church & State* 86, Autumn

Ellis, P. B., 2004, *Eyewitness to Irish History* (Hoboken, N.J., John Wiley and Sons)

Fitzpatrick, D., 1977, *Politics and Irish Life 1913–1921: provincial experience of war and revolution* (Dublin, Gill & Macmillan)

Fitzpatrick, D., 2012a, *Terror in Ireland: 1916–1923* (Dublin, Lilliput Press)

Fitzpatrick, D., 2012b, 'Dr. Regan and Mr. Snide', *History Ireland* 20, no. 3, May/June, pp. 12–13

Gray, C. S., 2012, 'Concept failure? COIN, counterinsurgency, and strategic theory', *Prism: A Journal of the Centre for Complex Operations* 3, no. 3, June, pp. 17–32

Gregory, Lady and Murphy, D. J., 1978, *Lady Gregory's Journals*, vol. 1, books 1–29, 10 October 1916–24 February 1925 (Gerrards Cross, Smythe)

Hack, K., 2009, 'The Malayan Emergency as counter-insurgency paradigm', *Journal of Strategic Studies* 32, no. 3, pp. 383–414

Hankey, M., 1961, *The Supreme Command, 1914–1918*, 2 vols (London, Allen and Unwin)

Harrington, M., 2009, *The Munster Republic: the Civil War in North Cork* (Cork, Mercier Press)

Hart, P., 1993, 'Class, Community and the Irish Republican Army, 1917–1923', in O'Flanagan, P., Buttimer, C. G. and O'Brien, G. (eds), *Cork: history and society* (Dublin, Geography Publications), pp. 963–87

Hart, P., 1998, *The I.R.A. and Its Enemies: violence and community in Cork, 1916–1923* (Oxford, Clarendon Press)

Hitchcock, F. C., 1988, *'Stand to': a diary of the trenches 1915–1918* (Norwich, Gliddon)

Hittle, J. B. E., 2011, *Michael Collins and the Anglo-Irish War: Britain's counter-insurgency failure* (Washington, D.C., Potomac Books)

Hochschild, A., 2011, 'John French and Charlotte Despard: the odd couple', *History Today* 61, no. 6, pp. 30–40

Holmes, R., 1981, *The Little Field-Marshal, Sir John French* (London, J. Cape)

Hughes, M., 2010, 'From law and order to pacification: Britain's suppression of the Arab revolt in Palestine, 1936–39', *Journal of Palestine Studies* 39, no. 2, pp. 6–22

I. O. (Street, C. J. C.), 1921, *The Administration of Ireland, 1920* (London, Philip Allan)

Ion, A. H. and Errington, E. J., 1993, *Great Powers and Little Wars: the limits of power* (Westport, Conn., Praeger)

Irish Labour Party and Trade Union Congress, 1921, *Who Burnt Cork City? A tale of arson, loot, and murder: the evidence of over seventy witnesses* (Dublin, Irish Labour Party and Trade Union Congress)

Jeffery, K., 1984, *The British Army and the Crisis of Empire: 1918–1922* (Manchester, Manchester University Press)

Jeffery, K., 1987, 'British Military Intelligence following World War I', in Robertson, K. G. (ed.), *British and American Approaches to Intelligence* (Basingstoke, Macmillan), pp. 55–84

Jeffery, K., 2008, *Field Marshal Sir Henry Wilson: a political soldier* (Oxford, Oxford University Press)

Kardahji, N., 2007, 'A Measure of Restraint: the Palestinian Police and the end of the British Mandate', MPhil thesis, Oxford University (available online)

Karsten, P., 1983, 'Irish Soldiers in the British Army, 1792–1922: suborned or subordinate?', *Journal of Social History* 17, pp. 31–64

Kautt, W. H., 1999, *The Anglo-Irish War, 1916–1921: a people's war* (Westport, Conn., Praeger)

Kautt, W. H., 2003, 'Militarising Policemen: the various members of the RIC and their response to IRA violence in Ireland, 1919–21', http://www.academia.edu/1686881/The_Auxies_Black_and_Tans_and_the_RIC_and_their_response_to_IRA_violence_in_Ireland_1919-21

Keane, B., 1986, 'The Church of Ireland decline in County Cork 1911–1926', *Chimera: the UCC Geographical Society Journal* 2, pp. 53–9

Keane, B., 2012, 'Ethnic Cleansing? Protestant decline in West Cork between 1911 and 1926', *History Ireland* 20, no. 2, March

Keane, B., 2013a, 'The Dunmanway Killings – murder, myths and misinformation – Protestant decline Cork 1911–1926 in context', http://The_Dunmanway_killings-murder_myth_and_misinformation-_Protestant_decline_Cork_1911–1926_in_context

Keane, B., 2013b, 'Protestant Cork decline 1911–1926, murders, mistakes, myths, and misinformation, updated 14 April 2013', https://sites.google.com/site/protestantcork191136/home/protestant-cork-decline-1911-1926-murders-mistakes-myths-and-misinformation-updated-25th-july-2012

Khalidi, R., 2001, 'The Palestinians and 1948: the root causes of failure', in Rogan, E. L. and Shlaim, A. (eds), *The War for Palestine: rewriting the history of 1948* (New York, Cambridge University Press), pp. 12–36

Kingston, W., 'From Victorian Boyhood to the Troubles: a Skibbereen memoir', http://durrushistory.files.wordpress.com/2012/09/memoir-of-willie-kingston-1885-1975-skibbereen-solicitor-and-historian1.pdf

Kostal, D., 2007, 'British military intelligence-law enforcement integration in the Irish War of Independence, 1919–1921', in National Defense Intelligence College, *Can't We All Just Get Along? Improving the law enforcement–intelligence community relationship*, pamphlet (Washington, D.C., NDIC Press), p. 138

Lane, J., 2012, *The Dunmanway Killings Curiouser and Curiouser …* (Millstreet, Aubane Historical Society)

Leeson, D., 2011, *The Black and Tans: British Police and Auxiliaries in the Irish War of Independence, 1920–1921* (Oxford, Oxford University Press)

Liddell Hart, B. H., 1972, *History of the First World War* (London, Pan Books)

Linge, J., 1994, 'British Forces and Irish Freedom: Anglo Irish defence relations 1922–1931', PhD thesis, University of Stirling

Lloyd George, D., 1933, *War Memoirs of David Lloyd George* (Boston, Little, Brown, and Co.)

Lloyd George, D., 1938, *War Memoirs* (London, Odhams Press)

Lyons, J. B., 1983, *The Enigma of Tom Kettle: Irish patriot, essayist, poet, British soldier, 1880–1916* (Dublin, Glendale Press)

Macardle, D., 1968, *The Irish Republic* (London, Corgi)

MacDonagh, M., 1917, *The Irish on the Somme: being the second series of 'The Irish at the Front'* (London, Hodder and Stoughton)

MacDonagh, O. and Mandle, W. F., 1986, *Ireland and Irish–Australia: studies in cultural and political history* (London, Croom Helm)

Mac Giolla Choille, B. (ed.), 1966, *Intelligence Notes, 1913–1916, preserved in the State Paper Office* (Dublin, Stationery Office)

Mansergh, N., 1991, *The Unresolved Question: the Anglo-Irish settlement and its undoing, 1912–72* (New Haven, Yale University Press)

Martin, H., 1921, *Ireland in Insurrection, an Englishman's Record of Fact* (London, D. O'Connor)

McDonnell, K. K., 1972, *There is a Bridge at Bandon: a personal account of the Irish War of Independence* (Cork, Mercier Press)

McKenna, J., 2011, *Guerrilla Warfare in the Irish War of Independence, 1919–1921* (Jefferson, N.C., McFarland and Co.)

McLean, I., 2010, *What's Wrong with the British Constitution?* (Oxford, Oxford University Press)

McMahon, P., 2008, *British Spies and Irish Rebels* (Woodbridge, Boydell and Brewer)

Meehan, N., 2011, 'Distorting Irish History 2, the road from Dunmanway: Peter Hart's treatment of the 1922 "April killings" in West Cork', *Spinwatch*, 24 May

Mitchell, A., 1995, *Revolutionary Government in Ireland: Dáil Éireann, 1919–22* (Dublin, Gill & Macmillan)

Moore, H. K., 1930, *Reminiscences and Reflections from Some Sixty Years of Life in Ireland* (London, Longmans, Green and Co.)

Morrissey, C. J., 2011, 'The Earl of Bandon and the burning of Castle Bernard, 1921', *Bandon Historical Journal* 27, pp. 32–43

Morrissey, C. J., 2012, 'The Bernards of Bandon: a County Cork landed family and their estate, 1639–1921', *Bandon Historical Journal* 28, pp. 49–65

Morrissey, J., 2006, 'A Lost Heritage: the Connaught Rangers and multivocal Irishness', in McCarthy, M. (ed.), *Ireland's Heritages: critical perspectives on memory and identity* (Ashgate, Aldershot), pp. 71–87

Murphy, B., 1998, 'The I.R.A and Its Enemies: a review article', *Month: Review of Christian Thought and World Affairs* 31, pp. 381–3

Murphy, B., 2005, 'Peter Hart: the issue of sources', Irish Political Review 20, no. 7, July, pp. 10–11

Murphy, B. and Meehan, N., 2008, *Troubled History: a 10th anniversary critique of Peter Hart's The IRA and Its Enemies* (Millstreet: Aubane Historical Society)

Murphy, G., 2010, *The Year of Disappearances: political killings in Cork 1921–1922* (Dublin, Gill & Macmillan)

Ó Broin, L., 1985, *Protestant Nationalists in Revolutionary Ireland: the Stopford connection* (Dublin, Gill & Macmillan)

O'Callaghan, S., 1974, *Execution* (London, Muller)

O'Donoghue, F., 1986, *No Other Law* (Dublin, Anvil)

O'Donovan, D., 2012, 'Some Ballincollig petty session reports', *Times Past: Journal of Muskerry Local History Society* 10, pp. 72–81

O'Flanagan, P., 1988, 'Urban minorities and majorities: Catholics and Protestants in Munster towns *c.*1659–1850', in Smyth, W. J. and Whelan, K. (eds), *Common Ground: essays on the historical geography of Ireland* (Cork, Cork University Press), pp. 124–48

O'Flanagan, P., Buttimer, C.G. and O'Brien, G., 1993, *Cork: history and society* (Dublin, Geography Publications)

O'Flynn, D., 2010, 'They missed the train and lost their lives', *Times Past: Journal of the Muskerry Local History Society* 9 (2010–11), pp. 63–4

O'Hegarty, P. S., 1998, *The Victory of Sinn Féin: how it won it and how it used it* (Dublin, University College Dublin Press)

O'Leary, D., 1975, *Kilmeen and Castleventry Parish, Co. Cork* (self-published)

Ó Loinsigh, P., 1997, *Gobnait Ní Bhruadair: the Hon. Albinia Lucy Brodrick: beathaisnéis* (Baile Átha Cliath, Coiscéim)

O'Mahony, N., 2010, 'The life and death of Canon Magner', *Times Past: Journal of the Muskerry Local History Society* 9 (2010–11), pp. 59–61

Pattison, G., 2010, 'The British Army's Effectiveness in the Irish Campaign 1919–1921 and the Lessons for Modern Counterinsurgency Operations, with Special Reference to C3I Aspects', *The Cornwallis Group XIV: Analysis of Societal Conflict and Counter-Insurgency*, pp. 88–103

Prendergast, J. P., 1922, *The Cromwellian Settlement of Ireland* (Dublin, Mellifont Press)

Ramakrishna, K., n.d., 'The Role of Propaganda in the Malayan Emergency: lessons for countering terrorism today', p. 8. Available at: http://www.rsis.edu.sg/cens/publications/others/ProfKumarPresentation.pdf

Rast, M., 2011, 'Tactics, Politics, and Propaganda in the Irish War of Independence, 1917–1921', PhD thesis, Georgia State University

Regan, J. M., 2011, 'The Bandon Valley Massacre revisited', paper presented at Trinity College, Dublin, http://www.academia.edu/1710059/_The_Bandon_Valley_Massacre_revisited_TCD

Regan, J. M., 2012, 'The "Bandon Valley massacre" as a historical problem', *History* 97, no. 325, January, pp. 70–98

Rogan, E. L. and Shliam, A., 2001, *The War for Palestine: rewriting the history of 1948* (New York, Cambridge University Press)

Ryan, M., 2003, *Tom Barry: IRA freedom fighter* (Cork, Mercier Press)

Ryan, M., 2005, *Tom Barry: IRA freedom fighter* (Cork, Mercier Press)

Ryan, M., 2007, 'The Kilmichael Ambush: exploring the "Provocative Chapters", *History* 92, no. 306, pp. 235–49

Sellar, W. C. and Yeatman, R. J., 1931, *1066 and All That: a memorable history of England, comprising all the parts you can remember including one hundred and three good things, five bad kings and two genuine dates* (New York, E.P. Dutton and Co.)

Shaw, G., 2012, 'The Casement Brothers, Ireland and South Africa', *Southern African-Irish Studies* 4, series 2, no. 1, pp. 15–24

Shaw, N., 1923, *The Air & Its Ways: the Rede Lecture in the University of Cambridge* (Cambridge, Cambridge University Press)

Sheehan, W., 2005, *British Voices from the Irish War of Independence 1918–1921: the words of British servicemen who were there* (Cork, Collins Press)

Simson, H. J., 1937, *British Rule, and Rebellion* (Edinburgh, Blackwood and Sons)

Sloan, G. R., 1997, *The Geopolitics of Anglo-Irish Relations in the Twentieth Century* (London, Leicester University Press)

Smith, J., 1996, 'Paralysing the Arm: the Unionists and the Army Annual Act, 1911–1914', *Parliamentary History* 15, pp. 191–207

Smith, R. N., 1997, *The Colonel: the life and legend of Robert R. McCormick, 1880–1955* (Boston, Houghton Mifflin Company)

Stafford, T. A., 2005, 'The Collapse of the Royal Irish Constabulary: policing insurgency in Ireland, 1914–1921', MA thesis, University of New Brunswick, Canada

Sturgis, M. and Hopkinson, M., 1999, *The Last Days of Dublin Castle: the Mark Sturgis diaries* (Dublin, Irish Academic Press)

Taylor, A., 2006, *Bonar Law* (London, Haus)

Townshend, C. (ed.), n.d., *The British in Ireland. Part 4, Police Reports, 1914–1921* (Brighton: Harvester Press Microform Publications)

Ungoed-Thomas, J., 2008, *Jasper Wolfe of Skibbereen* (Cork, Collins Press)

University College Cork, n.d., 'Multitext Project in Irish History Movements for Political & Social Reform, 1870–1914', multitext.ucc.ie/d/Movements_for_Political_Social_Reform_1870--1914

Valiulus, M. G., 1992, *Portrait of a Revolutionary: General Richard Mulcahy and the founding of the Irish Free State* (Lexington, University Press of Kentucky)

Walsh, M., 2008, *The News from Ireland: foreign correspondents and the Irish revolution* (London, I. B. Tauris)

Walton, C., 2013, *Empire of Secrets: British intelligence, the Cold War and the twilight of empire* (London, Harper Press)

White, G. and O'Shea, B., 2006, *The Burning of Cork* (Cork, Mercier Press)

Woodward, D. R., 1983, *Lloyd George and the Generals* (Newark, University of Delaware Press)

INDEX

MERCIER PRESS

IRISH PUBLISHER - IRISH STORY

We hope you enjoyed this book.

Since 1944, Mercier Press has published books that have been critically important to Irish life and culture.

Our website is the best place to find out more information about Mercier, our books, authors, news and the best deals on a wide variety of books. Mercier tracks the best prices for our books online and we seek to offer the best value to our customers, offering free delivery within Ireland.

A large selection of Mercier's new releases and backlist are also available as ebooks. We have an ebook for everyone, with titles available for the Amazon Kindle, Sony Reader, Kobo Reader, Apple products and many more. Visit our website to find and buy our ebooks.

Sign up on our website or complete and return the form below to receive updates and special offers.

www.mercierpress.ie
www.facebook.com/mercier.press
www.twitter.com/irishpublisher

Name: _____

Email: _____

Address: _____

Mobile No.: _____

Mercier Press, Unit 3b, Oak House, Bessboro Rd, Blackrock, Cork, Ireland